Travelling In, Travelling Out

Writer and publisher Namita Gokhale is the author of twelve books. Her first novel, *Paro: Dreams of Passion*, published in 1984, created a furor with its candid sexual humour. Other novels include *The Book of Shadows*, *Shakuntala: The Play of Memory*, *The Habit of Love* and *Priya*, a sequel to *Paro*. Gokhale has worked extensively with Indian myth. She has written *The Book of Shiva* and retold the Mahabharata for young readers. She has also edited *In Search of Sita: Revisiting Mythology*, a landmark anthology on feminine figures in the Indian epics.

A co-director of the Jaipur Literature Festival and of Mountain Echoes, the Bhutan literary festival, Gokhale is committed to showcasing literature from across the Indian languages. She currently curates Kitaabnama: Books and Beyond, a multilingual book show on Doordarshan.

GW00728043

Praise for *Travelling In, Travelling Out*

'*Travelling In, Travelling Out* is a collection of 25 travel stories by an exceptionally well-curated list of authors . . . Though the stories are so different from each other . . . there is a feeling of a dissonant unity that makes these stories a cohesive collective. [The book] does exactly what the title suggests. It lets our mind wander where our bodies can't take us. And the journey, I promise, is a marvellous one.' — Ira Trivedi, novelist

'To extend the meaning of travel beyond packing a suitcase and moving to someplace different, HarperCollins has come out with *Travelling In, Travelling Out* . . . [There] is much to browse through in this eclectic collection.' — *Hindu Business Line*

'This collection of essays, finely edited by Namita Gokhale, is not a travel book in the conventional sense.' — Bhaichand Patel, *Outlook*

'The horizon of the book is the world: its essays take the reader from Asia to America to Europe, discovering situations and different ways to travel . . . Gokhale has put together an eclectic collection of 25 stories that are surprising, moving and sometimes mysterious.' — Daniele Pagani, *The Hindu*

'A departure from the traditional travel narrative, this is a unique collection, an anthology for an armchair traveller.' — *The Times of India*

'Namita Gokhale's latest travel anthology examines the word and the world through distinct perspectives. [The book] . . . is a compilation of surprising finds.' — *Bangalore Mirror*

'The readers can cherish the book and this will certainly be a value addition to their collection.' — *The Telegraph*

Travelling In, Travelling Out

A BOOK OF UNEXPECTED JOURNEYS

Edited by Namita Gokhale

HarperCollins *Publishers* India

First published in hardback in India in 2014 by
HarperCollins *Publishers* India

First published in paperback in India in 2015

Anthology copyright © HarperCollins *Publishers* India 2014, 2015
Introduction copyright © Namita Gokhale

Copyright in individual pieces vests with the
respective contributors

P-ISBN: 978-93-5029-145-0
E-ISBN: 978-93-5029-824-4

2 4 6 8 10 9 7 5 3 1

The views and opinions expressed in this book are the contributors' own
and the facts are as reported by them which have been verified to the
extent possible, and the publishers are not in any way liable for the same.

All rights reserved. No part of this publication may be reproduced,
stored in a retrieval system, or transmitted, in any form or by any means,
electronic, mechanical, photocopying, recording or otherwise,
without the prior permission of the publishers.

HarperCollins *Publishers*
A-75, Sector 57, Noida, Uttar Pradesh 201301, India
77-85 Fulham Palace Road, London W6 8JB, United Kingdom
Hazelton Lanes, 55 Avenue Road, Suite 2900, Toronto, Ontario M5R 3L2
and 1995 Markham Road, Scarborough, Ontario M1B 5M8, Canada
25 Ryde Road, Pymble, Sydney, NSW 2073, Australia
195 Broadway, New York, NY 10007, USA

Typeset in 12/15 Goudy Old Style at
SÜRYA

Printed and bound at
Thomson Press (India) Ltd.

Contents

Introduction

Orientations

NAMITA GOKHALE

As a disclaimer, this is not a travel book in the conventional sense. There are few 'voyages of discovery' to be made in our times. The analytical and adjectival traditions of examining 'foreign' cultures have been diluted by the all-knowing interconnectedness of our age. Google Maps has brought the world into our backyard. It's a smaller world, with enforced cosmopolitanism and cheek-by-jowl multiculturalism changing the way we think about faraway peoples and places. The essays in this anthology are more in the nature of everyday explorations and encounters, as also cultural mappings, musings and meditations on the nature of travel.

We are all travelling, all the time. As our small blue planet continues its trajectory around the sun, migratory birds use solar and stellar cues to intuit the magnetic field of the spinning earth. Other migrating animals, like whales and sharks and porpoises, use the unseen magnetic grid and the position of the sun to orientate themselves.

The invention of the compass was perhaps one of the breakthrough moments for the human race. It let sailors navigate by day or through dark cloudy nights, leading to the voyages of discovery and the relentless cycles of trade and conquest which mapped a new economic and political geography.

Clouds too are great travellers. Kalidasa's magnificent *Meghdoot*, literally 'Cloud Messenger', is an early example of fantastical travel writing. Composed around the fourth century CE, it invokes the geography of India with remarkable acuity and poetic perception. It observes its topography, flora and fauna through an aerial view of the landscape from Ramagiri, near Nagpur in central India, to Alakagiri in the extreme north. An exiled *yaksha* sends a message to his wife, using the conceit of describing the sights the compliant cloud will encounter as it wafts towards the high Himalayas:

> Having rested at a bower enjoyed by the forest-dwelling women, then travelling more swiftly when your waters have been discharged, the next stage thence is crossed. You will see the River Reva spread at the foot of mount Vindhya, made rough with rocks and resembling the pattern formed by the broken wrinkles on the body of an elephant . . .
>
> . . . Your showers shed, having partaken of her waters that are scented with the fragrant exudation of forest elephants, and whose flow is impeded by thickets of [snow?] apples, you should proceed. Filled with water, the wind will be unable to lift you, O cloud, for all that is empty is light, while fullness results in heaviness.
>
> Reaching the capital by the name of Vidisha, renowned in all quarters, you will drink the sweet water of the Vetravati river, which roars pleasantly at

the edge of her banks, rippling as if her face bore a frown . . .*

There has been a great deal of scholarly scrutiny of Kalidasa's geography: 'Far in the North, Himalaya, Lord of the Mountains, spanning the wide land from Eastern to Western sea.' These early travel writings often found their sources in the sacred literature of the Puranas, which mapped the landscape of ancient India and South Asia in factual and mythical detail.

Devdutt Pattanaik's essay, which opens the book, is about the ancient Indian concept of travel, 'from place to place and thought to thought'. He writes about the 'parikrama', the ritual circumambulation that mimics the movement of the cosmos and the sacred symbol of the wheel.

To quote:

The Tirthankara is visualized as not wearing clothes. He is Digambar, the sky-clad, a euphemism for naked. Alexander is said to have met a gymnosophist or a naked wise man when he came to India. We can speculate if he met the Tirthankara. Finding him seated, at peace, on a rock, staring at the sky, Alexander asked him, 'What are you doing?' The gymnosophist replied, 'Experiencing nothingness. What about you?' Alexander declared, 'I am conquering the world.' Both laughed. Alexander laughed because he thought the gymnosophist was a fool for not travelling, for not having ambition, for living a life without a destination. The gymnosophist laughed because there are no real destinations in the world. Seated or moving, we are always travelling. And when we keep travelling, we end up returning to the place from where we started: the *parikrama*.

---

*From PoemHunter.com.

Her Majesty the Queen Mother of Bhutan, Ashi Dorji Wangmo Wangchuck, writes about another pilgrimage, a journey into the very soul of the Himalayan mountain kingdom. In 'Village on Treasure Hill', we travel to Nobgang, perched high on a ridge above Punakha Valley, and get a glimpse of an ancient and rooted local culture and way of life.

This is very different indeed from American writer and journalist Marie Brenner's mischievous look at the stereotypes of India as a spiritual destination. 'A Retreat to Holy India' looks at the cushy comforts demanded by the modern mystical tourist. The Sri Lankan writer and television anchor Ashok Ferrey also evokes exotic India in a charming cameo which is a fantastical, farcical, but all too probable story about the imaginary Maharajah of Patragarh.

On a different note, M.J. Akbar's evocative prose takes us to the land of seven hundred hills, at the heart of the Saranda forest, to Singhbhum, the Koyna Valley—through history and geography to the sociology of a new and exploitative greed. 'The beauty only adds to the pain: that there should be poverty in the core of so much that is so gloriously beautiful—the sky, the forest, the land, the laughter, the heart, the sharing, the openness,' he writes.

Akbar's poignant piece was penned in 1986, but it heard the prescient echoes and footfalls of what was to come. Rahul Pandita's powerful piece, excerpted from his book *Hello, Bastar: The Untold Story of India's Maoist Movement*, reports on the displaced idyll, the violent, ideologically fraught landscape of a conflicted present.

In 'A House for Mr Tata: An Old Shanghai Tale' Mishi Saran transports us to no. 458, Wulumuqi North road, an eight-storey office building, across the road from the Shanghai Hotel. She writes:

The office building had sprung up on the site of what used to be, circa 1935, Avan Villa, a grand family home, housing two generations of a Tata clan. The cluster of four smaller villas behind what used to be the big house, accessed from inside the next-door Lane 468 still remain, at nos 24, 26, 28 and 30, and these are what I had come to see.

Traversing the geographies of the past, from Surat to Shanghai to San Francisco, we are introduced to Jehangir Bejan Tata, born 1919, and learn of his Parsi roots and the extraordinary entrepreneurial history of his forebears. The Parsi community, keen shipbuilders, had been deeply involved in the China trade of opium and cotton. This delightful essay journeys across the atlas in search of lost times and places.

At the heart of the book we find the disorienting, somehow disturbing black-and-white images of the Taj Mahal juxtaposed with the Eiffel Tower, the Sistine Chapel and the Statue of Liberty by the famed photographer Dayanita Singh. These pictures were captured at the pandals set up during Durga Puja celebrations in Kolkata. The pandals, a vastly popular form of public art installation, bring the world to their doorstep through tableaus and imaginatively crafted representations. They are another form of travel, both naïve and genuinely questing in scope and concept. Dayanita's genius in rendering the familiar unfamiliar questions the veracity of place and geography, and is a salute to the accidental tourist whom this book celebrates.

The no-man's land of the human imagination is pitted against the barbed wire of political hostilities and high-voltage suspicions of the state machinery. The trauma and paranoia of the security state have vitiated the joys of travel as an experiment in freedom. In 'Fear of Flying', bestselling novelist Advaita Kala recounts her experience of 'being picked up for a pat-down' at JFK. She explicates:

Much like a bug trapped in a jam jar, I stand in the plexi-glass fortified cabin placed for maximum humiliation in the middle of the terminal. But, thankfully, it is decided that I need company and a disgruntled airhostess from our national carrier is escorted in. Yeah, smart pick, Sherlock, like these ladies need another reason to be pissed off.

In 'Lost Without a Trace', Aveek Sen continues in the same vein of dystopian travel tales: 'I needed an American visa . . . The studio was right next to the visa office on Ho Chi Minh Sarani, a schizophrenic street that can't decide whether it is in Calcutta or Washington.' Summoning the visage on the visa photograph, he tells us how he got his 'face back . . . from the man at the computer. Twelve copies, six each of two different sizes, and a reference number for future use.'

Ali Sethi, Pakistani writer and journalist, engages in an introspective examination of the multiple identities implicit in the immigrant experience. 'The Foreigner's Situation' summons the spectres of 'all those who come from outside'—Pakistanis, Arabs, Turks, Afghanis, Somalis—to Copenhagen, 'who had brought their village ideas of social organization and held on to them here, even as they worked the machines in Danish factories and laid out Danish roads, and earned wages which, converting wondrously from Danish kroner to Pakistani rupees, turned the villages they had left behind into towns, the fields into roads and the cattle into cars.'

The 'beloved witch' Ipsita Roy Chakraverti writes of the mysteries of psychic perception. Travel with her, and the Wiccan Brigade, to the haunted medieval village of Bhangarh, near Alwar in Rajasthan.

Aman Nath, prolific author and co-director of the Neemrana 'non-hotel' heritage hotels, illuminates different aspects of Indian aesthetics, including the enduring form and functionality of the *lota*, the brass water pot, 'its rim turned out so well that nothing ever spills as you pour out of it'.

In a story that is as moving as it is horrific, Urvashi Butalia's travel journal portrays the human dimensions of the partition of India and Pakistan, considered the largest cross-migration in history. The magnitude of the tragedy is drawn out in the course of a journey that Butalia undertakes with Bir Bahadur Singh, a refugee from the village of Thoa Khalsa, to the rural landscape of his long-ago childhood.

On 11 March 1947, Sant Raja Singh of Thoa Khalsa village in Rawalpindi district picked up his sword, said a short prayer to Guru Nanak, and then, with one swift stroke, tried to bring it down on the neck of his young daughter, Maan Kaur. As the story is told, at first he didn't succeed: the blow wasn't strong enough, or something came in the way. Then his daughter, aged sixteen, came once again and knelt before her father, removed her thick plait, and offered him her neck. This time, his sword found its mark. Bir Bahadur Singh, his son of eleven, stood by his side and watched. Years later, he recounted this story to me: 'I stood there, right next to him, clutching on to his kurta as children do . . . I was clinging to him, sobbing, and her head rolled off and fell . . . there . . . far away.'

In Butalia's tragic yet cathartic story, the trio of travellers does not ultimately make it to Thoa Khalsa.

Not that we did not try. We did, in a half-hearted way. But it turned out that Thoa Khalsa now fell inside the Pakistan atomic ring and was banned to foreigners. We returned to Delhi the next day, our journey done, the radio programme made, a sort of forgiveness asked and given, Maan Kaur's story once again relegated to the realm of silence.

Geographer and cartographer Manosi Lahiri speaks of maps and map-makers, from the early Indian cosmographers to Ptolemy's 'geography' and the Mecca-centric maps of the Arab world. She gently interrogates the straight lines of political borders. She enquires: 'How were the maps of the Partition of Pakistan and India made? How were the Radcliffe Lines drawn between West Pakistan and India in the west, and East Pakistan and India in the east?'

I myself am a lazy traveller, preferring to read and daydream about distant shores rather than trudge through the cobbled streets of historic towns and heritage sites.

By the law of contraries, I travel constantly, within India and around the world. Wherever I go, I encounter fellow writers, and listen to stories and ideas and arguments. I tend to take in new and changing surroundings with an oblique gaze, being careful not to startle the subject of my scrutiny. As a novelist, what I am seeking is both difference and commonality.

Many years ago, in the course of a reading, Salman Rushdie had declared that 'trees have roots, men have boots'. He was perhaps referring to the diasporic experience, but the phrase stayed with me, changing context and meaning in my mind. The joys of rootedness and the quest for otherness seemed part of a perpetual pendulum of internal and external experience.

The nature of travel, of one foot placed after the other, uphill and downhill, on horseback, or bullock-cart, palanquin or aeroplane, caravanserai or pilgrimage, stimulates both personal and economic growth, measuring out the miles on our spinning planet, rendering the world both a smaller and bigger place.

For my part, I offer some imagined treks through the high

Himalayas, part history, part fancy and intuition—paths I have travelled in my mind's eye.

These mappings will transport you to the heart of South Asia, with all its bewildering contradictions and unsaid truths. There are many jewels and unexpected treasures in this book, startling moments of self-recognition, exterior journeys, interior monologues, subtle shifts of perception. You may hear the click of the change-of-mode moment, sense an approaching epiphany.

Traveller, venture forth . . .

The Idea of Travel

From Place to Place and Thought to Thought

DEVDUTT PATTANAIK

In the Rig Veda, dated conservatively to 1500 BCE, a poet–sage wonders, 'What came first? What existed before the first?' Thus he travels, not physically but mentally, and explores new worlds. Ramana Maharshi, a twentieth-century mystic, reflects this sentiment when he said that from his abode in Arunachalam, he travelled the world. Travel then is not just physical from one place to another, but also mental from one thought to another. The outer journey made sense only when it was accompanied by an inner journey, at least to the rishis, the poet–sages of India, whose hymns make up the venerated Vedas. They were the seers: those who saw what no one else saw.

We do know that the rishis travelled a lot: they travelled from the banks of the River Saraswati in the west to the banks to the River Ganga in the east, when the former dried up; their songs celebrating that once grand river are found in the Vedas. They travelled south from the Gangetic Plains to the river

1

valleys of the Godavari and Kaveri, as we learn from the stories of Agastya and Ram, in the epic Ramayan. They were the first explorers. But they did not travel to conquer; they sought to understand the human condition. In the epic Mahabharat, when the Pandavas are exiled, they are told to follow the path of the rishis, visit holy places, talk to sages and strangers, so as to expand the mind.

Expanding the mind is a constant theme of the Vedas. The hymns constantly evoke the *brahman*, meaning 'the great' or 'the expanded one'. Eventually, the word came to mean God. The term 'brahman' comes from the Sanskrit roots 'brah', meaning to expand, and 'manas', meaning the mind. Brahman then is one of infinitely expanded mind. The brahmin (before it became infamous) referred to that which enables expansion of the mind. It referred to the scriptures that explained mind-expanding rituals, as well as the men who memorized the scripture and the details of the ritual.

The central Vedic ritual called the yagna was a journey that enabled the performer to travel to the realm of the gods, the realm of ideas, and experience ecstasy and immortality that was in short supply in the mundane world. It was perhaps what we now call an adrenaline rush! That is why the hymns simultaneously refer to the stars and the rivers and the forests, as well as to the mind and the senses and the heart. The divide between the physical and mental is so subtle that interpreters are not sure if the Vedic hymns refer to the mundane world or to the metaphysical world. Perhaps they referred to both: as one travelled from place to place, one also travelled from thought to thought. Destination of the long journey over highways, rituals, trade routes and pilgrim trails then was also enlightenment.

Travel acknowledges the impermanence of things: the rejection of the familiar, the constant embrace of the unfamiliar.

All his life, the Buddha kept speaking about impermanence. So it was ironical that after he died in the fifth century BCE, his relics, such as bone, tooth and hair, were placed under mounds of clay and cow dung, which were decorated with parasols and garlands of flowers and transformed into a stupa. People did not want him to go; they wanted the Buddha with them permanently. They walked around this stupa in reverence. This act of circumambulation involved movement without actually going anywhere. The point was to make the mind travel, go around the Buddha and his ideas, appreciate them better. It came to be known as the *parikrama*. This ritual movement of reverence gradually came to be explained metaphysically. For it mimicked the action of the cosmos: all things go around to come around. Everything is cyclical, like the seasons.

It was in the time of the Buddha that the wheel became a sacred symbol. He is visualized as a spoked wheel in early Buddhist artworks dated to 100 BCE. It symbolizes the mind that wanders out of suffering to bliss, out of desire to peace, out of bondage to freedom. The hub of this wheel represents stillness of the mind, and the rim represents awareness, both created through meditation based on Buddhist principles, represented by the spokes of the wheel.

The wheel has been part of ancient India since Harappan times. Pulled by donkeys, oxen and horses, it allowed people to move from place to place. It led to trade and it enabled imperial ambitions. And so by the Mauryan period, the wheel became the symbol of royalty. It indicated the wheels of the royal chariot that can travel freely to the edges of the world, for all that can be seen was under the control of the sovereign universal emperor, the Chakravarti, master of the wheel.

This was most evident in the activities of Ashoka, the Mauryan emperor who reigned in the third century BCE. Royal laws

travelled from the hub, his capital city of Pataliputra in the
Gangetic Plains, north to Gandhara, modern Afghanistan, and
south to Andhra Pradesh. The extent of his power is indicated
by his edicts that were carved out in stone. He encouraged
monks and nuns to travel to different parts of the world to
spread the word of the Buddha. Travel takes a new form: not
the search for a new home, not raids into other people's lands,
not the quest for trade, but the transmission of ideas.

The ideas of both empire and proselytization seem rather
alien to the Indian way of thinking, which has been more
inward-looking, and one wonders if these ideas were inspired by
the actions of Alexander the Great, who overthrew the great
empire of the Persian emperors and shook up the world of his
times. Perhaps he inspired the three-fold division of worthy
beings (*shalaka purushas*) of Jain thought: the heroic Vasudeva
who is action-oriented, the regal Chakravarti who is policy-
oriented, and the wise Tirthankara who is thought-oriented.

Tirthankara was the supreme sage of the Jain canon, who
conquers the mind and discovers 'tirtha', the ford that takes
one to the other side of the river. He travels differently, like the
Buddha, from the world of matter to the world of the mind,
from the realm of things to the realm of thoughts, from the
arena of conflict to the arena of peace.

The Tirthankara is visualized as not wearing clothes. He is
Digambar, the sky-clad, a euphemism for naked. Alexander is
said to have met a gymnosophist or a naked wise man when he
came to India. We can speculate if he met the Tirthankara.
Finding him seated, at peace, on a rock, staring at the sky,
Alexander asked him, 'What are you doing?' The gymnosophist
replied, 'Experiencing nothingness. What about you?' Alexander
declared, 'I am conquering the world.' Both laughed. Alexander
laughed because he thought the gymnosophist was a fool for

not travelling, for not having ambition, for living a life without a destination. The gymnosophist laughed because there are no real destinations in the world. Seated or moving, we are always travelling. And when we keep travelling, we end up returning to the place from where we started: the *parikrama*.

Should we sit then, or should we keep moving? Should we be in repose or should we be restless? Should we root ourselves or should we travel? The hermit was advised to never stay in one place for more than a night, except during Chaturmaas, the four months of the heavy rainy season. The householders stayed in one place, in the village, but were advised to go on a pilgrimage at least once in a lifetime.

European scholars have always argued that India as a concept does not exist; it was created by the British. They are thinking materially, as is the Western wont. But the idea of Bhaarat (the land of the Bharat clan) is an ancient one, known to every Indian. It is not a political entity, but it is certainly an economic entity well known to pilgrims and traders. It was created by the pilgrim trail and marked by mobile marketplaces or *melas*, where people came together to worship, bathe, trade and talk. This diamond-shaped land was described as Jambu-dvipa, the continent shaped like a roseapple. The Persians called it Hind, located beyond the River Hind, which the Greeks called Indus. It was a land watered by rivers, foremost of which was the great Ganga and its many tributaries. It expanded south beyond the Vindhyas.

In the ancient chronicles (contrary to beliefs of European Orientalists), there are no tales of people migrating from the west of the Indus to the east of the Ganga, but there are many tales of kings and sages, even mountains and rivers, travelling from the north to the south. The Bhagavat Puran describes how Krishna migrates from the Gangetic Plains to the coast of

Gujarat. The Ramayan describes how Prince Ram leaves Ayodhya and travels to the shores of the sea and beyond. It also describes the travails of a sage called Agastya who makes the Vindhya bend as he moves southwards. Agastya carries with him a pot containing the waters of the Ganga; a crow tips the pot and out comes the River Kaveri, which then in essence becomes the southern version of the Ganga. Shiva lives in the north, atop Mount Kailas and his son, Kartikeya, after a fight with his father moves south where he mourns the absence of the mountains. And so his mother, Shakti, sends him mountain peaks, carried south on a sling by the rakshasa Hidimba. The mountains of the south thus become southern versions of the Himalayas. On the southern tip of India stands Kanyakumari, the eternal virgin, waiting for her groom, Shiva, to make the trip south and marry her but the gods prevent this—for as long as Kanyakumari stays virgin, she will remain rooted to the tip of the land, preventing the sea from overwhelming the sacred continent.

Dotted across India are temples of gods and goddesses, sages and kings. When one visits one place, one is asked to visit another, as if one relative feels the other should not be neglected. So when you travel north to Badari where Vishnu resides, you have to travel to Kedar where Shiva resides, or if you travel south to Tirupati where Vishnu resides, you must travel to Kalahasti where Shiva resides. Along with the pilgrims, the gods travel too: Vishnu bathes in Rameshwaram, holds court in Dwarka, meditates at Badari and eats at Puri, the four dhams or sacred locations associated with his worship. Shiva travels to the twelve *jyotir-lingas*, his sacred spots, every month on Shiva-ratri, the last day of the waning moon.

When the gods do not travel, the world comes to an end. Thus Vishnu's sleep on the coils of the serpent Shesha marks *pralaya*, the end of the world, before its regeneration. An abbreviated form of this happens during Chaturmaas, the four months of the monsoons, when the gods sleep and travel stops. When Vishnu wakes up, he climbs upon Garuda, the eagle, and travels across the world solving problems, restoring order and ensuring the world functions normally. Sometimes he has to descend (*avatarana* in Sanskrit) and take forms (*avatar*) as various animals and humans to set things right. Thus the gods are always on tour.

This idea is ritualized in temple festivals. For most of the year, the devotee goes into the temple to visit the deity. But at least once a year, the deity comes out and travels through the city, in every lane, visiting the houses of devotees. This is called the *digvijay yatra*, the conquest of the cardinal and ordinal directions, by the god-king who ensures that all his subjects are happy and at peace. The deity travels with his consort either on a palanquin or on a chariot. The grandest of these travel festivals is the *ratha yatra* of Jagannath Puri in Odisha which takes place at the start of the monsoon season. The deity, Krishna, with his siblings, elder brother Balabhadra and younger sister Subhadra, travels on three grand chariots to the house of his aunt and he stays there for ten days before returning home to an angry wife, Lakshmi, who is furious he went on a trip without her. To pacify her, he has to give her gifts.

The chariot wheel is always rolling for the gods. Krishna travels out of Vrindavan on the chariot of Akrura. Ram travels out of Ayodhya on the chariot of Sumantra. Devotees hope that one day, God will come back. Krishna does not keep the promise; Ram does.

No essay on travel is complete without considering Narad, the travelling sage, who moves between heaven and earth, gossiping with gods and kings and sages, never restful, always moving, constantly creating conflicts, stirring emotions, and compelling all to engage with the world.

The story goes that he was born of Brahma's imagination. He was therefore called Brahma's *manas-putra*, or mind-born son. And as soon as he was born, he saw no point in being part of the material world. He sought wisdom and liberation from material bondage and encouraged all his brothers to do so. Thus creation came to a halt; all of Brahma's children refused to engage with life. Brahma was angry. He cursed Narad that he would be forever trapped in the material world; he would have to keep moving from one realm to another until the world comes to an end. And so he travels up and down, here and there, restless and anxious, entertaining himself by provoking people and hoping they will realize that life has a bigger picture, with many more paths, not just the one they tread on, with many more destinations, not just the one they seek, each one valid to someone.

His appearance in a tale marks the beginning of some mischief. He tells wives about the adulterous dalliances of their husbands. He tells kings about the glory of other kingdoms. He warns people about the intentions of their relatives. And his well-meaning conversations make people envious or angry. As emotions are spurred, decisions are taken, often foolish decisions which lead to quarrels that only God can resolve. Thus God has to travel down from heaven to solve the problem and that makes Narad happy. Brahma may have stopped his journey towards God but he can get God to come to him with all his pranks.

The existence of a character like Narad draws attention to the eternal conflict in Indian thought: What is the point of life? Is it achievement? Is it time-pass and entertainment? Or is it about understanding and wisdom? No clear answer is given. What is demanded is engagement—the ascetic has to travel either mentally or physically. Stillness is rejected and movement favoured. The mind has to expand, the experiences have to broaden; we must appreciate the billion stars in the sky and not be satisfied with a single constellation.

And for that, it is important to leave the comforts of the palace and travel to the forest and return to the palace. The story of the Buddha tells us of a sheltered prince who has known only luxury and pleasure in his life. In his first journey outside the palace, he sees for the first time old age, disease and death, and this transforms him. Full of agitation, he seeks an answer to the misery of life. This compels him to abandon his newborn child and wife and go to the forest, where, after years of search and contemplation and conversation and meditation, he discovers wisdom to become the Buddha, the enlightened one. He travels out of the palace and finds liberation.

In Jain tradition too we have stories of kings and noblemen renouncing the palace and going to the mountains and caves to become sages.

Hindu stories are different: there is the journey of the king to the forest and then return as a wiser king. In the Ramayan, Ram is exiled and he returns home after fourteen years, after defeating Ravan, and ascends the throne to be a great king. He returns a different man, for the forest teaches him what the city cannot. He learns how rules and boundaries do not exist in the forest and how they do in cities and how their existence benefits the weak, as also that they can create victims who are crushed by the system. In the Mahabharat, the Pandavas are forced to spend thirteen years in the forest, and when they return they are stronger, smarter, humbler and wiser, having learned from sages, tribals and animals the meaning of what it takes to be good kings.

Thus the parikrama from the point of origin back to the point of origin transforms us. But this takes place not once, as in Western hero myths such as the Odyssey, but again and again. For Hindu thought is eternal and cyclical. Ram does not live his life once; he lives the same life again and again as the wheel of time rotates. Neither death nor wisdom has a full stop. There are only commas—no destinations, only waiting rooms.

Hindu gods keep travelling. And so they have mounts: Shiva travels on a bull, Brahma on a goose, Durga on a tiger, Ganesha on a rat, Kartikeya on a peacock, the sun on a horse, the moon on an antelope, Indra on an elephant, Ganga on a dolphin, Yamuna on a turtle.

The Ramayan speaks of travelling from Ayodhya through Chitrakut, Panchavati, Kishkindha, Rameshwaram to Lanka. The Bhagavat Puran speaks of Krishna travelling from Mathura to Gokul to Vrindavan to Madhavan to Mathura again and then to Dwarka, Hastinapur, Indraprastha and finally Kurukshetra. Shiva travels from Kailas to Kashi. We humans are also travelling. When we die we cross the Vaitarani and enter Pitr-loka, the land of the dead. And when it is time to be reborn we cross the river once again to be reborn through the wombs of our mothers.

Life then is a travel. Across India is the belief that to be born human one has to pass through 8.4 million wombs of various creatures. This makes human life special. And the point of human life is to travel from ignorance to wisdom. In ignorance there is fear. In wisdom there is peace and tranquillity. For that we have to engage with the world, form relationships and break them, buy and sell in the marketplace, leave the palace, go to the forest and return to the palace. We have to let the still serpent uncoil and rise up from the base of our spine through the spinal cord until it unfurls like a lotus with a thousand petals on top of our head. And when we reach the mountain peak, lest we assume we were there first, we will be told the story of Bharat, the first Chakravarti, after whom India is called Bhaarat. When he reached the top, his so-called destination, he saw flags of other kings who had reached there before him, and he was shown another horizon awaiting conquest. It will never end—there is always somewhere to go in this limitless universe.

The Maharajah of Patragarh

ASHOK FERREY

INTRODUCTION

Some years ago, I took my wife on holiday to the Golden Triangle in Rajasthan. It was her birthday treat. Having seen the Taj Mahal, both in the evening and at dawn—when it seemed to float magically in the mist, defying gravity—we headed off to Jaipur. Several days later we drove back to Delhi, visiting various small Rajasthani forts along the way. It must have been at one of these that the seeds of this story planted themselves in my mind. I was napping in the car on the way back when this story was born, almost fully formed, sentence upon sentence, phrase upon phrase. It is very rarely that this occurs to a writer, and when it does it is nothing short of a miracle. And that is probably why this story holds such a special place in my heart. Back in Delhi I scribbled it down in an exercise book and brought it home to Colombo.

A writer always asks the question: *What if?* He takes reality as it is presented to him in the farmyard, wrings its neck, and watches its headless body screeching around the yard, flapping its wings, making an unearthly racket. And it is this dance of death that interests him—not the actual truth itself, which is alive and boringly well, and probably settling in for the night back in the chicken coop.

So if there is any maharajah out there, living in a small castle in Rajasthan, who thinks this story is about you, I do apologize unreservedly. It is *not* about you; though it so easily might have been, if only I had had a say in the unfolding of your fate!

(Colombo, 2012)

THE MAHARAJAH OF PATRAGARH

The Maharajah of Patragarh was dreaming again. He sat on the roof of his sandstone castle taking in the early morning sun on a splendid reclining chair. The chair was curved in an elongated S-shape, rather like a magic carpet about to unfurl in preparation for flight. And in a sense this is exactly what it was, for when the maharajah sat there, it allowed his mind to roam far and free over the eight long centuries of his family's existence.

And what an existence! How many invasions there had been in that time! The Mughal emperors of Old Delhi, the English viceroys of New—Patragarh had turned its back firmly on all of them. His richer, grander cousins—rulers of neighbouring states—had cosied and cuddled for all they were worth, the taste of Cherry Blossom on their lips, reaping honours and rewards far beyond their wildest dreams. How they had squabbled among themselves over the order of their precedence, the size of their gun salutes! A classroom of overgrown schoolboys before their imperial schoolmaster.

The Maharajah of Patragarh had asked for nothing. And that is precisely what he had got.

While he slept the maharajah's mind flew free as a bird over the remaining extent of his property. It wasn't a large castle, an acre at most, surrounded by a moat. But it was built in the purest Hindu style with splendid bo-leaf battlements, and pinnacled domes inside each turret. There was no flirtation here with the prevailing Islamic Mughal fashion, the white marble with its inlaid pietra dura that had so easily seduced his cousins. None of the tawdry tinsel, the gaudy mirror work that adorned their bigger, flashier palaces. His small rooms were mostly painted in the slightly sharp, high colours of the eighteenth century.

His cousins kept abreast of the times. (It was easy to do when you had the money.) They had air-conditioning. He had cross-ventilation. As far as *he* was concerned, it was enough. His household froze in winter and baked in summer. But they had been freezing and baking for eight centuries. It was nothing new.

The maharajah sighed in his sleep as his mind's eye saw the cracked sandstone slabs of his roof. The dome in one of the turrets had been demolished in his father's day to make way for a galvanized iron water tank. It gave the castle a curiously lopsided air. How he longed to rebuild that dome!

But the moat was dry now. A single bedraggled peacock picked disconsolately at the weeds in its bed. It was all so difficult. If you were a maharajah, by virtual definition you were fabulously wealthy. So how could you tell people you were down to your last castle? They would laugh.

The Maharajah of Patragarh stirred uneasily and opened his eyes, and as he did, the chimes of a Meissen clock floated up from the courtyard below. Nine o'clock. He rose with difficulty to his feet. He was not as young as he used to be and every day it got more difficult. But then he remembered eight centuries of the bluest of blue Hindu blood coursing through his veins and his back straightened imperceptibly.

'*Show time*,' he said.

The young Sri Lankan couple was in India on honeymoon. Five nights and six days in the Golden Triangle the agent had advertised. He had unaccountably failed to mention the average age of the tour which was about eighty-seven. Five nights and six days of detailed and non-stop discussions on arthritis and bowel movements, hip replacements and incontinence. Even at the Taj Mahal, in the heart of the no-pollution zone, talk had very quickly descended to the sordid matter of Mrs Marawila's loose motions. It had been a relief to pay extra and get away for the day.

The white Ambassador car bumped across the dry moat and came to a stop outside the immensely high doorway studded with iron nails.

'I wonder if some loony old maharajah will come roaring out with a loaded shotgun?' the boy joked with the girl. But in the event the small doorway cut into the large one was opened by a dignified old retainer in a smart red coat and turban.

He bowed. 'The tickets are twenty rupees each but you can pay at the end. Let me take you round first.'

'The sort of *cook-appu* every decent house should have,' the girl whispered.

They took in the small throne room with its faux gilt furniture, overlooked by the narrow gallery curtained in muslin where women of the house sat in purdah. They were shown the little Chinese desk from which the maharajah had run his country of a few hundred square miles. There was a table for sixteen in the dining room, but the furniture was of that plain serviceable sort you find in up-country estate bungalows. Strangely, there were no photographs anywhere.

They ascended the narrow ramp to the roof.

It was the splendid chair that first attracted their attention.

'Oh look!' the girl said to the boy. Then they noticed the elderly figure in jam-jar glasses snoring gently, his face turned towards the weak rays of the mid-morning sun.

'Is that . . . surely it can't be the . . .?'

'Certainly not,' said the old retainer rather quickly. 'That's Nath, his faithful manservant. His Highness is away at one of his other palaces.'

'Can I take a picture?'

The retainer put his finger to his lips. 'Of course. But please don't wake him up. At this time of his life he really needs his sleep.'

They looked out over the battlements at the town, a sea of small dust-coloured houses with flat roofs. A little boy on a neighbouring roof waved at them.

'Girl!' he shouted in thin, clear, piercing tones. 'Girl! What your name? Where you from?'

'Where exactly *are* you from?' the retainer asked them.

'Sri Lanka,' the boy replied.

'Oh, I remember . . . I remember His Highness telling us. When he was up at Cambridge as a young man, he had a Sri Lankan friend. He went over there once for the holidays, to a house in Colombo. And he was so impressed with Sri Lankan hospitality he gifted them a Jaguar when he left.'

The boy laughed. 'And the jaguar gobbled up every living creature in the house, I suppose?'

But the old retainer was lost in thought for a moment. There was water in his rheumy eyes. 'It was a Jaguar motor car,' he said softly.

Downstairs they paid the forty rupees for their two tickets. The old retainer wouldn't hear of a tip. But the young girl with her sharp Sri Lankan eyes had noticed the nondescript furniture. She had seen the enamel basins put out to catch the leaks in the sandstone roof.

'Please,' she said. 'I'd like to contribute something to the upkeep of this amazing building. I know it can't be easy.'

'His Highness wouldn't hear of it,' was the sharp reply.

The girl shrugged and turned to go.

'But if you really want to help, there's Nath up there. You noticed the glasses he was wearing. Cataract in both eyes. We're raising a collection for the operation.'

'Of course, my pleasure!' The girl handed over a thousand-rupee note.

The Ambassador bumped away over the rutted track carrying the young couple back to civilization, and the Problems of Incontinence in Sri Lanka Today. The retainer watched them go. Then he mounted the ramp to the roof.

That was the worst about living in a castle. The heights. Every year the climbing got a little more difficult.

He reached the sleeping figure on the roof and stood over him for a moment, watching. But the sleeper woke with a start and in one fluent movement that belied his advanced years he sank to the ground.

'Maharaj-ji, Maharaj-ji,' he mumbled, kissing the other's feet and the edge of his red coat. 'It's so good of you to let me sleep up here in your chair all day, in this the evening of my years.' The other touched the top of his head, the signal that he could rise in the royal presence. 'Go down to the kitchens,' he said gently. 'Your lunch will be getting cold. Oh, and you can take off those ridiculous glasses now. You'll go blind if you wear them too long.'

A Retreat to Holy India

MARIE BRENNER

Her swami said everything she needed was within, but along the way Marie Brenner also discovered the cushy comforts of holy India for the five-star set.

THE YOGA OF IMPERISHABLE REALITY, 5 MARCH 2008

Okay, I am trying to practise stillness. It is my first morning at Shreyas Retreat, a yoga resort about an hour from Bengaluru. I am late for chanting class. I am trying not to hyperventilate. On the flight from Kochi I had resolved to give up my wheelie bag of wants, desires and judgements. I am, I tell my yogi, Krishna Prakash, going to dedicate myself to the benefit of all sublime living beings. I am going to get way beyond my sense of ego and self-centredness. But can Krishna arrange a driver to get me through the rutted roads to Puttaparthi, to the Mahashivaratri celebration at the Sai Baba ashram? Tens of thousands are expected to show up for the ageing holy man, who still packs them in, and I don't want to miss it. 'Madam! Shiva's birthday today! Impossible to get prayer pass at Sai Baba's temple. Sai Baba producing a lingam from his mouth! He promises a miracle! He has a need to be colourful. Madam! Roads are impossible. Sai Baba is four hours away.'

'So many wants, no wonder you are lost.' The voice of the universal yogi plays like an endless spool in my head. I collapse on a mat. 'This morning we are mastering the chanting of the bee,' an instructor announces, speaking in the odd, formal style of the subcontinent, a low mumble of marbles in the mouth. The Bhramari, he explains, is a breathing technique favoured by holy men and hedge-fund managers from Mumbai feeling much stress about the crash in the Indian stock market. 'Great relief in this noise,' he says, 'a long vibrato and chant that buzzes and vibrates up the nostrils, through the ears.'

Bzzz bzzz, bzzz bzz bzzz. Bzz bzz.

The banging and the car horns and the drums from the local village shatter the morning stillness. I try to keep my mind focused on the buzz and the breathing and the nearby grove of banana trees and shut out the *vritti*, the monkey mind of conflicting thoughts such as, 'How long would it take to drive to the city and check out the new designer department store Folio?'

After class I walk with Krishna down a long path towards the organic garden. 'Who was your teacher?' I ask him. Was Krishna a follower of the distinguished late Swami Rama? Or the late Swami Vivekananda, who cruised the West towards the end of the nineteenth century, sharing the teachings of the Bhagavad Gita? Or a more current swami, the eighty-two-year-old cricketer Parthasarathy, who identifies himself in his brochures as an esteemed YPO resource? Or perhaps Amma, the hugging saint?

There is silence. Then Krishna fixes me with the opaque gaze that expresses a kaleidoscope of emotions and explains that his teacher was Sri Shankar Narayan, whom he met in 1997 in Delhi while completing a postgraduate degree in business management. He tells me he is self-publishing a new book on the Gita. 'I have a unique title!' he says. 'I will deliver it to your room.'

THE PULL (AND PUSH) OF INDIA

To get to Shreyas from the Middle East, I had landed not at Bengaluru's international airport but in Kochi, formerly Cochin, in the glorious south of India. It is March. India is perhaps the only country where the landing card has three boxes to choose from in the Purpose of Trip category: Business, Tourist, Spiritual. We drifted down to the tarmac into a rosy sunset and an uplifting sight—a line of white Ambassadors with drivers holding up signs: CHATTERJEE, BANERJEE, SHARMA, SINGH, HOLY BIBLE ASSOCIATION, WELCOME!

The pull of India immediately took me across. For the past few years I have been filling notebooks with scenes of the new globalization. But in none of my previous trips to India have I ever been to an ashram. Not the traditional dusty holes where the mice scramble over your feet and you are awakened at four in the morning, where you sit for twelve hours chanting and scrub toilets to get to holiness. Nor to five-star retreats like Shreyas in the south or Ananda in the Himalayas where, it is said, Richard Gere, Russian oligarchs and Bollywood beauties can be found. So I leapt when my editor at *Departures* shot me an email with the following assignment: 'Hey, how about *Eat, Pray, Love* for the hot flash set?'

On the road to Shreyas, child barbers with neatly appointed stands share the sidewalk with powdered-paint vendors ramping up for the Holi festival, the mass paint fight of Dhulendi and spring celebration that overtakes the country every March.

India is defined by its villages but also by the roads that connect them. Blow-horn trucks covered in vibrant murals compete for space with motor scooters. Women in pink-and-yellow cling to the drivers, their dupattas sailing in the wind. Pigs, oxen, yellow-green autorickshaws like bright beetles scurry home. Diesel fumes and dust mix with the fragrance of incense sticks and moist flowers from the temple down the road. We pass villages of grey cement storefronts and square brick houses, men napping on woven cots, and women carrying bundles of dried dung cakes, used for fuel, on their heads.

In the cities the zooming young professionals and intellectuals watch news analyses and talk shows on news channels and use the word 'deracination' at dinner parties to define their fear that all the sweeping changes will strip India of its cultural identity. The term you hear everywhere is 'branding'. Big-name Western status symbols have kept the middle class in a buying frenzy.

Some of the country's elite are wary of—even snobbish about—Western-style consumerism, though. There's a movement to fight the shopping malls, the branding, the invasion of Bottega Veneta, the luxury conferences and the Louis Vuitton cakes that are this season's chic centrepieces for Delhi hostesses. In a recent column in *Time Out Mumbai*, the economist Gaurav Mishra described his own personal backlash against materialism. He resolved to give up everything he owned for a year ('All the accumulated acquisitions of an intellectual yuppie'), along with his sea-facing house and fast-track job, in order to negate the corrupting addiction to the things that accompany prosperity.

Most Indians are not burdened with an excess of consumer goods, of course. Yet, at the moment here, there's a troubling fad of reinterpreting Holy India for the five-star crowd. There has always been a thriving centre of rationalist entrepreneurs, scientists and secularists who know how to turn trends into quick profits. How else to understand the empires established by the platoons of nouveau billionaires: the geniuses behind computer giant Infosys, call centres, Bollywood, vast industries of pharmaceuticals, and Amma, the plump hugger of Kerala who tours the world and, more than twenty-five million hugs later, has built hospitals, schools and computer centres with the profits.

Now Shreyas has adopted the empowerment slogans from the West. The journey of self-discovery replaces the Sanskrit terms that have always lured seekers. What we are talking about is cashing in on *turiya*, the highest state of consciousness, much favoured by the poet Allen Ginsberg, who was in and out of the ashrams of Rishikesh before the Beatles were. It is a state most recently explored by the writer Elizabeth Gilbert, who details her experience in the captivating memoir *Eat, Pray, Love*. Surely, a glimmer of turiya is worth the twenty-two-hour flight. But all this way for something I can get in California?

Close your eyes at places like the Oberoi resorts outside Jaipur and Udaipur and you are on a Bollywood set, the texture of India replaced by the unnerving, ersatz, Americanized cartoonishness of lawn sweepers in Kerala costumes, with bowing staff in kurtas and turbans raining namastes on the Butterfield & Robinson crowd. These new resorts remind me of a scene in a Broadway musical: *Kerala!* They are posh, for sure, but they are India without the Indianness. The ragged joy and dusty grandeur and inconvenience are smoothed out in Pixar colours.

At first I find it disconcerting to pull into Shreyas, one of the Indian destination resorts touted by swanky specialists. It rises like a tumour of the new globalization, a Golden Door amid the rubble of villages. Nearby, trains on their way north to Punjab howl past. Hundreds of passengers hang off the trains, a timeless scene. A long beige wall separates Shreyas from the chaos of the road, then a gate opens to reveal vistas of gardens, staff gliding quietly to lead me to my room. I arrive at night. There is an arc of silence, as if I have wandered into an ashram in mid-darshan. 'Where is everyone?' I ask Krishna, who walks me down a path by a pool.

'Madam, it is a little quiet right now,' he replies.

'Am I the only guest?'

'There are two others,' he says, 'but they leave tomorrow for two days.' Mystery surrounds this announcement.

My room is comfortable but not luxurious, with a devotional from the Bhagavad Gita on the wall. In the bathroom is a vase of tuberoses and a view out to the pool, a stack of books on the Gita, and a few suggested yoga classes and massage sessions. The next morning the staff knocks frequently to see if I want another glass of freshly squeezed juice. Across the road the village of Nelamangala is preparing for the Shiva festival that will take place the following day.

There is nothing casual about the event. The place will shut down for two days, and the clamour of horns and drums breaks the morning meditations, interrupting our flow towards brahmacharya, the exalted state in which I must learn to shun all thoughts vulgar and all things mundane. I try not to think of the moral implications of trying to get to this high state of consciousness at a resort that costs $500 a night, more money than millions of Indians make in a year of hard labour.

Krishna is one of the millions in the new India who are scrambling, driven by big plans. The phrase you hear to describe them is Nobel Prize-winning economist Amartya Sen's 'the Jews of the next century'. He could be thinking of Krishna, for whom the Bhagavad Gita, a central text of Hinduism, presents a path not just to inspiration but also to aspiration. Krishna is not daunted by the fact that in Delhi today there is a geyser of new books on the Gita, with its principles of holy non-attachment and prayer reinterpreted into work-is-worship themes to suit the country's new busyness. In some segments of India, devotionals have been almost eclipsed by concerns of global ambitions. The hot-button mantra is 'work'.

The new Indian Tony Robbins figures—Swami Parthasarathy, Sadhguru J. Vasudev of the Isha Foundation—fascinate me with their hard sell, which has morphed for today's global economy. You see and hear them at conferences, flying with their entourages in white kurtas to YPO sessions at the Aspen Institute and the World Economic Forum in Davos.

'I don't read the Gita,' Sadhguru told me the first time I met him. He was staying with a large group way outside Delhi near Gurgaon, a sprawling new city of malls and corporate headquarters. I found him in a golf club development that was being thrown up by a property lord. He's a golfer and a schmoozer who brags about his perfect memory and sports a Santa Claus beard, rapper sunglasses, a T-shirt, and a definite weight issue. All around him baby boomers and yuppie Indians were hyperventilating into a trance with a breathing technique perfected at his foundation. Would I like to attend a $1,800 VIP session for three days in California to learn it? 'I just turned over my property to Sadhguru,' one man said at lunch. 'I feel so cleansed. I am proud he has a centre in what was once my home in Delhi. And that my family and I can be of service.'

Krishna's eyes shine with parallel possibility. When we meet he had been up for days, typing PowerPoint presentations into a computer from the tiny office at Shreyas. There is nothing in his particular circumstance—a small house, unpaved streets— that will stop his wellspring of driving hope and ambition, the centre-of-the-universe engine that propels the new India into the middle class. It is a small leap into a bright future fuelled by dreams honed in tiny houses and small schools where students eat a government meal of daal and chapattis off banana leaves and plot how to ace a standard exam to qualify for Banaras Hindu University.

THE JOURNEY BEGINS, CA 2004

Back then the Chanel boutique at the Imperial hotel in New Delhi had not yet made its way to India, but malls and luxury brands were beginning to appear.

'They want me to go white-water rafting in Rishikesh! What do I wear?' I hear the voice in a tiny sports shop in Khan Market, near an exclusive residential area of Delhi. We are in the early days of the new globalization and the puppy (Punjabi urban princess) is out shopping with her mother-in-law and husband. Outside the market the drivers of Delhi ladies wait by their cars. On the sidewalk the guy with no legs and a dhoti cruises up and down on his wheelie board greeting strawberry sellers. I have gone in search of a bathing suit, which was still kept then, for modesty's sake, out of sight, wrapped in plastic in the storeroom. The puppy frets about what is appropriate to wear for rafting down the Ganges. 'I will get soaked!' she says. 'I have read about this practice!'

The first signs of India about to Diet are just on the horizon. For generations the traditional workout for elite women here has been yoga asanas and slow walks around the park. The notion of exercise, of body obsession, was limited to Bollywood stars and anyone who came in and out of the West. No one minded the pillowy midriffs that peeked through saris on the buffet lines.

'What is this white-water rafting, madam?' I watch the sombre clerk pinwheel into incomprehension, then offer a voluminous pleated tracksuit that went out of fashion in the early days of disco. 'Something like this, madam?' he asks.

I cannot stop myself: 'But you'll get drenched! Wear a bathing suit with a shirt over it.' I am met with a polite, icy silence. Uh-oh, I have stepped over the forbidden line. She offers her credit card and walks out with yards of nylon, moving slowly, as if through gel.

The following year the first of a new breed of weight-training studios are set up in Mumbai. A small spa opens with a flourish in the centre of town. A line of beggars is outside the door.

The interior is impeccable, practically antiseptic. A woman in white touts 'the first wheatgrass juice machine in India!' With great fanfare she opens a nearby refrigerator to show me wheatgrass imported from the West, vacuum-packed like beluga caviar. Could luxe yoga retreats be far behind? Shreyas, with its screening room stocking complete sets of *Frasier* DVDs and a flatscreen that beams in CNN India, is a long psychic journey from the mass twelve-hour in-breath, out-breath sessions that once tortured *vipassana* acolytes in spartan cubicles looking for enlightenment.

THE ONE-POINTED MIND, 9 MARCH 2008

I have been up late at Shreyas, reading the Ishopanishad, one of the shortest of the Upanishads, a classic text of Vedanta. It has been left by my bed, and inside it someone has circled the definition of *nishkama karma*, action without desire for rewards. This state, according to Swami Rama, is made possible by selflessness and the feeling of oneness with all. So I am trying to get out of my New York habit of looking around this spa and trying to understand why I am, more or less, the only guest.

There is a card in my room that says, 'The prime purpose of your stay at Shreyas is (a) to learn yoga processes or (b) to learn more about integrating yoga in your life.' How to explain to Krishna and the well-meaning Shreyas staff that within a five-block area of my Manhattan house there are classes all day long in every kind of yoga—Ashtanga, Vinyasa, Bikram—in a dozen studios? That there is an entire world of women who practise power yoga and warrior flow and that the industry in America is thriving? Ahead of me at Shreyas is a four-day schedule of Ayurvedic possibilities, a few gentle Vinyasa classes (a workout in which I will try my headstand with the staff), languorous strolls to the local village to serve meals at the government school, and a cooking lesson from Rajan, a superb organic chef who was once employed by the Indian embassy. Like all chefs, even in the new India that officially shuns the caste system, he is surely a Brahmin, barefoot in the kitchen, the shrine of holy food.

I soon fall into a routine, giving myself over to the lack of real activity. I avoid the tiny gym with its wheezing treadmill, opting for desultory jogs on the running path. Using any excuse, I try to lure Krishna to take me on walks through the rice fields outside the walls so I can take pictures of the murals of Air India jets, Hindi-English word charts, and the enigmatic smile of Gandhi decorating the local school. The high point is at 11 a.m. when the staff meets for yoga in their street clothes. I join and try to vanish into invisibility, hoping they will ignore the *firengi*, whom they ordinarily treat like a Ming vase. Then it is time for a Balinese massage in a small shack with an outdoor shower and, afterward, a real test of my lack of discipline, in the form of the lunch feast at a table set for one. The afternoon offers a stirring session of yoga *nidra*, a form of deep relaxation, and then the hard decision: do I lounge in the special gazebo in the vegetable garden or by the pool? The Shreyas magic begins to take over. I hear that voice again in my head saying 'Everything you need is within.'

Am I really going to be the only guest? As I write, I am being stared at by Santosh Kumar, who would be cast in a Bollywood spa drama as the Faithful Manservant Always by Your Side. He is driving me a bit crazy, I have to admit, though I am devoted to his care and his exquisite flower arrangements. Santosh seems to have an additional goal: Can the firengi gain four pounds in four days? At the moment, he bombs me with extra dosas that squirt butter, tempts me with the freshest chutney of grated coconut. My diet worksheets from Jordan Carroll, Upper East Side nutritionist, have slipped under the bed as I collapse under the shower of cashews and vats of cardamom rice pudding. At breakfast, lunch and dinner I cannot resist the long white table with rose petals strewn across the linen. Santosh, trained in hotel management at Bangalore Academy, stands at one side, waiting. More *dosas?* Cashews? *Chiku* fruit?

Santosh is not forthcoming about the rumoured other guests. But soon two slim Brits with shaggy hair appear, looking like sleepy puppies. They mumble their names, Zak and Sharna. I wonder, are they celebrity rockers hiding out from fans? At breakfast Zak mumbles again, 'I am a musician.' And Sharna sings. Hmm. No clues there. They mention this is their first trip to India, whomped up with two days' notice by punching 'yoga retreat India' into Google. Shreyas's was the first site to come up. And by the way, they are off to Sai Baba's retreat.

I fight off a powerful stirring of envy. How come them and not me? How do I get on his Shiva celebration list of VIPs? Zak turns out to be Zak Starkey, drummer for The Who and Oasis and son of Ringo Starr, whom he resembles. By the age of twelve he was performing publicly, a fact he announces softly, with hooded eyes. It is a clear signal to steer the conversation away from all matters Beatles. He and Sharna Liguz hide at Shreyas, preparing for the launch of their new group, Penguins.

'India is cool,' Sharna says. 'I never thought it would look like this.'

I wish them well in their time with Sai Baba. 'It should be amazing,' Sharna says as she bids me goodbye, off for forty-eight hours with the devotees and a road clogged with masses carrying devotionals and golden crowns of Shiva on their own heads.

'Madam, you will do much better to watch Sai Baba on YouTube,' Krishna says. 'There is much controversy that surrounds him.'

I follow Krishna to the office and for the next hour watch a mirage of materializations in the form of wads of who knows what coming from Sai Baba's mouth as he covers it with a towel.

A few days later Zak and Sharna stumble back from their trip to the ashram and collapse by the pool looking exhausted. On my last night at Shreyas, the three of us meet outside in the Sylvan Gardens. We lounge on pillows by an astonishing spread that Santosh has set up by the pool. Dozens of candles and roses and tureens of vegetarian stews cosset us, as does the deep quiet. As I leave, Krishna hands me a thick envelope. Inside is a pristine copy, just off the press, of *Fellow Seeker* by Krishna Prakash. 'I would very much like to come to your country one day,' he says as he hands me the gift.

SILENCE IS THE SIGN OF THE WELL-DEVELOPED INTELLECT, 11 MARCH

I have travelled north to Ananda in the Himalayas. I am on India time, which means that I am, unapologetically, late again. This time I do not hyperventilate on the way to Vedanta class. Silence is my operating instruction. After a week of luxury spa life at Shreyas, I have absorbed this expensive lesson. Or maybe it is the magic of Ananda, rated the world's best spa by a cluster of magazines. There is a reason for this. Nestled high in the

Himalayas on the grounds of the Viceregal Palace of the Maharaja of Tehri Garhwal, it has refined the international spa formula yet kept the essence of India at its core. Yes, it is pricey. And yes, the place attracts rich Manhattanites and Swiss bankers, but there is also a 21,000-square-foot spa with Ayurvedic massages that fill a three-page list. And there's the trainer who could compete with Equinox's. And there's his sense of absurdity as he details the exercise regimes of most upper-middle-class Indian women. 'Walk to the buffet. Rest. Tell the driver, "Home." Turn on soap operas. Ask the maid for tea and biscuits.'

My room has a picture window that overlooks the Himalayas and the Ganges. There is a jacuzzi and a peerless spa shower. You eat on a deck with the same vista and wander back and forth from spa to dining room. It is about as perfect a spa setting as is possible to imagine, and from the moment I see the books of the maharaja that are preserved in his library, I plot to extend my trip for as long as they will keep me.

We meet outside at seven in the morning on the yoga mats and watch the clouds play over the mountaintops, taking in the view of the Ganges and the frayed ashrams of Rishikesh far beneath. Yoga is conducted by stern taskmasters fighting for attention with an assembly of peacocks, which stroll near the mats. If it mists, your headstand will be interrupted by the sight of spreading tails.

Getting to Ananda requires rushing to the 6.50 a.m. Shatabdi Express train in Delhi, darting through the crowd of coolies balancing stacks of suitcases on their heads. Then the ride is four or five hours, depending on the condition of the tracks, in a luxury coach that seems to date back to the time of Mrs Indira Gandhi. The ride is a thrill. Mother India just out as you travel north into the peaks.

In a field there are women pushing oxen who look to have

been painted by Tagore. In Haridwar, a jumble town still a good hour from Ananda, painters work on a banner: WELCOME 3RD ALL INDIA OPEN RAFTING CHAMPION. And then the road, the hairpin turns up the mountain, passing through Rishikesh into a quiet landscape and the joy of another sign. I ask the driver to stop so I can photograph it. If you are a collector of evidence of the yin and yang and oddities of globalization, this one is a prize. A large boulder in the mountain, painted to catch the eye of the village population, reads: THE MAKERS. SPOKEN ENGLISH AND PERSONALITY DEVELOPMENT. CALL CENTRE INTERVIEW AND PREPARATION $$$$. RUN BY FLIGHT ATTENDANT VINAY BADONI (RTD.).

Late morning. The breeze riffles the pines on the grounds of the Viceregal Palace, once presided over by an oddball of a maharaja who produced an unsettling smattering of crypto-fascist literature, some of which is preserved in his library, now used as a computer room for the spa.

I resist the weakness of faint-heartedness on encountering a book called *Yisroel: The First Jewish Omnibus*. It sits on a shelf with strange books by German professors trying to explain the Nazi war machine.

Not entirely irrelevant is the question: Can you control the mind? You have to hand it to the Ananda staff: they have taken Werner Erhard's EST trainings from the seventies and fluffed them up to be as Eastern as they are Western. Erhard made his fortune with the quick and useful soundbite: 'It is what it is.' Jimmy Carter was in the White House, lines formed at gas stations, and the president from Georgia decreed no hard liquor be served at state dinners. At this ripe moment the spa industry took off in America and Erhard struck it rich even while insisting that his seminars run seven or so hours without bathroom breaks. His ride was swift and bracing before he crashed. So in the shining new India, why not test an Eastern version of EST in the misty Himalayas, the setting of eternal wisdom and so much want?

The ideas are presented by two dreamy followers of Swami Parthasarathy. They are usually found across the country in Pune, at the elaborate Vedanta Academy, run by the Vedanta Cultural Foundation. From the first, there is the echo of Erhard in their pitch: You must come! Can we call you? Put your name on the sign-up sheet. Can you send us your emails? We will follow up.

I admit, I am hooked. I like the dialogue. 'Likes and desires can drive you crazy.' 'The mind will jump from one thing to another.' 'We have to approach situations with no expectations.' 'When the ego asserts itself, go limp.' Soon I stop booking massages to be instead with the Pune Moonies at Vedanta class.

EACH DAY A DIFFERENT SIGN

What is *swadharma*? I fill my notebook with such terms, and this one, I will learn, is the notion of individualism, of one's own law of action, and it's one of the core concepts of the Gita. Or, to my cynical Western mind, a pathetic rationale propped up to explain why a significant portion of the more than 300 million middle-class Indians can seem oblivious to the almost 400 million others who are living on less than $1 a day.

I also have, as part of the curriculum, in my notebook the terms *tamas*, *rajas* and *sattwa*, classifications of personality. The tamas is the lazy sloth who indulges and refuses to turn away from dosas or Häagen-Dazs. The rajas type comprises the work-as-worship bling-bling crowd, busy all the time on their hamster wheels of pointlessness. And then there are the holy warriors of the sattwa type, struggling always, even at $600-a-night Ananda, for that arc of wisdom, that perfect Ayurveda moment, the understanding that Parthasarathy says comes with the idea of Western as Eastern. I take all this to dinner and sit next to an Indian banker from New Jersey.

'Do not be so foolish,' he says. 'The real gurus one never sees. And if you are making notes from the West, they will continue to hide from you.'

The Ananda staff are at their best when lecturing on how to manage expectations, using Swami's fifty-odd years of marriage as an example. I will paraphrase the story: 'Marriage? How do we do it? I wake up and I see my irritable wife. She has always been irritable. When I married her she was irritable. I ask her if she wants tea and she barks at me! I am happy! I know that I am in the correct house! I know that I am not lost! That I am exactly where I am supposed to be.'

Soon I sneak out of class and make my way down the pathway of the Ananda palace, go through the gate, and take in the vast panorama outside the cushy confines of the spa. For the moment, the clamour of the outside world stills. In my first days of wanting to understand India, Erhard was being set up in Los Angeles and I was studying *An Area of Darkness*, V.S. Naipaul's 1964 account of his travels in the country. I used his chapter titled 'A Resting Place for the Imagination' to understand the mysteries of a world unknown to me. I had written a note to myself, even then, that I later noticed jotted in a margin: 'The horizon is infinite and grand.' The lesson was within.

In Search of Lost Time

MAYANK AUSTEN SOOFI

At a height of 1,938 m, giddy tourists gratify themselves by boating on the lake, riding the ropeway trolley and shopping on Mall Road. That's Nainital, the hill station in Uttarakhand's Kumaon region, 330 km north of Delhi. The sensitive traveller goes back with memories of smog and crowd, trash and traffic, tipplers and honeymooners.

Most of Nainital is as scarred as other north Indian hill stations, like Shimla or Mussoorie. Mall Road, the principal promenade, is littered with plastic packets. The hill slopes are pockmarked with hotels. The mossy rocks are painted with ads. The tree branches are entwined with electric cables. Throughout the day, the hills echo with the sound of honking cars.

Old, pristine Nainital is preserved largely in people's memories; only the residue of that fabled past is there to see and feel. To those who grew up in Nainital in the 1960s, it was a place of innocence and privilege.

For centuries, the lake was held sacred by the hill people, but it was the British, homesick for England's cool climes, who built the first bungalows. As schools and shops came up in the colonial era, Nainital became the commercial and anglicized heart of Kumaon, in the foothills of the Himalayas. It was also the summer capital of British India's United Provinces. Muhammad Ali Jinnah went to Nainital for his honeymoon.

After Independence, the town came to be known more for its boarding schools. Students came from as far as Myanmar, Thailand and Africa. In the 1950s, three future Bollywood stars were studying in Nainital: Danny Denzongpa at Birla Vidya Mandir, Naseeruddin Shah at St Joseph's College and Amitabh Bachchan at Sherwood College. Film director Karan Johar's mother was a hosteller at St Mary's Convent. Two Anglo-Indian women, known as the Murch Sisters, became famous for adopting underprivileged children and enrolling them in the town's various colleges. One of the children, Marcus Murch, became an actor in Geoffrey Kendal's theatre company, Shakespeareana.

Education ran Nainital's economy. Coolies took the luggage of students up and down the hills. Barbers gave them haircuts. Tailors stitched the uniforms. Bookshops catered to their syllabi.

Tourism increased through the 1960s when the hill station became the summer retreat of the rich. In May and June, the social life of Delhi and Lucknow would shift to Nainital. The rajahs of Kashipur and Pilibhit and the nawab of Rampur were regulars, so was the Taraporewala family of Mumbai. The old-money clans bought cottages, or had their favourite hotels, sometimes even favourite rooms.

For two months, they feasted, walked, skated and danced. 'Our group would tie four or five *kishtis* (boats) with a rope and together we'd sail on the lake for two hours,' Zeenat Kausar of Delhi (her family owned the now-defunct *Shama*, an Urdu film and literary magazine), who always stayed at the Grand Hotel, told me one hot, smouldering afternoon in her apartment in Delhi's Nizamuddin West. 'A gramophone played K.L. Saigal songs.'

Of course, the upper crust were members of the Boat House Club, an establishment that had once denied membership to hunter–conservationist Jim Corbett for not being blue-blooded enough, but now admitted brown sahibs. The club had a bar, a multi-speciality restaurant and billiards rooms. It was famous for its live band, ballroom evenings and yacht races, which simmered with politics. Children were barred from the club after 7 p.m.

In the summers of the 1960s, Capt. Ram Singh of the Indian National Army, who was close to freedom fighter Netaji Subhash Chandra Bose, conducted a band playing martial music on a bandstand every day after 4 p.m. The bandstand was built in a part of Nainital known as The Flats—the offspring of a landslide. In 1880, this landslide had killed 150 people and destroyed buildings, including the Naina Devi temple. The debris from the hill covered a part of the lake, forming the gravelled ground.

The hawkers on The Flats sold *chana jor garam* and fruit like apricots, peaches, strawberries, pears and apples. In September and October, chestnuts came from Ranikhet. The popular dessert was the *bakse waali* pasty, or pastries stacked in steel trunks. Tourists and locals whiled away the afternoons watching hockey or football matches on The Flats.

Then, as now, the most important touristy ritual was the boat ride on the lake. In the 1950s, it cost two annas. Today, it is more than a hundred rupees. And the town's standards are slipping. The lovely rowing kishtis are giving way to swan-shaped plastic paddleboats. The souvenirs sold on the street are no longer hand-painted scenes of the lake town but nude, one-armed Venus candles. There is unplanned development. The hotels are shabbier.

In the 1980s, the rich abandoned Nainital for Kashmir, though then prime minister Rajiv Gandhi would often visit with his family. By the 1990s, then Union finance minister Manmohan Singh's economic reforms made it easier for wealthy Indians to carry cash to foreign locales. The Greek islands became the new Nainital. The original saw a demographic change.

In the 1980s, the Maruti 800 arrived. It was the affordable car that increased the mobility of middle-class India. People started coming to Nainital from towns such as Bareilly and Moradabad, while more and more middle-income Delhiites adopted the hill stations as a weekend getaway. The nature of what they looked for in a holiday was different.

While walking on Mall Road, these visitors look at the shops, not the lake. The locals call them NRIs, 'newly rich Indians'.

In summer these days, Mall Road is jammed with people. The Hindi swear words of weekend revellers can be heard from one end to the other. The well-heeled old snobs will be mortified by the presence of hundreds of identical paunchy men in tight T-shirts, women dressed up like Christmas trees, heads covered with 'look-I'm-on-holiday' straw hats, and constant jostling for a picturesque spot. And there are the children, running pell-mell, screaming for goodies.

In the 1960s, Mall Road was more rarefied. Young people in bell-bottoms skated and the glamorous gentry strolled. Women were dressed in chiffon saris and *jamawar* shawls; men in ironed suits and polished shoes. The shops had character.

Started by a Swiss woman, The Sakley's was loved for its pastries, éclairs and doughnuts. Huntley & Palmer, run by the

Arora brothers, had delicious English biscuits. Narain's bookstore, with a view of the lake, specialized in literary fiction. It was also the only place in Nainital to sell 78-rpm records of singers like Begum Akhtar and Rasoolan Bai. Ramlal & Sons were drapers and outfitters for students and bureaucrats. The best shoes were found in the shop of Mr Listen, a Chinese settler. Everyone who got married had photos taken in the Bakshi Brothers' studio. In Bara Bazaar, up Mall Road, there was the garment store of the Rais brothers, two extremely polite men who greeted customers with '*farmayen*' (yes, please say).

Dana Mian, a second-hand book dealer, walked the hills with a coolie who carried a book-filled steel trunk on his head. Until the 1962 war with China, Buddhist lamas freely crossed the border to sell precious herbs from Tibet. Chinese traders came with silk.

Occasionally, the 'season' was rocked by scandals. 'My father's younger brother fell in love with an Anglo-Indian crooner who performed at a restaurant on Mall Road. They fled to Rampur and got married,' lawyer and educationist Nilanjana Dalmia, who spent her childhood in Gurney House, once the residence of Corbett and now owned by her family, told me one rainy afternoon on the terrace of her lovely house. Although a private property, it admits visitors. The cottage has a gabled roof and period furniture. The rooms have been preserved as they were when Corbett sold the property in 1947. The shelves have books by Charles Dickens and P.G. Wodehouse. The rug in the living room is the skin of a tiger.

In the old days, nobody drove. People walked or rode on *dandis* (palanquins) or horses. Today, hyper-energetic day trippers leave before sunset.

But old Nainital is not completely lost. Most of the landmarks are still there. The Sakley's bakery products rival those of any big-city patisserie. Narain's collection of books, both in English and Hindi, is extensive, though a decade ago the owner started stocking candles to survive. The lakeside municipal library— open to all—has a duck house below.

Like the town itself, the Boat House Club too has lost its exclusivity. Tourists are let in upon payment of Rs 415 'per couple'. Talking on mobile phones is allowed in the bar lounge, which has hanging lamps and heavy sofas. The windows look out on to the lake. The walls have black-and-white photos of the 1880 landslide. A clock chimes every hour. The piano is locked.

Nainital had three cinemas. Capitol Cinema and Roxy screened English films. Ashoka Talkies, near Town Hall, showed Hindi potboilers. All three have shut down. The Capitol, where one could watch foreign films such as *Ben-Hur*, *The Ten Commandments* and *The Picture of Dorian Gray*, was originally built on The Flats as an assembly hall to host grand parties for the British. Today, the portion where the balcony used to be is a factory store for designer candles. The part that faces the lake is a video-games parlour. The glass panes on the doors are broken.

Situated just above Narain's, the Grand Hotel has been standing since 1872. Every room has a clear view of the lake. Nehru liked dining there. The King of Nepal would check in with his own carpets and cutlery. When he stayed at the hotel for the filming of *Madhumati*, actor Dilip Kumar instructed the staff to serve tea to any fan coming to visit him. Today, the Grand's corridors offer the same view, but the furniture has changed—cane chairs instead of the old planter's chairs.

One thing is intact. The matches still happen on The Flats, the shouts of players wafting up and reaching the ears of lone men walking the deserted slopes of faraway hillsides. The bakse waali pasty vendors can still be sighted.

To get away from tourists, walk on Thandi Sadak, the cobbled pathway across the lake. It's the anti-Mall Road: no shops, no touts. One side faces the hill, the other looks to the lake. Or walk on the town's hillsides, which are as deserted as the Mall Road was in the 1950s. To climb into another world, climb a bit higher. Kilbury forest, 13 km away, is a different country—utter silence amid a dense cover of oak, pine and rhododendron trees. The slow-moving clouds are close enough to touch. You rarely see anyone except collared grosbeaks, brown wood owls and laughing thrushes. The forest has more than 500 bird species. Sometimes, the pathway runs over a stream. The enveloping clouds make the world as white as snow. Built in 1890, the Kilbury Forest Rest House is a perfect retreat.

The British-era Raj Bhawan, or the Governor's House, on a hill looks magical at sunset. With an entry pass of Rs 30, it can be viewed only from the grounds, for the interior is barred to visitors. Made of grey stone, this Gothic installation has 113 rooms. From the rear it resembles an English country house. On rainy days, the mist gets so thick that the building is reduced to a mere outline—its turrets look finer than any brushstroke by an artist.

The golf course, spread over forty-five acres, is within the Raj Bhawan grounds. If the sky is overcast, the golfers frequently disappear into the approaching mist. Tourists can play by paying Rs 250 for eighteen holes.

Despite being a Nainital cliché, boating on the lake is heavenly. Each kishti is like an island. The rhythmic splash of the oar on the water lulls you into sweet drowsiness as puffs of cloud drift down the hills and float over the lake. The view, so fragile that it is more like a state of mind, explains why some people nurture a passion bordering on mania for this town.

At The Bookshop in Delhi's Jor Bagh market, the owner, K.D. Singh, who studied at the hill station in the 1950s, has recreated his own Nainital. Only friends with a 'Nainital connection' know the secret geography. The new releases are displayed behind the glass display in 'Tallital', your entry point to Nainital. Older books are exiled to 'Mallital', the region beyond Mall Road. Classics are stacked up on 'Snow View', the ropeway ride's destination. Singh himself sits in the 'Boat Club'. The desktop image on his computer is of the lake. Nainital, 0 km.

Travelling to the Hills in Search of Myself

BULBUL SHARMA

It was a bleak, wet morning the first time I saw Shaya. The hills were covered with a dull grey mist and patches of muddy frost lay under my freezing feet. I could see the slate-roofed hut far down below, hidden behind a grove of leafless apple trees. It was not the dream cottage in the hills I had imagined, with rose bushes, blue butterflies and frolicking lambs, and I skipping along like Heidi among sparkling mountain streams and old deodars.

I walked downhill, slowly dragging my feet like a prisoner of war. The cottage stood at the end of a winding, rocky path not far from a gushing stream. The path was slippery with tiny white pebbles, and as I clung to the small bushes, I tried not to look down at the steep rocky cliff. I was breathless even though I was walking downhill and as I stood there listening to the sound of the rushing water, my eyes watering and nose dripping in the freezing February wind, suddenly, as if the mountains wanted to surprise me with a gift, a flock of rosefinches flew down to greet me. At that moment, thirty years ago, I fell in love with Shaya.

The journey to this little village in Himachal Pradesh has been a long, wonderful, enriching and difficult one. We have had so many disasters like mini-floods, forest fires, an invasion of strange winged insects, ghosts, snakes, roof leaks, no-water and no-electricity days, wall collapses and the worst of all—an overflowing septic tank. I have lived through it all with my long-suffering family and a few close friends. We have emerged stronger and more tolerant, better equipped to deal with life's nasty little surprises.

Then there have been magical days. Sunshine on a peach tree laden with red-gold fruit, giant peacock butterflies dancing in the mist and hundreds of wild flowers beneath our feet. I have found secret groves of deodars hundreds of years old and magical circles of the delicate 'lily of the valley', a rare flower. I have seen golden eagles soaring in the sky searching for unfortunate field mice and flocks of red-billed blue magpies—the robber birds—chasing ravens around trees.

Shaya, like all mountain villages, has a totally different story to tell each season. I have seen it at its worst in February but still loved it like you love an old friend despite his or her defects. Summer, the hills are green and more green; rainy season, the green becomes deeper with patches of emerald too and then as autumn creeps in, the colour changes to brown and red-gold. The only colour that remains the same is the dense, dark green of the deodars in the forest beyond the orchard. The ancient deodars, their thick trunks covered with soft moss, stay a dark, mysterious green-blue all through the seasons, standing steadfast and true like old, trusted friends.

In winter the Shaya village, which has only fifty-odd houses, wears a desolate look. It seems as if all the people in the village have gone to sleep like the characters in *Sleeping Beauty*. Occasionally, I catch a glimpse of a village woman outside her hut, clearing the snow from the cowshed. Sometimes I see children sliding down the hillside on tin sheets like makeshift sleighs, skidding dangerously close to the steep hillside.

When they were young, my children wanted to join the village children in their games and my son would often rush out and join them but I would drag him back. 'No, too dangerous,' I would say.

In those early days I found everything dangerous and life-threatening about village life and would keep warning my children.

'Don't drink the water unless it is boiled. It has tiny insect eggs in it. If you swallow them, they will hatch in your stomach.'

'Don't go outside after sunset. There are leopards here. The other day a leopard ate up our neighbour's dog.'

'Watch out for snakes in the grass. They will kill a man in two-and-a-half minutes—children take less time.'

'Wash your hands with Dettol after you touch the goats.'

Both my children, now in their thirties, tell me that they did everything I told them not to do. They drank water from the stream, played in the thick grassy meadows right next to where the grass snakes dozed and once saw a leopard catch a dog in broad daylight. They helped clean the cowshed and even milked the cow once.

I am glad now that they did all this and wish I had the courage then to jump in too. But to this day I am nervous about hill cows and always cross the road if I see one coming my way. But I have learnt how to recognize wild edible plants, cure a wart with juice from a particular leaf and sip nectar from rhododendrons.

Shaya has taught me so much over the years. I can see myself standing on a rock on a cold, wet morning and laugh. So much has changed, not in Shaya, but within myself. Shaya has remained almost unchanged as I grow old and discover various aspects, hidden shades of green and gold on the mountains like a favourite book you reread over and over again to find new shades of meanings.

Over the years I have learnt so much about village life. Like most city people who have never lived in a village, I had sentimental views about simple village folk mostly gleaned from Hindi films. Premchand's stories told me they were honest, hard-working and innocent. They are all this but much more. They have a mischievous sense of humour, a cunning sense of survival and an incredible amount of knowledge about their land. They almost always look down upon city people and consider us stupid, helpless and amusing. Slowly, very slowly I have become friends with a few women from the village. It took a long time for them to accept me—this strange woman from the city who thinks she knows everything by reading books, washing her hands all the time and scared of the cows and spiders. They found me peculiar and treated me like a child—foolish and helpless. They loved to feel the texture of my synthetic fleece jacket, try out my shoes and look with horror and fascination at the women's magazines I read.

They have taught me how to crochet, make pickles and weave a bag with string and an empty packet of chips. They have told me stories about their childhood and about the village they have heard of from their mothers. But best of all, they have shared their secrets with me. These strong, self-reliant women know who they are and are quite content with their lives. They are so rooted in their day-to-day life, their family and land that they see no reason to change them. Sometimes maybe they wished their husbands helped them a bit as they toiled from morning till night, or had a little extra money for small comforts like new shoes, a thicker blanket or a new cow, but they would shrug off these little wishes and desires and get on with life.

The men in Shaya have a strong opinion about every aspect of life, especially politics and sport, very much like men all over the world. They sit in the sunlit corners of the road and smoke and chat while the women work in the fields, digging, watering, clearing and cutting. The only thing the women do not do is plough the fields. This is still a man's job and they do it with pride, riding the plough like their ancestors had a thousand years ago.

The pattern of farming in the villages of Himachal has remained unchanged for centuries, except that now they have many more orchards in place of rice fields. Many grow flowers for the market too and make huge profits.

Though the women do all the work, I am not sure if they share the profits with the men only because it is still the men who go to the market to sell the produce. Most women have never left the village and have very little desire to do so. The only time they get into a bus to go to the nearest town is when they have to go to the hospital which, fortunately, is very rare.

They find life in the village self-sufficient and gradually I find that too. The circle of mountains seem to protect me from the cares of the city and what had seemed so important in Delhi last week suddenly disappears into the mist. Though there are moments when you suddenly wish for some city delights like a good film, or a glittering shop window or a hot, buttered toast.

We have a little shop in our village that keeps everything from bras to boots, from hammer and nails to wild rice, but no bread since none in the village likes it. They eat thick chapattis with home-made butter made with the milk from their cows, and delicious rajma just harvested from the fields. Sometimes they eat sweets made from marijuana seeds which they claim to be harmless. I have yet to try it.

But there are other excitements here too. Simple things become thrilling as you spend more and more time in the village. A village fair causes great excitement, a helicopter landing on a hilltop makes you rush up the hill to see it.

Every now and then, a man in flowing robes comes by selling honey he says he has gathered from the forest, but it turns out to be coloured sugar water. Another man with beautiful grey-blue eyes comes over the mountains, from China, my neighbour whispers, and sells us pretty plastic slippers.

I sit on my sunlit veranda under the magnolia tree laden with blossoms and buy all kinds of things I do not need. Rubber shoes, plastic tablecloths, hairclips, ribbons, rough wool in garish colours, beautiful cotton dupattas, hand-knitted woollen socks and brass bells for mules. I had been kicked by an irritated mule the previous week, so I thought I would make friends with it by bribing it.

I have learnt to store everything here and my house is full of old trunks filled with junk. 'Everything comes handy one day,' they say in the village, and it is true for them.

Women colour their walls with leftover ink, make rugs from plastic bags, weave bedcovers from torn clothes and string. I am ashamed at what we discard recklessly in the cities. Women here would find a use for the smallest object and treasure it.

One day I found Geeta, my neighbour and friend of thirty years, running down the hillside waving an umbrella. 'Look what I found—remember?' she shouted, her face flushed with joy. It was an umbrella, a pretty one with pink and blue stripes that I had lost ten years ago.

'I saw this woman on the hill carrying it. I told her it was yours but she would not give it to me. I called the men and told them that you had lost this umbrella in that storm that hit the village ten years ago. "But I found it while I was cutting grass last year. It is mine," she said, but we shouted her down. Finally the woman gave it to me,' said Geeta and placed the umbrella, now a bit faded and torn, in my hands.

I wanted to give it back to the woman who had found it but Geeta would not let me. 'It is a matter of village honour now,' she said in a serious voice.

In summer the Shaya Hills become a vast green carpet with thousands of wild flowers blossoming in every corner. The stream flows with a loud song and the hill birds gather on the mossy banks to search for insects and seeds. The black-and-white spotted forktails, a pair of resident birds here, trail their long feathers as they hop gracefully on the slippery rocks, while the white-capped redstart, a small bird full of restless energy, flits a few inches above the rushing waters.

The marsh marigold, buttercup and wild ginger grow amongst the fern-covered nooks along the boulders. Sometimes I see a green grass snake sunning itself on the rocks before disappearing into the fields as if it knows I am watching it.

I almost got bitten by one a few years ago. I was sitting on the bench outside our cottage on a sunny, warm day, admiring the view. I got up to look at a blue peacock butterfly that had settled nearby when I suddenly heard a scream behind me. Then more screams and cries. A snake had bitten my friend. It had been hiding under the bench and when I got up, I must have disturbed its siesta so it rose in anger and bit the person closest to it.

He never let me forget it. In fact the entire village talked about it for years. But last summer my friend said that he had been cured of his knee pain and thanked the snake and me for it. 'Thank God it bit me and not you,' he said.

Apparently, snake venom has some medicinal properties. My knee hurts too and now I wait for the green snake every summer to emerge out of the shadows and give me a tiny nip. So far it has not obliged. Grass snakes I learn are not dangerous but their bite is merely painful, unlike that of scorpions here which can kill a man.

While I wait for the grass snake I watch my lavender plants grow. I had got the seeds from Provence, which is the lavender centre of the world, and at first they sulked about leaving their beautiful home in France and refused to grow in my wild orchard. But this summer they have made up their minds to settle down in their new home. There are a few mauve-and-blue flowers too that seem happy to see the sun. Lavenders hate water and I am worried what they will make of our monsoon. The villagers are not impressed with them, but when I tell them we can make oil from the flowers they show more interest.

The people of Shaya know a lot about flowers and many of them grow marigold, lily, chrysanthemum and gladiolus to sell in the flower markets in town.

Life is not easy here in summer and they work all day in their fields to make the most of the warm weather. Once the rains come—and they come with a ferocious temper—the hillsides are flooded. Once it rained continuously for five days and we were locked indoors with no electricity. Bu we survived.

The journey to Shaya so many years ago was a turning point in my life. It shaped me and my children into becoming different people. If I had never set eyes on this small, remote village hidden in a circle of mountains, I would have been a different person. The forests of deodar tell me stories, the stream is my friend in all seasons. I have learnt to enjoy being by myself here which I could never do in the city.

I walk on the mica stone path to the ancient temple with its gleaming slate roof. Once a year the *devta* is taken on a journey over the mountains to another village right on top of a peak to visit his brother. The entire village turns out for this great occasion and the men trek up the steep, rocky path carrying the devta's palanquin. Women are not allowed to go, so we stay and watch the men snaking their way up to the peak. We can hear the drums and their cries of victory as they reach the summit.

The pillars around the temple with intricate wood carvings from a hundred years ago talk to me. There are mysterious inscriptions etched on the stone walls that date back many centuries, and I always touch them for good luck as I pass by. I too should carve my name on a rock by the stream for people to see after a hundred years. I believe Shaya will always remain the same. A small village in the mountains with its head in the clouds and its feet firmly in the green, snake-ridden ground when all of us have ended our journey.

Village on Treasure Hill

HM THE QUEEN MOTHER,
ASHI DORJI WANGMO WANGCHUCK,
KINGDOM OF BHUTAN

Nobgang is perched high on a ridge above Punakha Valley. It was founded by the ninth Je Khenpo, Shacha Rinchen, who was the chief abbot of Bhutan from 1744 to 1755, one of the most revered and learned religious leaders of the country. Legend goes that while he was in meditation in a remote retreat in the mountains above Nobgang, he noticed a sparkling light, like a brilliant star, in an area that was then a jungle. He sent a monk to investigate, and the monk was astounded to see a stone radiating light. The monk promptly took the stone to his master who declared it a gemstone ('nob' in Dzongkha). So he named the place Nobgang, literally meaning 'treasure hill', and built a temple called Tsolokhang there. He interred the luminous treasure inside the image of the Buddha in a chapel on the third floor of the temple.

There is a powerful legend attached to this image. In the 1950s there was an epidemic of smallpox in Nobgang and several neighbouring villages. Many people succumbed to the dreaded disease, but after the first death in Nobgang, a curious thing began to happen to the statue—its outer layer began to blister and peel off, and there were no further smallpox deaths in the village. The people of Nobgang believed that the Buddha had absorbed the disease in order to spare them the worst of its ravages. Later, this image was repaired and given a new coating of gold. But, to this day, a small dot like a pockmark remains on the face of this serene Buddha. The dot moves its position every few years—earlier it was on the cheek, now it has emerged on the upper lip. No amount of gilding can cover it up.

Some years after the Tsolokhang temple was built, the tenth chief abbot of Bhutan built another temple facing it, the Zimchu Gomo temple, where the exquisite idol of Goddess Tsheringma is housed in the inner sanctum. People from far and wide come to pray to her for daughters and good husbands. The village of Nobgang grew around these two temples. Had my mother been born thirty years earlier, she would not have been born in my grandmother's house in Nobgang but in birthing shacks located on the outskirts of the village. For in those days, strict monastic rules had to be followed by the residents of Nobgang. No animals were allowed to be kept in the village, not even birds. Only a lone rooster, that served as the community's alarm clock, had the privilege of living there. Neither weaving nor farming, the usual occupations in villages, was allowed. A monk with a fearsome leather whip ensured that these rules were observed. Despite the restrictions, however, people were attracted to settle there because as a monastic village Nobgang and its inhabitants were exempt from the compulsory labour tax then prevalent in Bhutan.

There were more than fifty houses in Nobgang, strung out in a line along the ridge. Our house, situated on the highest point in the village, was a large double-storeyed one, with a walled outer courtyard and a smaller inner courtyard. It was made of rammed earth and stone, with carved wooden windows and lintels, and a broad, pitched roof covered with wooden shingles, weighed down with stones. From our house on the crest of the hill there were wonderful views of the snow-capped peaks to the north, and the wide and fertile valleys of Punakha to the east.

Running the entire length of the village was a water channel, made of hollowed out logs, propped up on wooden poles. The source of the fresh water which flowed through the channel was a spring above the village, shaded by a large tree entwined with gourd creepers—these were lovely to look at but not to eat. The gourds, hollowed out and dried, were used as ladles in every Nobgang house. Being the first house in the village, we were the first to collect water from the channel. We would store it in great copper urns in our courtyard, as would households further down who would tap it at the point closest to them. If people wanted to quench their thirst, they simply had to put a leaf into the channel to divert the water towards them. This water channel was the daily meeting point in the village, where people would gather, exchange news and pass on messages. The channel came to an end at a chorten at the far end of the village, where people living in the lower half of Nobgang would collect their water. It was not only our lifeline, it added character to the whole village and knit it together.

It was to this unique and beautiful village that my father came as my mother's husband sixty-six years ago to live with her parents. He was twenty-four, she was eighteen. His parents had bought a house in the village when they returned to Bhutan, after eight years of self-imposed exile. The exile was political in nature, owing to the assassination of Shabdrung Jigme Dorji, who was my father's maternal uncle. Shabdrung Jigme Dorji (1905–31) was the sixth reincarnation of Shabdrung Ngawang Namgyel (1594–1651), the founder of the nation state of Bhutan.

My father acted as the midwife when I was born in 1955. He cut my umbilical cord with a sharpened bamboo, before handing me over to my grandmother. By then, my father was an experienced hand at this task, for he had delivered my two older siblings as well. During the worst of my mother's labour pains, my mother would beat my father on his head, so that he too could experience a bit of the pain she was suffering, and my father would submit to this bashing with perfect good humour. For two months after each childbirth, he would chop logs for firewood to heat a gigantic cauldron in the outdoor bathhouse for my mother's twice-daily baths. The boiling water would be poured into a wooden tub and allowed to cool naturally to the right temperature, and then my father would carry my mother from the bedroom to the bathhouse, bathe her and carry her back to bed. In those days everyone in Nobgang believed in the curative powers of warm baths, and maintained that women should rest completely for two months after every delivery, as this would ensure that they stayed strong and youthful. Modern medicine might scoff at these beliefs, but my mother, who has borne and brought up nine children, is a remarkably youthful eighty-one year old.

The joke in our village was that if a man came as a husband to a Nobgang woman, he had to come with his sleeves rolled, with an attitude of 'I can', to take on any task assigned to him. That my father did when he fell in love with my beautiful mother and came to live in her house. My mother was the only daughter of her mother who was a figure of authority in the village, and of course, the unquestionable boss of the house. It was an education for me to see how my grandmother tackled people with a mixture of diplomacy, command, accommodation and fearlessness to get her way. She not only managed to make people accept her point of view but end up thinking that it was originally theirs as well.

You may have gathered from what I have written so far about my upbringing in Nobgang that women enjoy positions of equality with men in Bhutanese society. Women often inherit their parents' property, and their husbands often live there with them. Women are free to marry whom they choose, and to divorce and remarry without any social stigma. And household tasks, including childcare, are shared by the husband and wife. My earliest childhood memory is of my father carrying me on his back when I was three, securely strapped to him with a *kabney*—a long woven cloth knotted across his chest. Sometimes my baby sister Tshering Pem would be strapped to his back along with me. This left my father's hands free to do other chores around the house, while we were safely with him and out of harm's way. We would peep over his shoulder, watch what he was doing and eventually fall asleep nestled against his back.

As I grew older I would gather wood, fetch water, help harvest maize and vegetables, and often take the cattle out to graze. I especially loved milking cows. I was a tomboy, and felt more comfortable in my elder brother's knee-length *gho* than in the ankle-length *gochu* (tunic) that small girls wore. My gochus were stitched by my father, as were my long boots, with cloth uppers and leather soles. He was very skilled with his hands, as most men were in those days, able to stitch clothes and make shoes for his family, repair everything from farming tools to the house roof, as well as do fine woodwork, carving lintels and window frames—these last tasks, though, were saved for the winter months when there was little work in the fields. And, of course, he was skilled in delivering babies (the practice of men acting as midwives still continues in remote villages in Bhutan).

My father used to be gone for long stretches of time, loading our family horses and mules with rice, chillies and *zaw* (toasted rice made by my mother and grandmother), to barter them for dried fish, salt and tea in Phari, in Tibet. He would also go once a year to Kalimpong in India to buy cloth, sugar, soap, edible oils and betel nut. We would count the days until his return with toffees for us, and marvel at the factory-made fabric that he would bring back, to be stitched into new clothes. For the rest, we were self-sufficient. We ate what we grew; our oil for cooking as well as for lighting the house came from mustard seeds that we pressed ourselves; we made our own butter and cheese; and brewed tea from plants that grew nearby, such as the hypericum (St John's Wort), now recognized all over the world for its medicinal properties. Every household had basic knowledge of herbal remedies, and many villages had a skilled traditional healer with an encyclopaedic knowledge of medicinal plants. But, of course, they were not able to save lives in cases of serious illness, where surgery or antibiotics were required. We had no access to modern medicine.

At harvest time, it was the custom for all the villagers to pool their labour and work on one person's fields at a time. When the work was done, the owner of the field would host a feast for all those who had helped him, and this was always a jolly occasion, when many romances flowered amongst the young people. It was the same system of communal labour whenever someone in the village was building a house—everyone would chip in. The presence of many hands made light of work at these times.

One of my most vivid childhood memories is of a gramophone record in my paternal grandparents' house. Uncle

Wangchuk, my father's older brother, had brought a hand-cranked gramophone with him from Kalimpong—a great novelty in Nobgang—and a 78-rpm record of just plain laughter. This was a particular favourite with the whole village, elders as well as children. Many were the winter afternoons when people would gather at my grandparents' house and ask for that record to be played. After listening to it for some time, the laughter would become completely infectious, with everyone listening falling into paroxysms of mirth, until tears flowed down their faces. This record, which brought fun and laughter to generations of people in Nobgang, is still in perfect condition in Uncle Wangchuk's house, who still lives there, the oldest person in the village, at the age of ninety-one.

Nobgang now has motorable roads running through the length of the village, where we once had the water channel. Today, every household owns mobile phones and television sets, which are eroding the Nobgang family tradition of eating meals by the hearth, listening to one's grandparents' stories. The village has transformed over time; a school and a basic health unit have been built. Village life has become easier with electrical cooking gadgets and other fuel-saving appliances. Nobgang still looks almost the same, with the old houses renovated but still standing in their original places, and the two temples as the guardians of the past and the future. Those of us who have moved away from our village long ago to live in Thimphu, the capital city of Bhutan, still return several times a year to reconnect with our roots and to seek the protection of our local deities, Tsheringma in particular, the Goddess of Long Life and Prosperity.

Whenever I return to Nobgang, memories of my happy childhood envelop me, with gratitude to my parents and grandparents, for having strived to give us the opportunities that have made us who we are today. My parents, who are still strong and spirited, live in Punakha in a house next to a chorten—a temple complex my father built some years ago as a nunnery which houses 108 nuns. This new tourist destination is on a hill a few kilometres away from Nobgang. Their nine children and many grandchildren give them reason for pride and comfort. They may have moved away from Nobgang, but Nobgang is in all their descendants.

Bhangarh: Of Darkness and Light

IPSITA ROY CHAKRAVERTI

In life there is nothing completely 'bad' or fully 'good'. The greatest joy is never unalloyed. The deepest pain may be consoled. Happiness and grief, laughter and tears, the sacred and the evil coexist. Often they blend and interweave, forming strange patterns in our lives. Perhaps that is why, following the scheme of things, there are places on earth where the dark and light energies come together or run side by side. We walk alongside them, often unsure where we tread. We refer to the land as 'haunted' or 'unlucky' or 'jinxed', not really aware of what we refer to. In esoteric parlance, this is the earth's magnetic grid, consisting of what are known as 'ley lines'. They emit electromagnetic currents and criss-cross the earth. At certain points, as they cross over each other, the earth manifests a restless energy. We do not fully know why some places should be more active than others, but the fact remains that there are sites on the planet where the energies run close to the surface, where the earth's awareness or consciousness seems to be palpable and its memories replay themselves for the person who is willing to see and listen.

It is said that Bhangarh Fort in Rajasthan and its immediate surroundings convey strange vibrations which can very easily be picked up and experienced by sensitive persons. These energies convey themselves to the human mind and body in different shades of dark and light. After a while, good and bad become relative terms. I was interested because I believe that everything in life is your perspective of it. Also, I am an adventurer at heart.

In January 2012, I picked a team of thirteen enthusiastic and bold psychic investigators from my group, the Wiccan Brigade, which researches the unexplained and studies the unknown. Including myself we were fourteen in number. We had decided to investigate the infamous reputation of Bhangarh, allegedly the most haunted site in India. Was there substance in its notoriety or was it merely a tourist gimmick? If anyone could discover the truth, I could. If any team was willing to take on the challenge, the Wiccan Brigade was. We travelled to Jaipur and on the 22nd of the month readied ourselves with sophisticated cameras, magnetometers and compasses. Researching Bhangarh promised to be a moving subjective experience but we meant to capture its secrets with the electronic eye also.

The Fort and the adjoining village lie on the Delhi-Jaipur highway, about 100 km from the Pink City. It is in the district of Alwar, on the edge of the Sariska Tiger Reserve. We chartered a bus and drove down to Bhangarh. The road seemed well paved but bumpy in places. It passed through mostly arid land, which got surprisingly green as one neared Bhangarh. It was an interesting point to note this span of fertile earth in the midst of desert conditions. It could also be the energy fields there. We looked around at the fields of crops and the rising, forested hills. Suddenly we were in a valley and the bus left a cloud of white dust as it drove down the road. A rather ramshackle sign said that we had reached the village of Bhangarh. A few people wandered about staring at our bus, but they seemed accustomed to tourists. There were a few marble-cutting shacks here and there; otherwise quiet prevailed. We had heard that Bhangarh village did not have more than 200 huts and houses in all. It seemed even less. The driver said Bhangarh did not have electricity. How befitting, we thought, for India's most haunted site.

Soon we reached the outer walls or ramparts of the Fort and paused at its iron gates. Here, the usual tourists and curiosity-seekers were wandering around. They watched us as we parked our bus and entered with our equipment as well as our food packets, for we did not mean to go hungry in the midst of our investigations. The impression one gets as one enters is one of a town once vibrant but now desolate. The fortress town covers quite a few miles of dusty tracks, interspersed with broken paved paths. Surprisingly, there is abundant greenery within the walls. The grass grows profusely on undulating slopes and ancient trees are swathed with leaves. However, the hills that surround Bhangarh are arid, covered with dusty bushes and scrub. One feels one is at the base of a bowl, strewn with ancient, strangely shaped rocks and trees. Old structures have caved in and stand at intervals gazing up at the sky which seemed to, every now and then, change hue even though the weather was fine and it was one o'clock in the afternoon. Temples, like the ones to Gopinath, Someshwar and Mangla Devi, were deserted but retained an air of worship conducted there centuries ago. We sat in the courtyard of the Someshwar Temple, which seemed potent with many vibrations and shapes from the past. There were rooms within where puja seemed to have been conducted not very long ago. Stone Shiva lingas and iron tridents were seen along with ritual markings on the walls.

There is a spring that percolates through the rocks nearby and flows in a narrow stream just outside the walls of the temple. It is difficult to decipher its source. On the way, we had passed a signboard that sketched out a rough map of the place. There were place names like Lahori Gate, Phulbari Gate and Ajmeri Gate. Also indicated were sites like Modon ki Haveli, Dancers' Haveli and a bazaar. The Archaeological Survey of India has put up a board that forbids visitors to stay within the Fort complex beyond sunset. I thought it interesting that they have chosen not to position their office on the grounds but about a kilometre away. Before going to Bhangarh, I had heard of people who had disobeyed these warnings and had later disappeared or been found roaming the grounds deranged. I could not help wondering what had caused these mishaps. Fear of the unknown, or some malefic presence that still haunts the place? These days, there is also a pillar near the gate which informs one that Bhangarh is an ancient site and a nationally protected monument. That is all. The rest you have to discover for yourself.

The history of Bhangarh adds to its mystery. It was established in 1573 by Raja Bhagwant Das, as a residence for his second son, Madho Singh, younger brother of Akbar's trusted general, Man Singh I. It is said that Bhagwant Das had found the site particularly pleasing and had been drawn to build here. However, happy times do not endure. It was during the rule of the next ruler, Chhatr Singh, who died in 1630, that the decline of Bhangarh started. One is not sure when the legend of Princess Ratnavati came into being, but many say that it was during the time of Aurangzeb when Bhangarh and its fort were attached by

Jai Singh II and made a part of his personal estate. He happened to be a believer in the stars and in destiny and this is where the story of Ratnavati comes in. Many claim that the beautiful princess, an adept at magic and the occult sciences, was installed by Jai Singh II as the ruler of Bhangarh in order to read the stars and ensure his success. She was young, but she was strong and intelligent. Unfortunately, Ratnavati came into conflict with the prince of the neighbouring kingdom of Ajabgarh, who was a master of tantra and the black arts. His name was Singhia and he had tried everything in his power to seduce Ratnavati but had failed. Hence his hatred for her. Finally, in a duel of magic, she caused a huge boulder to roll down from a nearby hilltop. It crushed Singhia but he cursed Ratnavati and Bhangarh even as he died. We can call it coincidence but there happened to be a war between Ajabgarh and Bhangarh the following year in which Ratnavati was killed. After that, the once beautiful town started on the long road to decline. Strangely, there was a massive famine in Bhangarh in the year 1783 in which all its inhabitants died. It has been a ghost town ever since, and allegedly haunted. No living person dares live within its walls. They also say that the curse of Singhia allows no soul who is trapped there to leave. There is a *chhatri* or a pavilion with a stone roof high up on one of the hills adjoining Bhangarh. The spirit of Singhia, it is whispered, keeps watch from there.

Our team walked on, towards the Fort which stands at a rise in the land. But on the way, we stopped to inspect a double line of broken-down and uniformly roofless rows of rooms, made of grey granite and embedded with quartz and sandstone. They stand side by side, facing a similar row of such cells. Some have narrow stone steps within, leading to non-existent floors above. The steps stop midway as if the builders had suddenly fled. The ASI says that these stone rooms without roofs, set out in a row, with open fronts, without a hint of doors or doorways, were at one time shops in a marketplace. I have my own theory.

I feel Bhangarh was at some point in history a seat of magic. A place where people came for physical and mental healing. They came to acquire power and achieve spiritual and material goals. The Ratnavati and Singhia stories confirm this theory. The fact that local villagers still come here to exorcize women from their community, who they claim are 'possessed', is another sad story, but it does show that Bhangarh is a place with a dark inner history. We saw in a secluded corner of the land, surrounded by huge trees, not far from the main Fort, a heavily veiled village woman, trembling with fear, being questioned by the male village elders. On being asked by us what they were doing, the men got hostile and fell silent. A few bystanders whispered to us not to interfere. She was 'possessed' by an evil spirit, they said, which was causing children in the village to fall sick. They were merely exorcizing her. Strange chantings went on. This seems to be nothing unusual in Bhangarh even now. Such rituals and 'exorcisms' are obviously the practice. We have since brought this incident up at public forums, but our society seems not much concerned about its women—even in the twenty-first century. It would rather witch-hunt.

In the meantime, Bhangarh broods over what has been and is. It conveys its dark memories through the crumbling structures, its sinister Fort, and through the old banyan trees that spread over the grounds. The trees seem to have an energy of their own. They have grown over the ages into strange, twisted shapes and have twined around ancient brickwork. If you look at them closely, you seem to see distinct human forms in macabre poses and faces with grotesque expressions. It was interesting to note that the needles of our compasses couldn't stop quivering and spinning near some of these trees.

We had decided to stop for a light lunch midway and lowered our food packets onto a stone slab—something like an old-time bench. At once, a contingent of langurs came swooping down, menacingly demanding what we had brought. We were more worried about our cameras and equipment than the food, but they seemed to have their priorities. Strangely enough, the looks they gave us were hostile as if they knew why we had come there. They were not in favour of any kind of investigative work. We gave away our food and walked on towards the Fort. They followed us for a while, glowering and snarling. Were these some of the angry, hungry, trapped souls of Bhangarh, I wondered. What seemed strange was that they didn't seem to mind other tourists munching sandwiches or chips. But they somehow knew the purpose of our visit and did not like it. Were they the present guardians of Bhangarh, or a manifestation of the hostile energies which Singhia the tantrik had once raised here? We proceeded onwards and neared the Fort. There were some broken stone steps to climb and then slowly and carefully, we walked up a short but slippery, cobblestoned incline. We came to an arched gateway and walking through that, we entered a grey stone quadrangle, overgrown with grass, open to the sky. Broken stones jutted out from what might have been once a path. We climbed more steps leading up to the palace itself.

The main Fort, as it stands today, is a double-storeyed building—dark, dank, sinister and with narrow flights of steps leading all the way to the roof, from where one can have a view of most of the complex. What is remarkable and deplorable is that people of various persuasions who fancy the occult still slink into some of the dark rooms to conduct rituals that seem to be of the secret and malefic kind. We watched some of these people as they squirmed uncomfortably with our cameras on them. We had not met a single guard or security person in the course of the entire day. Today, Bhangarh is being misused. There is no doubt it was once a seat of magical power—black or white, we need not specify. The old energy lies coiled up within its ancient bricks. However, the superstitious, the ignorant and the self-motivated are trying to tap into it today with no government agency present to stop the abuse of the place.

The team and I climbed up the stairs to the first floor and stood at the head of a threatening, but strangely inviting, arched corridor. It ran straight down and ended some forty feet away at a wooden portal which led into a dark room. From where we stood, that was all we could see. On our right was a blackened-with-age, stone-and-stucco wall and arches leading to a covered balcony on the other side. There seemed to be two rooms at the end of the corridor. This, I believe, is the heart of Bhangarh Fort, where the most sinister forces are present. Even with the sun shining outside and striking the balcony, the corridor seems draped in shadows. I would say that there are forces and influences there which can adversely affect the vulnerable. Not all our team members had come up to this corridor. Some had felt slightly unwell on reaching the quadrangle and I had dissuaded them from climbing the steps to this part of the Fort. About seven were with me now. I paused before walking down that stretch of dark stone and said a protective prayer for our team. We also readied our cameras and recording devices. I started the walk. A fellow team member came up behind me with his camera. The rest of the team followed as they looked around, alert to pick up unusual phenomena. I felt watchful eyes scrutinizing our every move and hostile forces trying to trip our steps. But that may have been merely my imagination. Nonetheless, the mood in that part of the Fort was heavy and menacing. It was the atmosphere of magic misused and gone astray. I would not advise anyone to linger in that corridor.

Midway down that strip of stone, I paused again. I felt a cold presence circling a pillar a few feet away on my left. It spewed forth dark energy. I brushed aside the feeling and walked on. My team members and I reached the end of the corridor and we stepped into one of the two dark rooms. They were small, not more than about ten feet by ten. The impression I got was that they were the rooms which had been used for invoking certain powers in the past. They were not rooms to be lived in. Their powers were obviously still being utilized. I found the walls darkened with soot and it led me to believe that, recently, fire rituals might have been carried out there. The room spoke of palpable evil. Interestingly, in the adjoining room, to prove me right perhaps, an occult ritual was being secretly conducted. Various props and tools were laid out as two men chanted and conducted strange rites with a child, a young boy sitting between them, looking bewildered and confused. They had a few women and a boy standing on watch outside the room. Our presence seemed to disturb and annoy them greatly. I feel that the time will come when the energies within Bhangarh, which are being abused, will rebel. They should be allowed to rest.

It was nearing 4 p.m. by now and by the rules of the ASI, we had one more hour to linger. I suggested to our team that we return downstairs and evaluate what we had seen and experienced. We needed to talk amongst ourselves and compare notes. We needed to check our cameras, which had very strangely gone blank and blacked out in certain spots. This had happened near a few trees and as we had approached the corridor. We had also been carrying the substantially large and heavy magnetometer, but somehow the compasses had come in the most handy, not just for showing the cardinal points but in reacting to unexplained energy spots.

As we looked back at the palatial structure from outside, the fingers of the slanting sun seemed to touch it and release a host of shadows within. We realized here was a place where strange forces are still at play. Perhaps the rise of land it stands on is partly responsible for this. Our instruments certainly reacted in inexplicable ways and would indicate criss-crossing ley lines underground. Any effect would be increased and magnified by the presence of subterranean water. We had observed a spring, with unknown source, not very far from there. Apart from that, the palace, obviously, had been built to be more than just a military fortress. It had connections with other dimensions. It was a place from where Ratnavati, the princess who knew the magical arts, had exercised her powers. But as I said, there is a very thin dividing line between the good and the bad. The light and the dark. This world and others. When one goes to a place like Bhangarh and dares to investigate its mysteries, one must be a bit reckless. We were.

We took photographs with the most sensitive cameras and were rewarded. There appeared on pictures strange lights and orbs, which have since been put up for inspection by experts in orthodox areas of research. These lights remain unexplained. Psychics have long claimed orbs to be signs of paranormal activity. There have been pictures taken by the team which show among the twisted trunks of a banyan tree an astral form. There has appeared a black shadowy figure, by a pillar, pointing at me as I walked through the corridor of Bhangarh Fort. I remembered the cold spiralling coil I had felt when I had stood there. We screened these pictures at a public seminar and discussed our findings on Bhangarh. It was in the March of 2012, in Kolkata, about two months after returning from Rajasthan. The audience was mystified. Strange light orbs glowed down from the screen and shades from another dimension challenged the non-believer.

Did we feel anything else? Or experience any other strange reaction? We did. Behavioural changes and disorientation amongst members after we returned that day from Bhangarh. One of our members had an accident and fractured her femur while getting off the bus. She said she saw the hydraulic door closing in on her as she made ready to alight from the bus at the hotel. Actually the door was swinging open. Did Bhangarh distort her vision, even if for a few hours? Ordinarily, she is completely grounded and strong and extremely intelligent. Another member, normally soft-spoken and mild, became aggressive and started quarrelling with her colleagues. I noticed visible signs of personality change in her, which subsided on our return to Kolkata. A third member, who is emotionally mature, very intrepid and generally an adventurous young man, suddenly started showing signs of inexplicable nervousness and wanted to return to Kolkata that very evening. Interestingly, he was one of the members who had entered dark nooks and tunnels clicking shots. Back at the hotel, we were mainly concerned about the colleague who had suffered the leg injury, but she put up a brave front. However, at dinner that night, there were thoughtful silences in a group which is normally full of high spirits. Some members appeared to be a trifle depressed. Others were edgy. I think it was their inherent sense of discipline, their loyalty to me and to the mission they were on that kept them together that night. Bhangarh had had an effect.

These reactions lasted till our return and then wore off in the natural course of time. Once more, we were engrossed in researching our evidence and even in psychic self-exploration. Would we return to Bhangarh? We would. We often talk of it. A part of ourselves seems to have been left behind there.

P.S. We did go back the following January for further in-depth research. We discovered a small, overgrown, stone-strewn quadrangle, surrounded by crumbling and arched rooms near the Gopinath Temple. I, along with a few team members, descended into one of the darkest rooms. In the dim light the ceiling appeared in bad shape but there had obviously been attempts at repair at some stage for a bag of sand and one of cement were stacked in a corner. However, the workmen had obviously fled for some reason. The whole area was deserted. One of the inner archways that led into an inner room had been walled up. Only a narrow opening remained at the top. We stood in this room and absorbed the atmosphere—dark and filled with a sadness which could not speak. A tragedy which had happened and was never ending.

I decided there and then that no matter whatever the personal danger to me, I would try to help these miserable entities locked within their prison. My team supported me without flinching. They were ready. And then I spoke aloud the chant for the release of souls. My companions did the same. We kept on repeating it. I held out my hands to the space in the bricked wall and told them to come away from the darkness and be free. We felt a response. My hands seemed to feel something swirling around them. Some members were taking still photographs from one side of the room. A video camera was also on. After a while a sense of peace seemed to descend. The swirling stopped. The darkness seemed less. I felt as if we had done what we could for these sad souls. Somebody told me later that there was a legend which related that some time in the future, somebody would come to release these souls from their agony and they would be at peace again. Maybe we had done what we had been sent to do.

When the developed pictures came back, there were dozens

of white orbs and pale orbs with face-like shapes within them, on print. They seemed to be surrounding us, floating towards my hands. We are not ones to be led by wishful thinking, flights of fancy or superstition. But we could not explain what the camera's eye had captured. We have since researched this phenomenon with technical experts, taking into account the work on the subject of orbs in psychic photography. I would consider Miceal Ledwith, DD, LLD and professor of systemic theology, who served as member of the International Theological Commission for seventeen years, and Klaus Heinemann, PhD in experimental physics, a researcher at NASA for many years and research professor at Stanford, the pioneers on the subject in the West. Their book, *The Orb Project*, examines the subject thoroughly. In this part of the world, my team and I are the first. I believe we conducted a kind of exorcism in that dark chamber at Bhangarh and released innumerable souls which had been trapped there for centuries. But then, that is what I believe.

The Land of Seven Hundred Hills

M.J. AKBAR

Saranda forest: Our guard of honour is made up of five small blue-and-yellow birds. They appear just a little after we enter the forest. They are sitting on the road when we near them and then for quite a while they fly in front of our car, hopping back on to the ground when they get too far ahead, and then again flitting through the air ahead of us as we catch up. A peacock, disturbed while pecking for food, looks up, pauses a little, and then walks away with quiet dignity. The dry brown crumbling leaves crunch with a loud crackling sound under the wheels, disturbed for the first time perhaps since they have fallen from the sal trees; not much traffic passes this way. The silence is broken by a noisy waterfall. It is getting dry now, with the onset of winter, but in the monsoon the hills echo and re-echo with the song of tumbling water. The evening sun sparkles through the branches of the tall sal trees. We are in the heart of Asia's biggest sal forest, Saranda, the Land of Seven Hundred Hills, and the protected home of the tribals.

Earlier on in the journey, a tree trunk slung across the road, and then locked to a stump, had stopped us at the edge of the forest, and we had to show our written permission before we were allowed in. Nature's Loveliest Poem Is A Tree and Tree Plantation Combines The Goodness Of All Religions—different ideas merged into single sentences by some poetic bureaucrat and painted on boards for public nourishment. These had become victims of time and lay broken in a corner. The caretaker at the barrier had smiled in relief at the written note from the sahib (he had got word of our imminent arrival, but there was no guarantee like the written word), informed us that he had heard from a truck driver that one *kutcha* bridge had broken along the way, and wished us luck on our thirty-kilometre trip to the Kholkabad forest bungalow in the centre of the seven hundred hills draped with the graceful sal.

The sal is the tree of life, the sustainer. Its seed is medicine and revenue; it cures dysentery, the killer disease; and when converted into fat it is sold to big factories which, among other things, produce Cadbury's chocolates with its help. The sal is the tribal's spirit and culture. When the government once tried to develop teak plantations in the forest, the tribals protested, and one day, men from about twenty villages gathered and simply devastated every tree in the area where teak had been sown. Broken trunks piled one upon the other in a sudden clearing in the jungle bore testimony to tribal anger and veneration of nature's loveliest poem. The high point of the year for the tribal is the festival of Sarhul in spring, when the sal flowers bloom. The festival must be held before the first touch of rain falls on the flowers and the date is determined by those who understand the sky. This year (1986), the tribal weathermen have determined that Sarhul will be early, before the end of February.

When the administration mounted its last campaign against her, among the things they accused Jyotsna of was working with the CIA to destabilize India and create a country of the tribals, Kolhanistan. If such indeed are her motives, then Jyotsna has disguised them well. On the walls of her office it might have been reasonable to expect pictures of Jesus Christ and the Pope, in respect of the faith she was born into, or perhaps Queen Elizabeth, in honour of the land which gave her part of her education and her teenage sustenance. Instead, there are large portraits of V.I. Lenin and Karl Marx.

Perhaps the best thing about her personality is that she is free of the ultimate sin of the reformer: pomposity. She takes her work seriously, not herself. She was born a Syrian Catholic in a small town in Alleppey, Kerala–Kuttanad. 'On the seventh day they baptize you with happiness and joy,' she says with a wry smile that suggests that one's options at that age tend to be somewhat limited. The family was devoted to the Church, and early in her teens she wanted to become a celibate and dedicate her life to the service of the poor. 'I would work for the poor. At least as I understood it then.' Instinctively she thought of Bihar–after all, poverty and Bihar have been synonymous for some time. 'We used to learn about Bihar through mission Sundays, when collections would be made; we began to believe that the poor only lived in the north, not Kerala.' A short laugh. 'I was fifteen or sixteen when I decided to join the Notre Dame mission.' She was sent to Britain to be a help to the delegation there. She learnt catering in Northumberland, and then taught in Liverpool. But it was not the poor of England she was going to dedicate her life to. After nine years she came back to Bihar, and started teaching in Patna. This was now 1970.

The mission school was useless, she says–it only concentrated on teaching the children of the elite, who in turn were only interested in learning how to eventually go abroad. She tried to awaken the consciousness of the children by taking them to visit slums, but everyone protested: the children did not want to go there, their parents were shocked, and the school administration angry. The school was happy to let her and four or five friends with similar ideas go. After three months, Jyotsna took leave of absence from the mission and went to live in a tribal village called Sonya near Chakradharpur. She was nervous and afraid, she recalls. But the people accepted her with love. The moment her leave of absence was over, she resigned from the mission and continued her individual work. 'I no longer had any fear. I was living with the people.'

Did she turn against the Church? 'Just then I was not taking a position against the Church. The Second Vatican had given hope, and I thought things would change. I had become anti-institution but not yet anti-Church . . . Later I discovered that the Church was itself anti-poor. The students of St Xavier's Church did not want to disturb the status quo. I lost whatever faith I had in the Church, or in any kind of institution for that matter.'

But not the institution of marriage? I point to the simple gold ring on her finger. 'Oh that! When we were in the Church, we used to wear a silver ring, so I put on a gold one after we left . . . And you know when you go back home to Kerala, they feel a woman must wear some ornament. And I am married now. Raj and I had been working together for so long, I felt, why not get married!' The laughter tinkles across the courtyard.

Singbhum derives its name from the Singh Rajas of Porahat who ruled the tribals, says one version, hence the *bhumi* (land) of Singhs. The second interpretation says Singhbhum is a corruption of Singh Ponga, the main god or spirit of the tribals of the district. The Singhs came over from Orissa to rule this neighbouring district through the classical syndrome—tribal jealousies led to division, and anger led to an invitation to the neighbouring feudal lord who soon took over every village. There are more than fourteen lakh tribals now living in this forest-and-hill-strewn district; not even one-fourth of the more than 4,500 villages have drinking water, and only 218 villages have electricity (thanks to their proximity to mining centres). The only real variation is in the levels of poverty. Get your measuring rod and find out who is how far below the line. There are some who still live in the trees. Birhor literally means 'man of the jungle'. About a hundred people of this tribe have been settled, thanks to the Tata Steel Rural Development Society, in a small colony about twenty miles from Jamshedpur, but most of them continue to live in the trees or in rudimentary huts that barely last a rainy season. Life determines what we become most proficient in. They make their huts out of leaves, and their skill is such that if a roof leaks, then the man who has made the hut is excommunicated for a month. He must show that he can build a perfect roof of leaves before he is allowed in society again.

The dam on the Koyna river catches the water in a pretty valley tucked in the middle of rising, wooded hills. The sun is just above the curving line of trees on the slope, mellow and tired after a long day's work. The sun—the single source of light—shapes the nature of the day. The moon and the stars and the kerosene lamp provide just enough light for a drink of rice wine, song, dance or a last conversation with a friend before it is time to sleep. As the sunlight thins and the cold breeze picks up, the women, as usual more hardworking than the men, begin the walk back home with bundles of *kundi* leaves on their heads, the result of a full day's work. They have been brought here to the middle of the jungle from Manoharpur by the contractor to pick these large kundi leaves. After the leaves have been dried and the weight of the moisture has evaporated, the leaves will be weighed and the women paid one rupee for every kilogram they have plucked. The money spent on the food they are given is deducted. They have pitched camp on an open space beside a running brook and built huts of leaves.

Public Carrier MPA 6581 is standing there when we reach, ready to take some women back to Manoharpur and perhaps replace them with others for the next day's work. The contractor's name, we learn, is Iqbal Hussein, and these leaves will eventually reach Chennai where they will become plates on which food will be served. Who says we are not a secular country? A tribal picks the leaf which is exploited by a Muslim so that a Tamil Brahmin may eat his vegetarian lunch in pristine purity!

Is one rupee per kilogram (less the money on the food) an average rate? No, even Orissa, not particularly famous for its benevolence towards tribals, has raised the wages for the same work to a rupee and a half per kilogram. Why could not Bihar do it too? Ministers decide these things . . . There are committees. And is it really wise, the man in power tells me, to suddenly raise wages so steeply? Might it not hurt the trade?

Fifty paise may be just a cup of tea in Kolkata or Mumbai or Delhi; in the jungle it is a 50 per cent rise in wages. But where is the government in Bihar to whom the woman plucking the leaves is more important than the contractor?

The Civil Procedure Code does not apply in tribal Singhbhum; it is still governed by the Wilkinson Rules. When the British finally subdued the Kohl tribals' revolt in 1832, the man sent to ensure future peace was Capt. Wilkinson, and he guaranteed the tribals that their way of life would be protected, that their systems of independent governance would be retained. So it is still.

The first proper administrator to rule from Chaibasa came, in fact, only in 1850. Lt J.S. Davis, a junior assistant agent to the governor general, was given the job. The position gradually grew in importance. The second district commissioner was Lt J.C. Haughton, a principal assistant rather than a junior assistant. By the ninth DC it was a lieutenant colonel who was the chair, and by the twelfth a full colonel. The Indian Civil Service proper came only with the arrival of the Right Honourable T.H. Renny on 8 November 1887, and the first Indian as late as in 1906 when Hira Lal Sen, a deputy magistrate, was put in charge, followed by Maulvi Saiyed Karam Husein in 1907 and Hira Lal Banerjee later the same year. The first Indian ICS was B.C. Sen, who was posted here in 1913. And then we have to wait till 1928 before Rai Bahadur K.C. Sarkar arrives for precisely four months. Babu M.L. Dutta is even less enamoured in 1933, and gets his transfer in just three months. National integration begins with K.V.B. Pillai in 1936, but our man from Chennai does no better than our men from Bengal, and is in office for just fourteen weeks. Khan Sahib G.Z. Abdin in 1937 can't take Chaibasa for more than ten days, while Rai Bahadur A.D. Banerjee in 1938 lasts out a full twenty before returning to the charms of Kolkata. N.P. Thandani goes six full months in 1938, but Rai Bahadur Rameshwar Singh restores the average by lasting only twenty-four days in 1939, and G.M. Ray creates some kind of a record by an official tenure of just four days in May 1944. K.N. Singh sees through Independence and our first IAS officer turns up in 1952, B.P. Prasad. Mr Prasad stays four years.

Chaibasa, to put it mildly, was not a place where the Indian sahibs of the ICS cared to spend their youth.

The discussion in the background, as I stare at the roll of honour, deals with how to govern tribals. The secret, says one babu, is that one should not show one's face too often, otherwise these illiterate tribals begin to lose their awe of the government. One has to keep them properly afraid. '*Ghar ki murgi daal barabar!*' he points out—the officer must be the occasional feast of chicken, not the daily daal.

Later, the next DC, a fine example of the IAS, a little cynical about good intentions but with reasonable commitment to liberalism and progress, describes the rationale of the Wilkinson Rules and the psyche of the tribal. 'When a child cries, and its mother does not hear, it will cry louder and louder until its mother responds. The tribal will not cry. He will keep his resentment pent up until one day it bursts.'

One small story.

The dispute between the workers and the management of the mine began, ironically, over the distribution of sweets. But all that is unimportant. We will limit our story to what Deepak Varma, the district superintendent of police of Kiriburu, did to teach some 'errant' tribals a 'lesson'. He whipped them in public and then dragged them on the streets after tying them to the back of a police jeep.

All right, another story.

Ganga Ram Kalundia was given a medal for bravery by the president of India for his services in the army. Upon his retirement he involved himself in work among his people, and became a leader of the resistance to the dam over the river Kharkai which is part of the Rs 350 crore Subarnarekha Project. In the early hours of 4 April 1982, the police knocked on Kalundia's door; he tried to escape; the police fired, a bullet hit his leg; the police bundled him up and threw him into the van and destroyed and looted his house. On the way, near the village Soso, they bayoneted Kalundia to death in the van.

The first thing you see upon entering Chaibasa is a dramatic advertisement for *Jaan ki Baazi*, showing at the Jain Movie Palace. (You would never suspect it, but the Jain family of Chaibasa is one of the biggest taxpayers in the country.) This is Tuesday, the day of the *haat* (market) and the city is alive with the din of commerce. Tribal women have brought sacks of rice, the men wood and woodcraft. This is their Sunday, and they are in their Sunday best: the hair oiled and the one sari or dhoti in their possession freshly washed. Down the road from the market is the stadium of the Singhbhum Sports Association. On the 21st, says an announcement, the semi-final match between the Damoria Block and the Khunitpani Block will take place— tickets fifty paise. Almost five years back, in March 1981, Narayan Jonko, Ashwini Sammaiya and Christ Anand Topno held a public meeting at this stadium at which they had demanded a separate country for the tribals, the state of Kolhanistan. Some of the promises made were fascinating: the proposed University of Kolhanistan, it was said, would be directly affiliated to Oxford (Topno and Jonko had just come back from a visit to England and Geneva where they had appealed for help at the UN and the Commonwealth Conference). Nobody took them very seriously to begin with—neither Delhi which had issued them with passports, nor Patna. There were a few scattered reports in the papers. But then, suddenly, one day the government awoke. Topno and Sammaiya were arrested; Jonko was discovered to have gone underground.

The cry was an exaggeration of a child long denied a mother's attention, and it did not achieve more than a passing impact. Jonko was the brain, and perhaps he was partly sponsored by those who would like to see a fragmented India. But the Topnos and Sammaiyas were manifestations of a long frustration, men fuelled by anger rather than mischief. Of course, everyone dipped their hands into the current to see what flotsam would come their way. The mine owners and the moneylenders who had robbed the tribals turned every protest movement into a CIA den; the political parties turned it into electoral games. But there was a residual benefit too. Suddenly there was recognition that some glint of development had to be taken to this bhumi. A simple decision like the mobile government shop can mean an enormous amount. Kerosene is sold by the mobile shop at Rs 2.3 per litre; the local shopkeeper charges Rs 5 or more in the interior. (Since there is no possibility of proper weights and measures, the soft drink bottle, with its measured capacity, comes in very handy.) The anger has provoked a trickle of change. And when you have not ever seen the miracle of clean water, the tube well can be a wondrous sight.

One leg. A beautifully clean, cylindrical body, lean and straight. A neck which is a rod. On its head a metal walking stick, curved at the top and curved at the tail. This is the Goddess of Water. The tube well. If gods and goddesses are symbols of need and fulfilment, fear and its containment, then perhaps the new deity of the tribals should be the tubewell. Wherever it has reached, its impact has been stunning. It is now the difference between the lifestyles of two villages. Kholkabad, the village at the foot of the hill on which is our bungalow, does not have a tube well yet, but Gope, our guide, is confident that a sanction will come soon. That is his ambition before he retires as *chowkidar* of the bungalow in three years—to persuade the big sahibs who come to stay there to grant a tube well to the village at their feet.

They make the stars differently in Saranda forest: in such thick and bright clusters that you feel that they might spill out of the sky at any moment. There is no moon that night as we walk down to the village, and the pool of shifting light formed by the torch seems an intrusion. We move towards the sound of the drum. A forest officer is with us, and doing all the talking. 'Want to see a dance?' he asks, hardly hiding the leer. Then he adds regretfully, '*Hum log ka* Ranchi *main hiyan say jyada* advanced *naach hota hai.*' What he means is that the women in the tribal villages around Ranchi show more of their breasts than here. I ask him if he could organize the sleeping arrangements back in the bungalow; he goes back looking very busy and useful.

> *When the sun was rising*
> *And the moon was large and beautiful in the sky*
> *At such a wondrous moment were you born*

There is great fun in their singing and dancing. The young people hold hands behind their backs, linking with one another in an affectionate, strong chain that goes back to the beginnings of their existence. Rice wine, warm and heavy and languorous, is being passed around. The presence of our guide, Gope, helps ease the tension which strangers bring to a family gathering. With some hesitation and then excitement we are offered the rice brew, the *handiya*. A lantern is placed beside me on a wooden log. A woman comes and sits down a little beyond the lantern: the light falls on her face and on the faces of her young children, the flame swaying slightly and forming patterns on the five faces—it is one of the most exquisite compositions I have ever seen. An old woman brings another leaf-cup of handiya, and teases, a little high herself, 'You should have come twenty years ago when I could have held you in my arms.' Gope translates and laughs. The banter is warm and wonderful; it is the ease of a confident culture that will always be outside the understanding of those who confuse 'advanced' learning with happiness.

> *I did not see you in the village, I did not see you in the market*
> *Should we go ahead and fall in love, stranger?*

The young man with the flute joins us. He has been standing outside the line of young dancers. No, no, he could not join them, he says: he is from another village, and if they ever hear that he has joined the dance here, it will be difficult for him to get married in his own village. We move away, and in the darkness meet a second group of young people. Just outside the line is Jugri, tipsy and jovial. 'Jugri is drunk,' Gope hears from his friend. Jugri sees us and shows off the transistor radio that he is holding and trying to tune (the batteries have clearly run out). 'This is a tape,' he suddenly shouts. 'I am going to tape this song.' Everyone laughs. 'Look at Jugri—he says he is going to tape!' Jugri is teasing us—men from the world of the tape recorder. He shouts again: 'Disco!' He looks slyly at us amid the renewed laughter. Then he runs into the dancers and begins flirting outrageously with one of the girls. His wife is on the other side of the dancing line. She steps out, takes firm hold of Jugri and walks off. 'That is the end of Jugri's adventures for the night,' Gope laughs.

The beauty only adds to the pain: that there should be poverty in the core of so much that is so gloriously beautiful—the sky, the forest, the land, the laughter, the heart, the sharing, the openness. Everything becomes the victim of hunger and disease. The mother points proudly to her daughter, about six years old, and says, 'Today she had medicine.' Doctors from Tata Steel had come that day on one of their periodic missions and checked everyone; and that medicine was like a feast, a sudden opening of the heavens—it was not something that the mother could ever take as her right from a modern society. 'There is no real conflict between the human being and wildlife in their claims on the environment', one of the rusted boards had said at the gates of the forest, this time quoting Indira Gandhi. Yes, but the vicious conflict was surely between the *co-aims* of man and man. What was the difference between man and animal? That man could laugh? Or that man could be both poor and rich, while every animal was equally rich or equally poor. Or should the analogy be different? Was it a conceit to call animals by different names and treat man as a single species? Was it not more accurate to admit that there were the same differences in the human race too: that some were the vegetarian, huge Brahminical elephants, jovial and learned, the *laddoo* in their palm, extremely equable when given their demanded place, and violent and roguish when angry; that some were lions among men, who had usurped, with their acquired might, the resources of the environment, who ate the flesh of others and proudly called themselves warriors and Singhs; that there were yet other men who were poisonous snakes, hissing their way through life, injecting the spittle of poison in communities, spreading lies and propaganda and their gospel of hate. And a caste of jackals, and then castes of the oppressed and the forgotten, denied by history and destiny their right to live as equals and as human beings, kicked, killed, smashed or simply spat upon, taunted and derided by the aggressors at the top . . .

Too much philosophy? Perhaps. But maybe one should be pardoned for a journey into thought when one reaches a forest where they make the stars differently.

Hello, Bastar

RAHUL PANDITA

The five men had been walking for days. They were exhausted, and the thought came to them that they might die without anyone ever knowing. The jungles of Bastar were unending. It was summertime and in the harsh sun, the five men walked slowly, drinking water wherever they could find it. But food had been scarce and they had not been able to eat for two days now. One of them was losing his patience.

The men had entered from Andhra Pradesh, and they knew that this was the life they had to lead now. Not for days, weeks or months, but for years. Or till a police bullet snuffed out their lives. They were one of the squads sent to establish a base in Bastar. But right now, they were worried about the gnawing hunger in their stomachs. Without food, they would not survive for long—this they knew very well. Even after hours of walking, they would rarely encounter a single human being. In some villages that fell on their way, the Adivasis would be so scared at the sight of them that they would run away and disappear into the jungle. In any case, the Adivasis had barely enough food even for themselves. One of the five remembers watching an Adivasi bring a handful of red ants and making a chutney out of it. The young man who was growing restless could not restrain himself any longer. 'If I don't find anything to eat in the next village, I am returning home,' he told his comrades. His four friends were too tired to try to convince him to stay back.

In the next village, the men found a chicken. They pounced on it, wrung its neck and devoured it after roasting it over a crude fire made of sticks. And they stayed back. The man who had threatened to return became one of the leading lights of the Naxal movement in this area. His name, however, is not known. In the complex history of the Naxal movement, some identities remain shrouded in mystery.

To begin with, the Naxals concentrated upon fighting the authority of the contractors and forest officials. Struggles also broke out against the management of the paper mill and contractors exploiting the forest produce. Massive struggles were waged to increase the rates for tendu leaf and bamboo collection. Within the first year, the Adivasis stopped paying taxes to the forest department. Large tracts of forest land were occupied forcibly for cultivation. Also, large portions of land occupied by traders and moneylenders were redistributed among the landless. Within a few years, thousands of acres of land were occupied through the might of the gun. The Adivasis, buoyed by the Naxalite presence, had begun to assert themselves. They would come out in hordes to press for their demands and, when required, forcibly occupy land.

The Adivasis had now tasted the power of the gun. In Gadchiroli, a woman comrade, Samakkha, took to task a forest officer who had grabbed a vehicle to confiscate forest produce from Adivasis. In front of a huge crowd of people he had dominated for years, the forest officer's collar was grabbed by a single woman, and he was forced to apologize. This left a big impression on the psyche of the Adivasi populace. The tehsildar in Alapalli, who was exploiting schoolgirls, was caught by the Naxal guerillas, beaten up and then tied to a tree. Then the women of that area were asked to assemble and instructed to spit at this face. One by one, the women approached him and spat on him. Some of them cried.

In many villages in Bastar, even the use of the plough was unknown to the Adivasis. The earth was considered as mother and using the plough, in the minds of the Adivasis, was akin to cutting through her chest. In fact, in the entire Dandakaranya region, only 2 per cent of the land was irrigated. To the Adivasis, even basic agricultural techniques such as weeding or usage of natural fertilizers like cow dung were alien concepts. The exploitation of women was rampant. In the forest, the Adivasis would store forest produce in isolated hamlets called *ghotuls*. These hamlets were used by forest guards to sexually exploit tribal girls. If the girls protested, they were threatened and in many cases evicted from work. In one such case, when the husband of the woman protested, he was killed by the forest guards and contractors. During a public meeting, this was brought to the notice of the Maoist guerillas. Immediately, the culprits were apprehended and publicly thrashed.

Because of such acts, many young Adivasis were attracted to the Maoist cause. In Gadchiroli district's *aheri taluka* was a young girl who grew up witnessing the exploitation of her people by the forest officers. Every year, they would come and take rice and jowar from her father. She would also hear stories of her friends being caught and sexually exploited by them. 'I would ask my father not to bow to their demands but he would catch hold of me and ask me to keep quiet,' she recalls. This was in the early 1980s and a Maoist squad had come to their village and set up camp by the river. 'We were not allowed to even venture towards that side since our elders thought the Maoists were dacoits and would kidnap us,' she says. But one day, the rebels caught hold of a boy called Raju and explained to him their aim and agenda. The word spread.

A few weeks later, the girl who was then fifteen went to the riverside where she met a senior Maoist leader she calls Shankar anna (big brother). By 1986, the girl had become a full-timer. Her first military action commenced seven years later when her squad attacked a police post.

Today, the girl is a woman and one of the senior Maoist guerillas, who goes by the name of Tarakka. She is a ferocious fighter, and in several press reports* she has been described as 'a woman known not just for her commitment to the "Naxalite cause" but also for her beauty'. Her name figures prominently in the October 2009 attack on police personnel in Gadchiroli's Laheri area in which seventeen policemen lost their lives. 'But I was not there,' she told me when I met her inside a Maoist camp, somewhere on the Maharashtra–Chhattisgarh border.

Within a few years of entering the Dandakaranya forests, the Naxals held sway over the whole region. Many landlords, contractors and tradesmen who tried to fight back with the help of the police were annihilated and their properties distributed among the peasants.

The biggest challenge the Maoists faced in this area was that of language. In some areas close to Andhra Pradesh, Telugu was spoken, but once they went deeper, they found that the people spoke only Gondi. The problem with Gondi was that it had no script. The Maoists worked on it gradually. Today, every Maoist guerilla in this region can speak and understand Gondi no

---

*Vivek Deshpande, *Indian Express*, 12 October 2009.

matter which part of the country he belongs to. The Maoists have been working on a script for the language and, in the schools run by them, they have tried to introduce textbooks in the language.

Gradually, the Maoists organized the tribals. Many protest rallies and strikes were held under the supervision of the Maoists in support for demands like better wages and better rates for forest produce.

In north Telangana, the movement extended to all the talukas of Karimnagar and Adilabad districts, except one taluka in each. In Warangal district, the focus developed from an urban to a rural movement. In the Dandakaranya forests, the movement spread to Gadchiroli, Chandrapur and Bhandara districts of Maharashtra; Bastar, Rajnandgaon and Balaghat of the then Madhya Pradesh; and Koraput in Orissa. In 1985 alone, in two talukas of Gadchiroli district, the Maoists liberated 20,000 acres of land from the government's or landlords' control and distributed it among the Adivasis.

The area had begun to turn into a guerilla zone.

A House for Mr Tata

An Old Shanghai Tale

MISHI SARAN

One blistering morning in early July in Shanghai, I stood on a busy street called Wulumuqi North Road, at no. 458. It was an eight-storey office building, across the road from the Shanghai Hotel. The ground floor appeared to house the Herbalife office.

The office building had sprung up on the site of what used to be, circa 1935, Avan Villa, a grand family home, housing two generations of a Tata clan. The cluster of four smaller villas behind what used to be the big house, accessed from inside the next-door Lane 468 still remain, at nos 24, 26, 28 and 30, and these are what I had come to see.

By the first week of July, according to the Chinese solar calendar, the period of 'xiaoshu' or Lesser Heat had just begun. Humidity suffocated the city and the cicadas cried ceaselessly in seeming despair. Even the briefest of outings left one's shirt drenched.

Inside Lane 468, after walking past the communal garbage

bins, past the lackadaisical guard at the main gate, I saw that subsequent additions to the properties—dividing walls, added rooms on top, haphazard tree planting in the inner gardens— had given the four semi-detached houses a higgledy-piggledy feel. Air-conditioning units that were installed later, external electricity lines, somebody's washing hanging out to dry added to the visual clutter.

The clean lines of the four original edifices had blurred with the add-ons.

The unresolved story of the Tatas' house in Shanghai whirled in my head.

Once upon a time, the entire estate before me—the office building and the four villas behind it—was cordoned off and a brass plaque indicated it was Indian property. At China's present property prices, the office building alone is now worth well over US $50 million, not to mention the price of the four homes behind it.

The story of Avan Villa tentacles through space and time: over the Pacific, to San Francisco in the present day and across the Himalayas to Bombay, over a hundred years ago. Geography and history collide in the diminutive, frail body of a persistent old Parsi, Jehangir Bejan Tata, born in 1919, now legally blind and prone to falls.

'They call me the fall guy,' he joked, sitting straight up on a sofa in his San Francisco house, holding close a walking stick. I had gone to see him in December 2012, and met his Russian wife, Lydia.

Mr Tata's English was courteous and old-world: 'with all due respect', and 'if you don't mind', and his sentence construction had a familiar coastal China hint. His voice was firm, despite its edge of an old-age tremor. He addressed me as 'Ms Saran'.

Before his vision failed, he could find his way to the local barber shop, staying on the safe side of the road. He could make a left and reach it. But no longer. Even when he gets out into the sun, he cannot see a thing. Then there are his falls, inside the house, and outside. He is not too vain to use a walker—he always uses a walker—but the pavement is cracked. Sometimes you get jammed on it, he said.

His body's inexorable decline has not prevented Mr Tata—who describes himself as quite an obstinate and stubborn man—from shaking his fist at history and demanding some answers about what happened to the Tata family property in Shanghai.

'They tell me you must get a lawyer, but all I want to know, *all I want to know* is what the status of our property is . . . the families of all my brothers are here and my twin sister is still alive. I just want to find out the status of our property. Why cannot the Government of India find out—what's the big deal . . .'

The Tatas live in north-west San Francisco's Richmond district. They live around the corner from a vast Russian Orthodox Church with gilded domes that float above ordinary San Francisco streets. When my husband turned the car onto Geary Street and we drove by the church on the way to see the Tatas, my heart clenched, for it was a replica of the Russian Orthodox Church in Shanghai's former French Concession; I recognized its curves and accents with a sort of spatial sixth sense.

Shanghai's former French Concession had been flooded with Russians escaping the 1917 Russian Revolution via China's northern border with Russia. They fled first to the city of Harbin and then, when Japan pressed into Manchuria, they moved further south to settle in Shanghai. Later, when life in Shanghai became difficult for foreigners under the Communists, many Russians migrated to this corner of San Francisco.

Their church is called the Holy Virgin Cathedral, 'Joy of All Who Sorrow', and its founder is St. John. His full name is the Archbishop St. John of Shanghai and San Francisco, for he arrived in Shanghai as a young bishop in November 1935 and became a leading light for the Russian community there. He, too, fled to San Francisco.

Lydia Tata remembers how Russian women in Shanghai would mutter about providing yet another pair of shoes for Bishop John, because, seeing a beggar, Bishop John once again had taken off his shoes and given them away.

Many of the Tatas' Richmond neighbours are families who once used to live in Shanghai. Such refugees often came to the United States with their China dream in tatters, entire fortunes abandoned in haste in 1949, when the Communists won the civil war against the Nationalists.

'I remember that it was all disarray as far as the business was concerned. Because my father really—with all due respect to everything—[my father] was a broken man when he had to leave Shanghai. He died [in Hong Kong] when he was not even eighty at that time—in my opinion, relatively young,' Jehangir said.

'Ms Saran, my father came to Shanghai in 1904. At that time, when Parsis came over, they usually stayed for life, you know . . . At that time he was with Ratanji Dadabhoy Tata['s trading company], then he went on his own. He was very successful in managing two cotton mills [with] over a few thousand workers total . . . and he managed the mills—buying the materials, raw cotton, to produce the actual yarn and bed sheets in those days . . . and everything in between. And then aside from that, he'd made some very good friends among the Chinese, he really made very good friends. And he also invested in the Chinese companies and all that. And then, in those days, when there was a contract, it was a twenty-year contract.'

The family shared with me a sepia-toned photo portrait of his father, Bejan Dadabhoy Tata, who was born in Surat, India, in 1874. In the photograph, he is dressed formally, in a collared shirt, a cravat, waistcoat and jacket. The ensemble is topped by a stylish fedora.

His bushy eyebrows—the right one slightly cocked—frame the top of round glasses popular at that time. The spectacles are poised on the bridge of a generous nose, then comes a wide philtrum and thin lips, set in a well-defined bow shape. The effect is of a man certain of his morals. A faint forward tilt of his shoulders hints at a yen for adventure. But his eyes hold a skittish look, as though he already suspected events might get the better of him.

Bejan Dadabhoy Tata was a distant cousin of his boss Ratanji Dadabhoy Tata (R.D. Tata), who himself was a first cousin of India's tycoon Jamshedji Tata.

In the summer of 1904, the same year B.D. Tata sailed east to help expand his cousin's business, R.D. Tata's French wife gave birth in Paris to their Eurasian son. They would name that boy Jehangir Ratanji Dadabhoy Tata—J.R.D. Tata.

The Parsis in India had been involved in the China trade of opium and cotton right alongside the British, as early as 1756. The Parsis were keen ship builders, they were financially adroit, and entrepreneurial to their bones. The China trade had even given rise to Parsi surnames like Chenoy and Chinai, and the traditional clothes that Parsi women wear to this day are exquisitely embroidered with Chinese motifs.

On 26 January 1841, the British planted a flag on Hong Kong soil. It was soil wrested from the Qing dynasty in the Opium War—though the treaty that would conclude the war and cede swathes of land in Shanghai and other ports over to the British had yet to be signed. On that January day, also present with the British were the Parsi gentlemen Pestonjee Cowasjee, Rustomjee Dhunjishaw and Framjee Talati. Right alongside the British, the Parsis made significant land purchases at Hong Kong's first land auction held in June that same year.

From Hong Kong, some Parsis soon migrated northwards to Shanghai, even before the French government had negotiated with the Qing dynasty for its own wedge of land that would be called the French Concession.

By 1854, the Parsis had established a Zoroastrian cemetery in Shanghai on Fuzhou Road. In 1866, right next to the cemetery, they built a fire temple at No. 538, Fuzhou Road.

Fast forward four decades and innumerable clipper voyages, to alight on Shanghai's riverfront, in the early twentieth century, right behind the house of the French consul general, at No. 8, Rue du Consulat.

Bejan Dadabhoy Tata has prospered in the east, he has married and had children; his wife Naja and their older boys have settled here in Shanghai. On 20 May 1919, Naja gave birth to her last two children, a pair of boy–girl twins, Jehangir Bejan Tata and Aloo Bejan Tata. The Chinese term such a birth dragon–phoenix twins, the best combination of all.

Around them, Shanghai was exploding with construction.

The British-dominated, de-facto government of this tiny slice of land was a body known as the Municipal Council. It was busy paving over winding creeks, expanding roads, establishing the infrastructure of a major city. The British slab of waterfront, the Bund, was the bustling hub of commerce. The park bordering the river was called the Bund Garden and a Municipal Council Orchestra, created in 1922, performed in a pavilion-shaped stage lit with gaslights.

Bejan Dadabhoy Tata and Naja hired a Chinese amah to look after their brood and take them to play in the park by the river. The Tata couple tried their best to impose their native Gujarati language at home, but their children answered in English. The youngest boy, the dragon twin Jehangir Bejan Tata remembers the Bund Garden, the music. He even recalls a fight.

'When I was about five years old . . . even younger than that, my twin sister (Aloo) and I . . . you know they presently call it the Bund, formerly it was known as the Bund Garden, and . . . I used to go with my sister, with the amah . . . They used to have a bandstand there, they used to play music, I don't know what kind of band—military music? This I remember very well . . . One day there was a sand box and we were playing and an English girl threw some sand in my face, this I cannot forget, but I got very angry and I did not say anything and when she wasn't looking, I put some sand in her sandwich. Then there was a big commotion . . . and it ended up with the amahs fighting each other . . . When we got home, I told my mother what happened and my mother said "Oh you naughty boy," and then the amah said, "No, she threw the sand first."'

Jehangir's mother Naja dominated the household. She did not speak Chinese, neither did his father, but there was no need, as the local Chinese staff spoke pidgin English. His father was kind to his children but he didn't fuss around the family much. Work kept him busy.

By 1926, B.D. Tata was doing well enough in China to think about acquiring land and building a home on it. He picked an area further inland, a district still developing on the western outskirts of the International Settlement. The total area, in Chinese terms, was over three mu, or about 28,000 sq. ft. B.D. Tata could rent the land in perpetuity.

B.D. Tata had a vision—an ancient Indian vision—of a main house, plus a house for each of his sons. In his mind's eye, he saw a large, gracious villa, with four smaller, semi-detached houses at the back. Lawns would surround the dwellings.

He hired prominent Shanghai-based British architects Davies Brook and Gran. The firm often favoured a style called Moderne—spare lines, curved-edge balconies, a streamlined look reminiscent of ocean liners and airplanes. The firm designed several Shanghai landmarks that are still extant, and a house for B.D. Tata.

The five buildings of B.D. Tata's estate were completed in 1935. He named the big house Avan Villa, after his mother. The Tata family moved west across the International Settlement, past the racecourse, into their grand new residence.

Jehangir Bejan Tata remembers every inch of the house:

'It was a seven-bedroom house with five bathrooms. It had three floors, the ground floor, first floor and second floor and the roof. The ground floor [had] parquet flooring, and as you entered the small hall [and turned] to the left, [there] was a bigger hall, then my mother had a prayer room. The first floor consisted of four bedrooms. My mother and father had a bedroom each with an adjoining passage, which served as a closet for clothes, and then my eldest brother had one there.

'There was a study, and from there, there was a large room—now we call it the living room—we used to call it the sitting room, and next to the sitting room was the dining room. And there were two beautiful murals, one known as a bas-relief, was like a sculpture on the wall, it was done by a [well-known Shanghai-based] Russian artist by the name of Poudgoursky. [The other] was a mural in the dining room. And I think that if these two things were still there, I think the murals in that would be worth in the millions. I'm not joking, Ms Saran, I'm not joking.'

'And we also had the servants' quarters too . . . off the

kitchen. The servants' quarters consisted of an area where the servants could dine and another floor where they had rooms, because we did have a boy, we did have a cook, and I believe we did have what was known as a coolie at that time. These were the permanent ones in the house.'

The Tata home with its roof garden and four semi-detached houses, with their elegant lines, located on Tifeng Road, as Wulumuqi North Road was called then, was featured in an architectural magazine at that time.

Rumbles of war in China began early, when Japan attacked Manchuria on 18 September 1931. It was part of a Japanese military plan to take over China, Southeast Asia and then the world. To prosperous, swinging Shanghai, the attack seemed a far-away nuisance in the north, until it reached their doorstep in 1937. The wider world only paid attention when Japan targeted Pearl Harbor, Hawaii, on 7 December 1941.

Jehangir was just finishing school in 1937 when the Japanese planes bombed Shanghai.

'I remember the Japanese barracks were right across [from] the school. You know, I must say [the situation] was not as bad as Hong Kong or Singapore. My father was concerned that we maybe would be put into [Japanese internment] camps, because we all had British passports at that time. I had a British passport, a lot of us had proper British passports.'

That meant the Tata passports were the real deal, not the second-class passports issued to citizens of British protectorates. But, the Japanese had classified all Indians, including the Tatas, as 'friendly enemies', and they were to be spared the prison camps.

In Shanghai, the Japanese confiscated the Chinese mills run by B.D. Tata and all work came to a halt. The young Jehangir, who had been working for his father out at the mills, was suddenly at a loose end. He focused on his hobbies—exercising, bodybuilding. He took singing lessons. He had a thought he might become an entertainer, as he was good at amateur theatricals.

To make ends meet in the war years, people did a brisk speculative trade in hard-to-find commodities. There was rationing of sugar, eggs, milk, flour.

Old orders around the globe collapsed one by one.

In China, under the Nationalist Kuomintang regime, led by Chiang Kai-shek, the foreigners' extraterritorial rights in the Treaty Ports, including Shanghai, had been abolished. The sole agency agreement that Jehangir's father had negotiated with the two Chinese cotton mills had to be relinquished.

Across the Himalayas, the Dominion of India dissolved and on 15 August 1947, India gained her independence.

Jehangir's older brother Sam, a photographer, had left Shanghai for India to document events there. At an exhibition of his work in Bombay in 1948, he met the already famous French photographer Henri Cartier-Bresson. The two men would become lifelong friends and Cartier-Bresson's revolutionary style of 'pouncing' with his 35 mm lens on unfolding, candid street scenes shaped Sam Tata's work. The two men worked together in India.

Sam came home to Shanghai and focused his camera on a turning point in China's history: the Kuomintang's downfall and the Communist troops entering Shanghai. When Cartier-Bresson arrived in Shanghai to help capture that same history in the making, he stayed with his friend Sam Tata, at Avan Villa.

Sam frequented the artistic circles that populated the French Concession, not far from the Tata house. That is where he met a lovely Russian teenager, Lydia, and invited her over, not knowing that she would later marry his younger brother.

The Tatas felt a new era lapping at their feet.

Jehangir's British passport was expiring, and he went to the British consulate to renew it.

'So I went to the British consulate and—I'll never forget—they refused. They said, "You are now Indian." They said, "India is now independent" and all that. So I took up the Indian passport—the whole family took up the Indian passport at that time . . . and to this day I still hold an Indian passport.'

Many of Shanghai's expatriate community refused to believe the Communists would win the civil war against the Nationalist Kuomintang army.

But Jehangir's father, armed with his fresh Indian passport, read the writing on the wall.

He and Naja left Shanghai in early 1949, in despair, looking over their shoulder at beautiful Avan Villa, the estate they had constructed with their blood and bare hands. Jehangir's father was unable to reconcile the enormity of what he had lost—an entire life built over half a century: impossible to pack up a villa and four semi-detached houses on 28,000 sq. ft of land, impossible to pack a lifetime of friends and adventure and take it with you on a ship. His sons stayed on to wind up matters.

A city dismantled itself.

Jehangir Bejan Tata's thirtieth birthday on 20 May 1949 was a non-event. He does not remember it. His parents had left town; tension and uncertainty swirled through the city as Communist battalions surrounded it.

Six days later, the People's Liberation Army (PLA), clad in their cloth shoes and peasant clothes, had taken over the grand, glittering cosmopolitan city of Shanghai. Things changed overnight, and the shining metropolis the Tatas once knew vanished under a layer of fear.

'My cook came to me with tears in his eyes, he had to report everything I [was doing],' Jehangir said.

Local citizens were forced to watch executions of landlords and capitalists. People were made to confess. Many committed suicide, jumping off buildings. Whole families jumped, for the children were forced to report on their parents.

Jehangir and Lydia began a tense, two-year struggle with the Communist bureaucracy to obtain a marriage certificate.

Sam and Jehangir wound up the Tata family affairs as best as they could. Sam took the precaution of photographing the property deeds on glass negatives, as the original deed had to stay in Shanghai. Many foreigners had abandoned their properties by default, due to the great hassles of complying with all the regulations.

Jehangir actually rented Avan Villa to the Public Health Bureau of the People's Government of Shanghai. He signed a tenancy agreement in Chinese and English, a document dated 17 September 1952.

At the end of 1952, Jehangir appointed a British company, Platt, Hanson & Co., as managing agent for the Tata property in Shanghai. Then Jehangir and his new bride boarded a ship for Hong Kong on new year's eve.

Two years later, in July 1954, the Tatas heard that by order of the Shanghai Municipal Government, all foreign real estate agencies had ceased operation.

That news must have shocked Bejan Dadabhoy Tata to his core. He died the very next month, in August in Hong Kong, perhaps engulfed in sorrow and foreboding. The realization must have sunk in, for him and for scores of others, that they would never return to China, that the dream was over.

The Tata heirs managed to locate long distance a Chinese man, Mr C.L. Tang, who used to work for the Parsis at the temple on Shanghai's Fuzhou Road and they asked him to take on the task of managing their estate. The appointment was approved by the Communist government's House and Land Control Bureau in December 1954.

It was that year, Jehangir recalls, that C. L. Tang said he had to submit all property deeds and land documents to the Land Bureau.

'And he submitted all the documents, some of them were copies and some of them were real, so I don't have any original documents at all, all I have are copies that I made before I left Shanghai . . . So my question is, somewhere along the line, they must have a record of our property, a file number, don't you think?'

All the Tatas have in hand is a copy of Sam's photograph, printed from the glass negative.

C.L. Tang regularly sent to the Tatas correspondence and statements of accounts, including rental income, land and property tax deductions that the House and Land Bureau's Rent Office had made, as well as details of repair costs. C.L. Tang was the guardian of the income—he deducted his own payment from that income—but not a single cent of funds was ever remitted overseas.

C.L. Tang, however, kept sending the Tatas information on their Shanghai property. The government, too, sent via the agent a stream of requests for documentation and payments, taxes, special assessments, repair accounts. Every time the income balance grew too large, the family noticed that a special tax or repair assessment was made on the property.

Still, Naja and her children, now scattered all over the world, complied with all the requests.

Then, a decade later, in 1966, all correspondence from C.L. Tang abruptly ceased.

Horrific news of China's Cultural Revolution trickled to the Tatas in Hong Kong. China was drowned in a political and social chaos that historians would later describe as China's lost decade.

It was clear to the Tatas that if their loyal agent had not already been killed, tainted by his connection to foreigners, he might be at any moment. An attempt to contact him might jeopardize his life. The Tatas decided that no matter how much they loved their house, and worried over its fate, it was not worth more than a man's life. They abandoned efforts to track down their home.

After a decade, the Cultural Revolution's madness ebbed. Ever so tentatively, a wounded China cracked open her doors to let the outside world back in.

Eventually, Jehangir contacted the Indian consulate in Shanghai. He wrote letter after letter, asking for news of his estate. His two girls, Claudia and Irene, grew up and went to college in the United States. They married and had children there.

Jehangir and Lydia moved to the United States in 1993 to be closer to Lydia's mother and to the girls, and Jehangir resumed writing his letters, faxing them across the oceans. Over the decades, his handwriting in the faxes gets smaller, and shakier.

In 2001, at the age of eighty-two, Jehangir Bejan Tata made a trip to Shanghai with his daughter Irene.

Incredibly, Avan Villa was still there.

Somebody had turned the ground floor into an antique shop. The upper floors appeared empty. The store manager quite proudly showed the Tatas around. He explained he was renovating the building, that the house had belonged to an Indian, that the four smaller houses were for his sons.

'I know,' Jehangir might have snapped.

Behind the big house, the Tatas met one Mr Wang, a tenant of the Tatas for many years. Initially, Wang's father had rented one of the back semi-detached houses—all of it. Then, in 1966, the Communist Party began jamming increasing numbers of families into each of the houses. The Wangs then shared the house with five or six other families. Wang said that for many years there was a plaque in the alley that said the properties were owned by Indians.

Irene Tata and her father finally managed to track down C.L. Tang—who turned out to have moved to New York City—but Tang was in his nineties already. He was dying of cancer, he suffered from asthma. He told his visitors that the Communists had arrested him in July 1966. The authorities had also seized all the papers and files and correspondence relating to the Tata property, as well as the rental income that he was holding.

C.L. Tang's brothers and friends who had dealings with foreigners were also arrested and sent to camps for hard labour. Tang was heartbroken, for his brothers had not made it out of the camps alive. He wondered why he was alive himself.

'So I did not press the issue,' Jehangir said. 'I don't think I have any right to press the issue, so he was there and every time on [Chinese] new year, I'd phone him up and wish him for the new year, but I couldn't contact him for the last two or three years and he passed away, unfortunately.'

A few years later—it must have been around 2004—a family friend returning from Shanghai told them that Avan Villa had been torn down and in its place stood a graceless box of an office building.

Jehangir protested via his fax machine. Nobody had asked his permission to tear down Avan Villa, let alone informed him the house was gone.

Jehangir Bejan Tata kept up his faxes to the Indian consulate to try and find out the status of his property, but consul generals come and go and his faxes are addressed to a whole succession of names.

He would still like to know what happened to his father's dream house in Shanghai.

In his old-world, courteous way, he is essentially saying, if the Communists were going to snatch away his property, at the very least, he'd like to have a receipt. He would like some sort of document to put an end to the torture of not-knowing. The Tatas say that some overseas Chinese have received significant compensation for their properties, or had them returned. Some British families, too, have received compensation, although the word is, the amounts were not nearly enough.

I'm in awe of this fragile man, in his tenth decade of life, pointing a finger at a powerful political regime and asking for accountability.

'The main thing is, would it show that it originally belonged to my mother and her five children? And the original names of the owner . . . Again I'm somewhat emphasizing on the fact that the ownership, the original ownership should be stated somewhere along the line.'

I telephoned a lawyer friend in Shanghai, and she put me in touch with an elderly Chinese paralegal who had experience with the tangled issue of old family homes taken over by the Communists.

The man spent days in mysterious offices I never knew the names of. He said he'd pulled numerous strings, called on contacts, seen documents, but could not possibly photocopy them to show me.

Only one thing was clear: Avan Villa belonged to the government.

A document? Could we see some sort of document?

He told me tales of senior, overseas Chinese who had escaped from Shanghai in 1949. Now they return and beg the Communist government for their homes back. The government shrugs and tells them, 'If you invest tens of millions of dollars in China, we might get your house back for you.'

But often the homes were inhabited by multiple families, for the Communists sub-divided single-family villas and parcelled out sections. They used complex rules of semi-ownership, or 'renting' or 'right to use' and gradually—ironically—China allowed its people to purchase property outright.

As for Avan Villa, there is still no sign of an actual file.

The family has a photograph of the big house, dated 29 June 1941, taken by a hired studio photographer on the occasion of a formal and lavish Shanghai-style Navjote ceremony celebration. Nearly 150 guests dressed in formal attire have collected on the grass. The Parsi women are clad in saris, the men—Parsi, Western and some Chinese—wear Western-style suits. Western female guests sport dresses and hats. Other Chinese men wear the *changshan*—a traditional collarless long gown with slits and generous sleeves. A row of children sit cross-legged in front.

It is a snapshot of the multinational mix the city used to be.

Behind them rises Avan Villa, with her airy, confident lines. A side veranda gives out on to the lawn, a capacious balcony graces the upper floor. The overhang above the balcony features the signature Moderne—curved edges. French windows give access to the balcony and some of them have been left open for the party. Their angled panes reflect the summer skies of seventy-odd years ago.

Meanwhile, Jehangir Bejan Tata has had another fall, Lydia Tata told me last week on the phone from San Francisco. He has lost a lot of weight.

In May 2014, Jehangir Bejan Tata will turn ninety-five. He has begun to talk about dying, which is terribly upsetting to his family.

'Hang on,' I beg him telepathically from across the oceans. 'We might find that piece of paper yet.'

This July, a typhoon crashed into Taiwan and South China, but its flicking tail swept Shanghai skies clean and the city is domed daily in silkscreen blue. A golden afternoon light dips amidst the roadside plane trees the French planted a hundred years ago and the cicadas, for the moment, are silent.

Jehangir Bejan Tata died in San Francisco in November 2013.

Through the Lens Darkly

PHOTOGRAPHS BY DAYANITA SINGH

TEXT BY NAMITA GOKHALE

THE HOUSE OF LOVE

These enigmatic and evocative images, conveying the mystery and strangeness of distant places, have been shot by acclaimed photographer Dayanita Singh at Durga Puja pandals in Kolkata.

Her mischievous photographs of the Taj Mahal nudge us to relook the very nature of cultural iconography and of mimic 'tourist' images. These photographs demand to be read, not just viewed. Her photographic fiction challenges preconceptions with its intensity and straight-faced irony.

The Taj Mahal, the 'House of Love', is a recurring theme in Dayanita's work, appearing as a dream motif, as a metal sculpture, as a kitsch souvenir, as a theatrical pandal installation and other such disconcerting interpretations.

The two photographs, especially the second one with its seemingly incongruous juxtaposition of the Taj Mahal, the Eiffel Tower and the Empire State Building—the wonders of new and old worlds—evoke the hunger of an expanded universe of familiar cultural significators.

Photograph Dayanita Singh

Photograph Dayanita Singh

Photograph Dayanita Singh

Photograph Dayanita Singh

SHOTS IN THE DARK

The public celebrations during 'Durga Puja', which include fanciful 'pandals', reverse the trajectory of travel and bring the destination home to the viewer. Dayanita quotes her friend Aveek Sen: 'In the night of the mind, my many cities become one . . .'

'This is the largest art installation in the world,' Dayanita comments. 'Every street crossing is transformed with a structure to house the goddess. Yet my interest is not in the goddess, but in the homes built for her.'

Among thronging crowds of Durga devotees, these pastiche museums of curiosities use bamboo scaffolding, thermocol and paper mâché to evoke the wonders of the great world. If dreaming is the best way to travel, the wraith-like nature of this faux evocation of the Sistine Chapel and the Statue of Liberty releases the inner essence of what they might mean to a local tourist or traveller.

Lost Without a Trace

AVEEK SEN

I needed an American visa. It was getting too late, and the fact that I couldn't put off applying for it any longer was making me feel resentful and a bit queasy. I knew I had pushed myself to a tight and risky corner. It was a hot day in the beginning of April. I thought I'd start with getting myself photographed, for there were elaborate, nervous-making instructions about the photos in the form.

The studio was right next to the visa office on Ho Chi Minh Sarani, a schizophrenic street that can't decide whether it is in Calcutta or Washington—and its name doesn't help. You had to enter through an antique gate and walk across a wasteland of demolition rubble to get to the studio. I went in through the swing doors into a tiny, sparsely furnished, but tidy room. One end of it was curtained off, where the pictures are taken. The air conditioning was perfect, the neons stark but not harsh, and there was music playing—Enigma's 'Mea culpa' on a loop. There was a youngish man working at a computer, and a younger fellow lolling semi-purposefully. I found myself relaxing immediately in this room. But I felt alert too, curious, almost a little turned on—not sexually, but inside my head and eyes. Switched on, more than turned on. Something will happen here, I felt, something mysterious but so quiet and fleeting that it would be like nothing. Yet, it could be carried away to the world outside and would stay with me. The older man seemed to know what I had come for, and gently asked me to wait.

Sitting there on a little stool, I was reminded of how, on a summer day in Rome many years ago, I had walked into one of those immense Baroque churches, just to take refuge from the stupefying heat, and seeing a row of latticed confessionals inside, had decided on an impulse to confess like a good Catholic. Waiting in front of that curtained-off space to be photographed reminded me of those fake, kinky, but calming moments of waiting for the priest. I had felt a peculiar blankness inside the church, as if the combination of pretence and having nothing to confess had reduced me to a kind of nothing in that space, an absence of identity that was oddly exciting. The anticipation of being photographed had exactly that feel of having misplaced an essential bit of myself just when I would be called upon to present it to somebody. It was like realizing suddenly that I had left my face behind at home. This did not fill me with panic but with excitement. Wouldn't it be fun to fake a face?

Then my eyes went to the large pinboard on the wall behind the computer at which the man was working, and I knew why this room made me feel switched on from the moment I stepped into it. It was a place of *darshan*: its everyday religion was that of the eye. (And how brilliant that this quintessentially Indian word yoked pure looking with nothing less than pure philosophy!) I dislike taking photographs myself, except tentative ones on my phone that I erase after a while. But I am happiest among photographs and photographers, as delighted to watch them taking and making photographs as I am to look at photos, play around with them, and use them as aids to reflection and writing. And I knew that what I saw on that workaday pinboard would keep me occupied for a long time.

Most of Calcutta's celebrities, I saw, patronized this little studio. So, when they come to make their passport and visa photos here, the proprietor enlarges these photos and puts them up on his pinboard after getting them autographed, one after another without any space in between. The result, quite inadvertently, is an ongoing photography show that somehow captures the strangely moving ironies of the human face. Like those little hidden cinemas in Paris that show offbeat matinees, so that you stumble into one in the middle of the day expecting something vaguely blue and then realize that you are watching great cinema, this mundane place next to the American embassy had quietly placed before my eyes a little theatre of human identity.

There were heroines, starlet-politicians, icons, sons and daughters of icons, heroes looking like gym instructors, gym instructors looking like heroes, ageing fashion designers, writers looking like ageing fashion designers, ageing footballers looking like writers, pop singers looking like ageing gym instructors, and others whom I could not recognize. They had faced the camera and flash full, wore no make-up, and had been forbidden to smile. All of them had that blank, washed-out look. The women looked battered, as if they had just recovered from a black eye or bruised lips. Enigma was still singing 'Mea culpa'. But it was as if these people had suddenly heard the Trump of Doom in the middle of a party, and had come, with a touching lack of resistance, to face the most pitiless and unblinking eye of all.

The young fellow called me behind the curtain, and in a few quick flashes finished his job. I came out and darted back to my seat. I hadn't finished looking at the pinboard. By this time, however, something else had started happening around me. A uniformed chauffeur had come into the studio with two little photos of his employers to get more copies made. The man at the computer took a second to identify them, and fished the files out of the computer. Then with five deft clicks of the mouse he reproduced five more copies of each, which the chauffeur put into his pocket before disappearing through the swing doors into the city. The whole thing took just a few minutes. The bringing of the photos, making their copies, printing them out, cutting them up, putting them into a numbered envelope and carrying them away were done with an automatic, synchronized, deadpan and wordless impersonality that held my attention. Soon, I got my face back too from the man at the computer. Twelve copies, six each of two different sizes, and a reference number for future use.

In the metro on my way back home, sitting among a sea of unknown faces, I steeled myself for a long look at my visa photos. In them, there wasn't a trace of the queasiness and the sweat and the wait in the studio, of the many things that had happened within, around, before, during and after. The photos were pure surface. They said nothing.

Fear of Flying

ADVAITA KALA

It didn't make it to the ticker, or even the radio, if only to juice up your daily commute, but I got picked up for a pat-down at JFK. There are many reasons why a person is randomly selected for a pat-down and I now find myself in august company. However this still doesn't explain: why me? I thought I'd check with Blogger Bob, the TSA's official blogger, on why someone like *me* would be picked out. But Blogger Bob turned out to be, in my opinion (and at the risk of being on pat-down lists for life), a bit of an exhibitionist and not quite personal enough. So I continue to be assailed by the 'why me' syndrome. Friends have attempted to rationalize the occurrence—it's because I am a nervous flier and nervous people can look suspicious. My family (extended included), who finds a reason to blame me for everything that doesn't quite work out in my life, suggest that I am a terrible dresser when I travel which quite obviously means I may be capable of a terror attack. Fair enough.

ABOUT TWO WEEKS AGO

Much like a bug trapped in a jam jar, I stand in the plexi-glass fortified cabin placed for maximum humiliation in the middle of the terminal. But, thankfully, it is decided that I need company and a disgruntled airhostess from our national carrier is escorted in. Yeah, smart pick, Sherlock, like these ladies need another reason to be pissed off. Of course the satirist in me tries to engage in some detainee kind of camaraderie—like when do you think we will get out? Been here before? Will the plane leave without you, it sure will without me? She has the been there, done that look and her response isn't even monosyllabic. She merely shrugs and the message is clear: I need to get serious.

So I return to my silent meditations of 'why me'. Could it be the flannel PJs squeezed into my overstuffed tote? Or the fact that I once lived in the Middle East? Or maybe they tracked my desperate calling at every store in the shopping arcade in search of the sleep-inducing Nyquil. Till a wily store clerk finally got what I wanted and suggested Tylenol PM—'It knocks you out' he assured me. For a drug run this was an overt but successful one.

It could have even been the fact that I waved a rather dramatic goodbye to my checked-in baggage. But then the baggage handler and I shared a corny laugh and exchanged banter on the efficiency of the industrial-size X-ray machines. I was impressed by the size but he seemed to disagree, saying they were too slow. Which they were. Maybe this conversation wasn't appropriate keeping in mind my nervous, shifty deportment or maybe even the colour of my skin.

As I watch backpack-strapped South Asian males stroll by, another bout of the why mes descend on me. But I am spared further introspection by the appearance of Yolanda (name changed). Yolanda announces her presence much like it's a Ben

Stiller film, her fleshy hands reaching for the ceiling as she snaps on neon-blue latex gloves. And suddenly the 'why mes' are replaced by two other words: 'Cavity search'! Or, as a rather amorously challenged friend puts it, *getting some*.

Yolanda articulates for me, in a tone that swings between officious gynae examination speak and kinky foreplay, all the things that she is going to do to me. Cavity search not included. She asks if I am all right with doing it right there. Not one for public displays of affection and completely aware of the inconvenience it would cause her, I say absolutely not. I needed privacy. 'Of course,' she sighs and says, 'Follow me, hon.' Her manner not quite living up to her stated courtesy.

She picks up the tote and declines my offer of help—I am not to touch my belongings. I apologize for their heft as she calls for help to carry the rest of my things. Although secretly pleased I maintain a solemnity—with my gate a few miles away, I am grateful for any lugging that I am spared and follow meekly.

The examination is to be conducted in a storeroom, not really as impressive as I would have imagined or expected. It just doesn't make me feel like I am enough of a 'person of interest'. I was thinking of a more sterile, steel, cold glass-and-white light kind of ambience. And here I am in what looks like a boys' locker room with abandoned luggage and is that an old sock in the corner? We soon have company—Yolanda's friend squeezes into the room, her hair a shocking carrot orange, the result of a bad do-it-yourself home dye job. The kind you have to live through, before dyeing your hair again, lest it all fall out. Yeah, I've been there. I feel instant pity, before I realize that the principle of the two is in action (never be alone with a suspect). This is getting serious. I offer to remove my fleece hoodie but the overture is regretted with an askance: 'No! Leave it on!'

As Yolanda delivers on her promise, she also updates me on

life on the other side of the body scanner. You see it's not like it's easy or fun doing this pat-down stuff. And despite my self-indulgent forays into the reasons why I was picked out, I realize that I could have quite simply been the sixteenth or the seventeenth in line. This truly could be random. And if one were to forget the controversy and the accusations of 'GATE RAPE', national outrage and racial profiling, and look at it from another's perspective, it's sort of a pain-in-the-ass job. As Yolanda put it, 'He [the evil boss] insists on putting me in the pat-down. I walked nine blocks in the snow today. Nine blocks to the ATI to get on the six. And he done put me in pat-down duty. I've gone busted my knee. I can't bend no more. You know, I be doing it. But my heart ain't in it . . ."

And just like that, it was over. I have to admit it was anti-climactic. After being privy to the many headlines and arguments that parenthesize the debate on the propriety of the pat-down, I was expecting a little more.

ABOUT NOW

And now when it's in the past, I question my lack of serious outrage and indulgence in silly musings. It may be explained by the fact that I fail to instantly identify as a race or gender. I have had experiences that shape me just like the next person, but I don't attribute them as a direct consequence of either. Which they very well might have been for a person of more perception and a greater sense of their place in the world. Not for a person who is more embarrassed than outraged by the idea of racism or sexism, and considers it a personal failing to be perceived as a victim of either.

Maybe there will be a delayed epiphany and I will feel the outrage and not an overriding of reason by the residual memory of the sadness I felt as I stood out in the balcony of my apartment with its view of what were the World Trade Center towers and the WTC cranes necking with each other (a subject of many a cute newspaper headline). Or the memory of a boy I once knew and workplaces that were considered home, a time before lasting images of a burning dome took away that sense of safety.

Maybe the anger will wash up one day at these acts like *random checks* that possibly widen and deepen the chasm. Instead, I still grapple with the helplessness and the daily reminders that are the gateposts of our reality, the landmarks of our collective legacy—that of a political violence that is conveniently labelled terrorism. A war with no foreseeable end or borders.

A day after my return, a suicide attack was carried out at the busiest airport in Moscow. It took me back to Yolanda, crouching on the floor, her body weight resting on her busted knee, tapping at my ankles. Did she think it was a waste of time? I know she did and so did I, *at the time*. But as I turned away from the television and the headlines, muting the sound of screeching ambulances, I was glad we did it anyway.

The Foreigner's Situation

ALI SETHI

Every morning, minutes after Faisal drove up to his kiosk in
Copenhagen and undid the shutters, Uncle came down from
his apartment in the brown brick building across the street. It
took Uncle a while to reach the kiosk: he was an old man now,
his hair gone white and his frank square face turned leather-red;
he walked with one hand behind his back and the other clenched
around the handle of an unopened umbrella that he used as a
walking stick. His walk was shivery and erratic: he took quick
steps, had to stop, then took another few steps. Sometimes he
had to turn his head to one side and smack the back of his skull.
It was a condition, Faisal knew, a shutting down in a part of the
brain that caused the slow and painful loss of a man's extensions.

Uncle didn't care; it didn't stop him from painting, which
was all he'd ever wanted to do. Faisal, who was only thirty years
old, who took kick-boxing classes on the weekend and wore
bright polo shirts (nowadays with the collar turned up) but had
always done work of a decidedly unartistic kind, found this to
be a little incredible. There were many Pakistanis in Copenhagen

but no one in Faisal's purview who lived with this kind of abandon.

Uncle considered it his achievement. He had told Faisal that he came to Denmark in 1961, long before the other Pakistanis arrived in droves, and he came not to make money but to pursue his love for a white girl. That didn't work out; a few years later Uncle married another girl, also white, and for years they lived together in the building across the street. They had an apartment upstairs and a room in the basement for Uncle's paintings. Faisal had been inside this room. It was small and damp and hung with watercolours and pen-and-ink drawings of fruit and pottery and landscapes but also stark-naked women lying about in easy attitudes. The one big table in the room was crowded with empty beer cans and over-full ashtrays. Though Faisal sold alcohol and tobacco in his shop, he would never take them into his clean, spare apartment in the suburbs, where the walls were devoted to Quranic ayats and golden-framed portraits of the House of God, and the only people in the pictures were Faisal's Pakistani wife and their three small children.

Still, despite these differences, Uncle and Faisal got along and could converse on just about anything—Faisal standing behind the counter of his kiosk and waiting for customers, Uncle sitting on a stool by the colour-flashing jackpot machines to one side.

That was how I found them on the morning I walked into the kiosk. Uncle introduced me as a grand-nephew who was visiting from Pakistan.

Faisal shook my hand.

'And this guy,' said Uncle, meaning Faisal, 'is the only Pakistani I talk to over here.' (I already knew that: Uncle had told me the night before that he stayed away from most of the city's Pakistani immigrants because he had found them to be irredeemably backward.)

Faisal, hearing himself described favourably, grinned now and looked away. But later, when he and I were in his car, he let out a long sigh.

'Uncle is not like other foreigners,' he said with dismay and tenderness.

His breath was musty. He was fasting; I was to go with him at sundown to a Pakistani restaurant for the iftar meal.

'Foreigners?' I asked. 'You mean Danes . . .?'

'I mean us,' he said. 'Pakistanis, Arabs, Turks—all of us who come from outside.'

'Are those the only foreigners here?'

'No,' said Faisal. 'There are also Afghans and Somalis. Lots of Somalis in recent years. You know, because of what's happening in their country . . .'

'When did we—I mean Pakistanis—first come to Denmark?'

'From what I know,' he said, 'Uncle came before all the others. That was fifty years ago. Then—I think ten years after Uncle—came the other Pakistanis. But,' and this was what had confounded Faisal, 'there was hardly any contact between those Pakistanis and Uncle.'

I wondered if Faisal knew about Uncle's background. Uncle had come from Lahore, then Pakistan's only big city, from one of a handful of well-to-do English-speaking families of teachers and civic administrators. He could afford to embark at the age of nineteen on a sightseeing tour of Europe with his friends, rebellious youths like himself who were sharpened at British-made schools and had the cock to drink imported whiskey all through the PIA flight to London. Uncle's mind was loaded with the names of famous European artists—Monet and Van Gogh and Degas and Gauguin—who had given him a simple but powerful idea of the artist's vocation: one had to break free of one's setting and experience the world's pleasures; and one had to do it in the style of the Europeans.

The Pakistanis who came a decade after him were peasants. Though in Pakistan their houses—mud huts in a village—were only 300 km away from Uncle's, their circumstances were entirely different. The peasants didn't speak English or Danish, didn't know about Europe or its art. They left their country expressly to earn a living: they worked in Denmark's factories, on its roads and at its construction sites, and they sent the money they made back to their families in Pakistan. In those days the Danes were more relaxed—they needed labour and weren't full of suspicions—and the labourers took advantage of this laxity and began to summon their relatives to Denmark.

Faisal came in 1999. He was a teenager then. But his relatives, travelling with the first wave of immigrants, were settled here and prospering. It was their earnings that had provided for Faisal in Pakistan: he had been to an English-language school in a small city whose many shops and cars were underwritten by money remitted from abroad. By the time his turn came to emigrate, it wasn't hard for Faisal—many had done it before him and were waiting for him on the other side. He wasn't frightened of the plane he boarded, wasn't intimidated by the forms he had to fill out at Copenhagen airport. He already spoke English and, after a few months at a language school in the new country, he could speak some Danish too.

'Still,' he said, 'Copenhagen was very different for me. I was shocked when I got here.'

He drove a taxi for the first five years. The landscape was strange, the people even stranger. There was no sun for weeks, and when it came out it occasioned an extraordinary display of devotion: at once people stopped what they were doing and went out of offices and homes and threw off their clothes and lay down in parks and even in the streets to commune with the special sun, the same sun that in Pakistan was over-abundant, that chased and burned and even killed people.

'I felt there was a difference in the people's temperament,' said Faisal.

One day a white woman got into his taxi and began to tell him about her childhood. 'My meter was on,' said Faisal. 'I was worried she would yell at me for asking her to pay. But she told me to keep the meter on. She was paying me to listen.'

The woman described to him her childhood home, her many cousins and the intricate games they had played with one another. She described these things with longing and affection. But then her parents had died and her cousins had gone their own ways; and like this, over many years, the woman had lost touch with all the people she had known and loved. 'She was weeping in my taxi,' said Faisal. 'She paid me just to witness her grief.'

From this and other experiences Faisal had gathered that loneliness too could be a disease, a kind of sickness of the soul. 'Basically there is this pressure here to be free. People come under it at the age of eighteen, when they are forced to leave their parents' house. Everything they do now must be for freedom: they must have it in their marriage, must have it even in the raising of their children. The jobs they do must make them feel free. But at forty they are hit by panic: have they really been free? Isn't their freedom about to end? So they go out again and attempt freedom. They drink and dance and have sex. Their children start to hate them. In the end they have to talk to strangers about their childhoods.'

It had happened like this to Uncle: he had shunned community and gone for freedom, but in his old age, his freedom exhausted, he felt the need for a witness. Now he spent a lot of time telling Faisal about his childhood in Pakistan, describing again and again the Partition of India in 1947 and the bodies that came floating down the Lahore canal, and all the things he knew about Pakistani politicians and actors and singers, making sure to mention their amorous entanglements. Faisal knew he was a help to Uncle, a reliever of the old man's burdens. But he was also compelled by Uncle's stories and found himself committing them to memory as if for later use, as if he were looking, albeit from a permanent distance, at a life that might have been his own.

'Uncle stayed away from the community,' said Faisal. 'He wanted his freedom. He paid a price for that. I have seen how his daughter talks to him. She can be so rude. Once she was very rude to him in my shop. Uncle couldn't say a thing. He was so helpless that I had to intervene.'

Faisal couldn't tell whether Uncle was relieved or pained by his intervention.

'This is what happens,' continued Faisal, 'when you marry a white woman and let your child grow up all Danish. You are neither here nor there.'

I asked him about his own children.

'I was lucky,' said Faisal. 'I learned my lessons early. I am teaching my children respect. I want them to grow up with a knowledge of their culture.'

'But they will live here,' I said.

'But you can live here and have a balance,' he replied.

We drove past an algae-covered pond. Behind it were beige Renaissance-style buildings with gabled roofs. Bicycles went by on the streets, the cyclists tall and blonde and white: a picture of civic harmony and eco-friendliness, a simple balance between old and new, between the well-preserved landscape and its conscientious perusal by Denmark's proto-youngsters. But then we took a turn and went into a narrow lane and the buildings became small and workaday and grimy, the shop signs in Arabic and Turkish advertising halal meat and cheap calling cards and special packages for the pilgrimage to Saudi Arabia. Black graffiti—this in Danish—was slashed across the walls.

'This area belongs to foreigners,' said Faisal. 'Whites don't come here. Even the police are afraid to enter this neighbourhood.' He was excited. 'It looks all calm right now but if you started an argument with someone, you would be surrounded in minutes. These guys,' he continued, indicating with a nod the group of idle-looking men sitting on a pavement, 'they are selling powder.'

'Cocaine?' I asked.

'Everything,' he said. 'The foreigners sell all kinds of drugs.' Then he clarified: 'Actually the suppliers are whites. But the dealers are foreigners. And it is the dealers who get caught by the police, so the reputation for drugs is awarded in the end to foreigners.'

He also said: 'The whites love giving us a bad name here.'

I asked, 'And among ourselves? Is there interaction between Pakistanis and Arabs and Turks . . .?'

'More and more,' said Faisal. 'But there are limits. You must have heard about Ghazala . . .'

I had: she was the big-eyed nineteen-year-old daughter of a Pakistani taxi driver in Copenhagen. Some years ago she had told her mother that she was in love with a Pashtun boy and wanted to marry him. The mother was appalled: she beat Ghazala and locked her in the house. But Ghazala managed to escape with her lover and married him in a small Danish town. Her family heard about it; they made contact with her and offered to forgive her. A few days later, at the railway station where the family reunion was to take place, Ghazala's older brother brought out a gun and shot her to death.

'I knew the brother,' said Faisal. 'He used to drive a taxi. A kind boy.'

I asked, 'What happened to him?'

'Oh,' said Faisal, and he sounded surprised, 'you mean why did he do it? The community blocked him out. Not just him— his whole family. The Pakistani community here boycotted them when Ghazala ran away. It was like the family had to be punished for what had happened. The girl's brother couldn't take it any more. In the end the whole family consented to her killing.'

In all nine people—family members and friends—were found guilty of planning her murder. The Danish court awarded what were by its own standards severe punishments, including a life term for Ghazala's father, sixteen years for her brother and permanent expulsions for the plotters who were not Danish citizens.

The ruling showed that it wasn't possible to restrict the blame for such a crime to a single individual.

I said, 'Would you say that the community killed Ghazala?'

'Exactly,' said Faisal.

'But she had married a Muslim . . .'

'Yes,' said Faisal, 'but the community doesn't think like that.'

Later he told me that his own marriage to a Pakistani girl of his choice was seen within the community as a provocation. There was the fact of their 'love marriage'—still a taboo among the foreigners—but there was also the matter of caste: Faisal descended from warriors and land tillers and his wife from cattle rustlers. And such distinctions still mattered to people who had brought their village ideas of social organization and held on to them here, even as they worked the machines in Danish factories and laid out Danish roads, and earned wages which, converting wondrously from Danish kroner to Pakistani rupees, turned the villages they had left behind into towns, the fields into roads and the cattle into cars.

Faisal had grown up on that money in those unevenly changing places. For him, as for many others like him, some of the old ideas had lost their meaning, while new ones, arising out of new experiences, had come into focus: when he married his wife, Faisal was marrying a girl who, like him, had lived in both Pakistan and Denmark, wore Western and Pakistani clothes and spoke Danish as well as English and Urdu. He was marrying one of his kind.

But in other ways he continued to be a land tiller and she a woman of cattle rustlers, their clan identities parting and sharpening as they turned into their ties to people and properties back home, and onwards into their respective abilities to influence feuding politicians. Those were persisting realities in Pakistan. And those realities had followed them here, into this apparently tie-less land, where Faisal and his wife lived and worked from the beginning among their kin.

Faisal's marriage, then, had occurred both inside and outside his community. That he had managed to stay within the community even after his transgression showed that the community was changing. Indeed, Faisal's survival showed that he was, in many ways, living an intermediate life, positioned somewhere between his community's past and future.

Sitting with him in his car, I began to wonder what words like 'integration' and 'isolation', thrown around so frequently to describe the state of Muslims in Europe, could mean to someone in Faisal's position. Could he only 'integrate' into European society by breaking from his community? And, if he did that, what could he do next? Could Faisal, who was not raised on dreams of Degas and Gauguin, find integration in an art museum? What if, after quitting his community, he continued to meet Pakistani friends, eat Pakistani food and say his prayers in Arabic? Would that take away from his integration? Did he have to find a Danish girl and live with her in an apartment in order to feel integrated? Wouldn't such a life make Faisal feel isolated instead? And then I thought: but doesn't he already live in an apartment, and isn't his wife, who grew up in Denmark and speaks Danish, Danish?

In fact, the experience of Faisal's life was not an easy one. I could hear it in his voice when he told me that behind his back some Pakistanis still raised objections to his out-of-caste marriage; and he knew that Danes looked upon him in the street with their own suspicions. For someone in that position, I imagined, it would have been hard to belong anywhere.

And later, when I mentioned it to Uncle—Uncle who had married a white woman and kept his distance from the Pakistani community, Uncle who appeared to have quit one society and fully embraced another—I found him giving a harsh view of Faisal's foreignness. 'I pity them,' said Uncle. 'Their problem, you see, is that they are neither here nor there.'

The Ramadan fast was extra long in Copenhagen. The sun rose a little after 3 a.m.—the sehri meal had to be consumed at this time—and it set as late as 8 p.m. That could make a seventeen-hour fast. Walking with Faisal around the old part of the city, its cobblestone streets filled with tourists and the many hot dog and ice cream stalls that fed their cravings, I was reminded of a line I had memorized as a child in Pakistan: 'The breath of the faster is sweeter to Allah than the fragrance of musk.' In Pakistan, where everyone fasted during Ramadan (or appeared to, fearing censure) and everything shut down for the duration of the fast, the words had sounded solemnly righteous, even sinister, like a command for nationwide musk-breath. But on this overcast afternoon in Copenhagen, the light lingering faintly and temptingly over the food-filled streets, the same words felt vital and original: they promised to transform the faster's depletion into his nourishment, his singular suffering into an especial and unlikely attainment.

'How many hours?' I asked Faisal.

'Still a few,' he said.

To pass the time we decided to visit Ibrahim, a friend of Faisal's who had a travel agency in the city centre.

Ibrahim's shop was surrounded by others of its kind. From the outside it didn't stand out: the window had dull printout pictures of various landmarks—the Taj Mahal in Agra, the Faisal Mosque in Islamabad, the Shaheed Minar in Dhaka—with corresponding airfares jotted underneath. The international theme continued inside the shop: a mounted poster for PIA was hung between larger ones for Incredible India and Turkish Airlines.

'Never exclude,' said Ibrahim. 'That is the first rule of business.'

A slim man with bright eyes and a dark, shadowy face, he was sitting in a rotation chair, wearing a pinstripe blazer over a shirt and trousers. At once the clothes set him apart from Faisal, who was taller and bulkier but in his T-shirt and jeans now looked less worldly-wise.

'What do you think?' queried Ibrahim, making half-rotations with his chair. 'Am I not right?'

He said this after every big statement.

I said, 'I think you are right.'

But he said he hadn't always known this rule. When he came to Denmark many years ago he was just another immigrant, a man with an untenable diploma from a small-town Pakistani college and no money. 'For five years I suffered,' said Ibrahim.

'I was knocked around. They were hard, those five years. But one thing I will say: in this society, being knocked around is beneficial. Ask how. I will tell you: it makes you familiar with the society. Once you are familiar with this society, once you have understood its many games, big and small, you can convert your understanding into money. That is the tragedy of Pakistan. You can be knocked around for many years, you can acquire a deep understanding of the people and their ways, but you can do nothing with that knowledge unless you have connections. Am I not right?'

It was a Pakistani connection in another travel agency that got Ibrahim started in Copenhagen. He learned quickly: immigrants were unswayable when it came to attending weddings and funerals in the mother country and often had to make last-minute bookings on international flights. Ibrahim resolved to provide this service: first he got in touch with PIA's Karachi office—that was where the airline stored its information. 'Suppose there are 300 seats on a plane and 275 have been sold. Now the PIA officials who keep that information will say that the whole flight is booked. They will announce this. Those last twenty-five seats will disappear from their computer screens. If you called the airline to ask for a seat you would be told there was none.' But this was where the travel agent stepped in: he negotiated with the airline officials for those last few seats. 'Of course the passenger pays a little more for his seat,' said Ibrahim, obliquely acknowledging the yield for himself and the PIA official. 'But he gets the seat in the end. He gets to go home and do the rites. That satisfaction has no price for the foreigner, whose heart is heavy with longing and who yearns to show his relatives that he has not forgotten their ways. Am I not right?'

This yearning was common to all foreigners, Ibrahim had found, not just to Pakistanis. 'Indians have this feeling,' he said.

'Bangladeshis have it too. And Turks. I have many non-Pakistani clients.' That explained the different posters in his shop; it also explained the name Ibrahim had given his travel agency*—an ancient word that was common to many Asian languages and evoked a continent instead of a country.

'It is a name for everybody,' he said. 'If you are a Pakistani or Afghan and pass this shop, you will come in. If you are an Indian and pass this shop, you will come in. If you are a Turk, you will come in.'

He also said: 'My relationship with my clients here is based on trust.'

Connections in Pakistan, connections in Denmark, and of different kinds: Ibrahim was a man of many worlds, applying his knowledge of them to good effect.

And he had grown with his knowledge: soon after starting the travel agency he had branched out into the business of money remittances. ('It's about trust, the same trust.') This gave him a rare insight into the foreigners' finances. The big money was in restaurants—one Pakistani restaurant owner sent as much as 50,000 kroner every month to his family in Pakistan. Slightly smaller amounts came from the kiosk owners, who saved money by making their way around Denmark's high taxes. (Faisal had done this many times: you bought the goods in Denmark but took them to Germany, and there you claimed a tax refund. Then you drove them back to Denmark and sold them in the kiosk at full, tax-inclusive prices.)

'What happens to that money when it gets to Pakistan?' I asked.

'Waste,' said Ibrahim, contempt creasing his nose. 'We earn here and our relatives spend it there.'

---

*The name has been withheld so as not to identify/locate the characters.

'On what?'

'On hobbies. These days there is a craze for imported dogs. You know the Great Dane? That's the one. Just a few months ago my brother-in-law took one from here back to Pakistan. He *had* to take it *from* Denmark. He even took a Danish cage for the dog. It broke at the airport.'

Apart from spending on expensive pets (the well-bred horse was another must-have animal), the foreigners' relations in Pakistan spent money on houses, weapons, gadgets, cars, clothes, jewellery and furniture. Some of the remitted money was used to buy agricultural land to lease out to farmers, or to build plazas that were rented out to merchants, or to set up brick kilns that were run by hired labour. But these brought easy incomes to already comfortable lives.

Ibrahim had seen this happen to his own family. Where once they had lived in huts, they now owned a big concrete house with cars and electrical appliances and imported dogs. But beyond the high walls of the new house lay a haemorrhaging country, where power and gas shortages occurred with maddening regularity and there was still no health care or public education to speak of. The immigrant's prosperity had come; reform in the motherland hadn't.

Ibrahim blamed this retarding of Pakistani society on 'biraderi-ism', that old business of caste-and-clan affiliations. Politics in Pakistan, he felt, was just an extension of biraderi-ism: the mainstream political parties were still the personal properties of the old landowners and industrialists and their children. And what was the military's unquestioned control of foreign policy if not a clan privilege? Was the old enmity with India not like a clan interest? It kept up defence spending and kept out commerce between the merchants of the two countries. 'Over here,' said Ibrahim, 'I sell to Indians all the time. Why can't I do it in

Pakistan? Let me control the borders. I have thought about the money . . .'

We talked like this, moving from the promise of the future to the obstacles of the present and then into the deep past: the Jhelum river, on whose banks Ibrahim and Faisal grew up, had given birth to Hindu civilization. Its waters still flowed in ancient Sanskrit texts. And that early language of the Indo-Aryans lived on in the Punjabi we were speaking now in Ibrahim's shop.

'If I had stayed in Pakistan,' said Ibrahim, 'I would never have known these things.'

But here, on foreign soil, the man in the middle could look in many directions, his situation allowing him hindsight as well as foresight.

Two years ago Ibrahim had heard about a box that mediated between an Internet connection and a TV set. Suddenly you had hundreds of channels from India, Pakistan, Afghanistan and Bangladesh, as well as channels run by Asians in the West. So there were music channels from the UK; there were channels run by 'modern' Afghans in California; there were Iranian channels for speakers of Farsi and Dari. There was also a YouTube channel, and one for Facebook was on the way.

It was the foreigner's future in a box.

Ibrahim sought out its makers and offered to sell their product in Denmark. He showed them his travel agency, with its roster of clients from different communities; he wanted nothing less than a franchise. The box-makers were impressed. And Ibrahim went to work. In the last two years he had sold more than 1,500 boxes.

'What do Pakistanis like to watch?' I asked.

'The news,' said Ibrahim. 'And comedy shows.' The most popular of these had a man in suspenders doing take-offs of public figures, including a well-known politician from Gujarat.

'All the big Gujarati politicians,' said Ibrahim, 'they come here to meet us. They need our support now. They all have offices here.'

It had come to this: the landowners and industrialists of Gujarat going out of their way to meet and enlist in their parties the people who only forty years before had fled their lands for the 'good work' of Danish factories and construction sites. Viewed like this, it was the greatest measure of these immigrants' success, a sign of their integration in the other direction, into the power structures of the country they had had to leave but kept in their hearts. It was *because* the immigrants had held on to Pakistan that they were now able to tell this story of spectacular growth, which was not a story Uncle, with all his paintings in a basement, could tell about himself.

Strange, then, to have to return to the narrow subject of Muslims in Europe, and to the even narrower situation of Pakistanis in Denmark. As the hours passed and the light outside the shop began to fade, I found myself probing Faisal and Ibrahim about the very things that had marked them out as strangers for many Danes. How had they reacted to the Danish newspaper's cartoons of the Prophet? (Both were outraged; they were working in their shops on the day of the big protest in Copenhagen, but their friends and relatives had been in the rallies.) And how did they feel about Anders Behring Breivik's massacre of their fellowmen in next-door Norway, his idea of a protest against the 'Pakistanization' of Europe? (Ibrahim said, 'I think it's a good thing. Now they know there are fanatics other than Muslims in this society.') As we left the shop and stepped into the cold street, I thought I saw my companions turning into foreigners: Faisal walking with his chest out and shoulders swinging, one leg limping like a gangster's as he spat with casual force on the sidewalk; and Ibrahim walking beside him with an exaggerated slouch, his head bowed and eyes lowered, his hands deep in the pockets of his trousers.

For the iftar meal we went to a Pakistani restaurant. It was brightly lit and crowded; people sat in groups at tables laid out with napkins and cutlery and bowls of mixed treats: there were Arabian dates and Indian samosas, as well as apples and grapes and bananas, fruit grown so widely now as to have overcome their origins. A poster on the wall showed the smirking, confident face of a Pakistani man who was contesting Denmark's next elections for the Socialist People's Party.

Four schoolgirls were sitting at the table ahead of us. Two were Pakistani-looking and the other two were Arab or Turk. Three were in jeans, one in a long skirt; one of the girls in jeans also wore a hijab. But in this setting they seemed unconcerned with those differences: they were huddling around the table, giving identical smiles and taking pictures of their group with a flashing camera.

Ibrahim said, 'They are going to put those pictures on Facebook.' Then he leaned back and gazed around the light-filled room. 'For the next generation,' he said, 'all these things will be easier. Am I not right?'

F for Dharavi

JERRY PINTO

Dawood is twenty-eight years old. He drives my friend's car. When my friend is in the car with me, I sit in the back with her. When I am alone in the car with Dawood, I sit in the front with him. I think this is my way of saying to Dawood and to the many car-owning people who may see me in the car, 'I do not own a car. I just know someone who does.' But I also know that this is a false position. I belong somewhere between the front seat and the back seat. I grew up in Mahim, in west Bombay, where I still live. Dawood grew up in Dharavi, or Mahim east, as many residents there have taken to calling it.

'*Mera bachpan yahaan hi guzar gaya*,' says Dawood. It is as if someone were to say, in English, 'My childhood slipped by in this place.' There is a romantic resonance to this, a phrasing that sits uncomfortably on the busy intersection where we sit in an SUV waiting for a light to turn as we cross between Mahim west and east. Or, is it really uncomfortable? Bollywood once belonged to the masses. There are no masses so massed as those in this patch of land. Thus the surface refinements of Urdu probably belong here, spillovers from the many mini-theatres of Dharavi.

Dawood grew up in the 1980s, on the cusp of the great changeover in Indian entertainment, shifting the locus of Bollywood from the movie theatre to the home.

By that time, televisions had become accessible to all Indians. Colour had burst into the grimy monotones of our sets, and the first video cassette recorder arrived on our shores. Ever early adopters, televisions crept into every shop and stall in the city.

But not everyone could afford a television set or a video cassette recorder. The middle class solved this by hiring the player by the day. You put down a deposit, you picked up your recorder and went to the local film library and got 10–12 films. The libraries were ubiquitous by then. My circulating library started hiring out films and books, and the chemist across the road slashed his shelf space in half in order to cash in on the latest craze. Then everyone piled into their living room and watched movies until their eyes bulged. Sometimes the men went off for a nap when a tear-jerker played for the women. Then the women napped when an action thriller was playing for the men. Everyone was served but Bollywood was the staple.

Dharavi solved this problem in its own fashion. It set up the first of the mini-theatres, seating between 30–50 people. No one remembers when the first one came into existence. One day they were there and soon they were seen to be undermining the Bollywood economy. A single video cassette could be bought for about three hundred rupees. (Specials such as *Sholay* were sold in double cassettes and at roughly double the cost.) This could be played endlessly and yield no dividends to the producer or anyone else because there was no accounting for the number of eyeballs that squashed into these small shacks where you sat on chairs and watched a film play on a television screen. 'TV-

video bahut hua, sab ke sar mein dard hua,' sang Amitabh Bachchan in Ketan Desai's *Toofan* (1989)—it was not so much of a statement of the zeitgeist as it was a desperate plea. Don't let piracy take away our Mercedes Benzes.

Dawood does not remember going to one of these mini-theatres until he was fairly old. When he was young, he simply stood outside a tea stall, which he thinks was called the Makhdoomiya Tea Centre. It played Hindi films on a television set in a corner. You could either buy a cup of tea at the ordinary rate and drink it and leave, or you could pay two rupees and stay for the length of the film. As a youngster, Dawood would crawl up to the shop and position himself under the counter to watch a film. When he grew too big for that, he would simply stand outside until the owner drove him away with a flick of the cloth he used to clean the counter.

Dawood would wait a little while and come back again.

I decide to ask a stupid question, a class-inflected question. Didn't he have the money to pay?

Dawood is unsurprised and not offended. Or at least, he does not seem to be surprised or offended. His answer is pragmatic.

'If I had had two rupees, it would have gone into my stomach. Or to buy marbles. Or kites. Why would I pay for what you can see for free?'

Dawood soon learnt to time his movements so that he could come and go between ad breaks.

'I developed a great sense of timing, a sound judgement about when the film was about to begin again and I would come back right in time,' he says.

This meant that he would see films in bits and pieces. Did this bother him?

'Films are for time-pass,' he says.

In the city that produces the ultimate in time-pass, one can never be sure what the word means. It is a Mumbai chameleon that changes its hue, depending on its position. If I say I am doing time-pass, I mean that I am indulging in some harmless activity that has no useful purpose or end. If I say you are doing time-pass, I may mean the same thing for you. But if I tell you not to do time-pass, you must understand that I think you are wasting my time. If I say someone is a time-pass, I mean I like him and I think he's fun but he's not to be taken too seriously.

The communal experience of movie watching still holds in Dharavi. In one of the miniature theatres on Fortyfoot Road, I watch as Govinda begins one of his signature fast-talking sequences. There is much clapping and laughing and stamping of feet. At the end of the sequence, the audience calls for it to be played again. 'Once more,' they shout.

'Once more' is meant for live performances, but all over India cinema is a live performance. In Nagpur, where I watched my first 'adult' picture, *Dharmatma*, at the age of ten or thereabouts, the audience demanded replays of every song, and got them. In Kolhapur, I watched *Qurbani* on a rerun and understood that there may be subaltern ways to make money out of the fantasies spun out on screen. Every song or 'scene' (including the one that has Zeenat Aman running out of the sea in a bikini) was greeted by the patter of small change hitting the screen. If no money was forthcoming, the scene would not be played again. In Dharavi there was no charge but some scenes would be played on fast forward to make up for the lost time.

In the middle of a song that is being played on fast forward because it has no audience appeal, one of the young men in the audience shouts:

'*Rukh, rukh. Hilaaegi abhi.*'

(Stop, stop, she's going to shake her booty.)

The film is slowed down to the usual pace, and soon enough Karisma Kapoor obliges.

'*Abhi tu hilaa*,' says his friend to him, deliberately loud. (Now you shake yours.)

I did not see a single woman in the mini-theatres I attended in Dharavi. I asked the cashier in one of the theatres why there were no women.

'They come,' he said, 'Why won't they come?'

I had no answer to this and let it go. He was on the defensive.

Just as Dawood saw films in bits, often piecing them together, so the audience here seems to come and go. Phone calls summon them away and they rise and leave. Some mini-theatres allow you to reclaim your seat if it is available. Others say, '*Gaya to gaya.*' (If you're gone, it's gone.)'

'It depends on how well they know you,' says Shaleel, who describes himself as an office worker. On the day I first met him, he gave me a Muslim name. Then he told me that I should refer to him by a Hindu name if I were going to write down anything he said. He did not mind which Hindu name so long as it started with an S.

'What are you doing here?' he asks, when he feels he can, after two or three encounters. I try to explain what I am doing.

'*Paagalpan*,' he says briefly. Madness.

I wait for an explanation.

'How can watching a film here be different from watching a film somewhere else? Even if you sit in an armchair with a soft drink at your elbow and a full screen and you pay three hundred rupees, it is the same film.'

It is.

'*Baat baat pe Dharavi. Baat baat pe Dharavi* (Again and again, it's Dharavi),' he says and he sounds angry. I ask him if he is.

'Everyone gets rich on Dharavi. Everyone wants to see

Dharavi. Everyone wants to write about Dharavi. They even made a Hindi film with that name.'

Indeed they did. It was not a film marked by much, except for the glorious presence of Madhuri Dixit, then the reigning goddess of the silver screen, who made a guest appearance as the fantasy figure who haunted the dreams of Om Puri.

'*Tu kyon jal raha hai?* (Why are you getting jealous?),' asks Rinku Kumar, a friend of Shaleel's who works at a club and says his age is '20–30'. '*Tu yahaan rehta bhi nahin abhi.* (You don't even live here now.)' Saleel does not look embarrassed at being outed as a non-resident of Dharavi. 'Does anyone ever leave?'

The influence of Bollywood is everywhere in Dharavi. It does not seem to have waned even if the film industry now no longer considers its residents as important. Manmohan Desai, one of the greatest of mainstream directors of the 1970s, often said that he had to make sure he delivered value for money because his audience often paid in blood for their tickets. This was literally true. In the time before AIDS, you could sell your blood at a city blood bank. And the price of a pint was about the price of a ticket in the stalls. Blood banks reported a spike in 'donations' whenever a Manmohan Desai picture was released. Raj Kapoor, who made his fortune playing an immigrant to the city (in the 1955 blockbuster *Shree 420*), also often spoke about how cinema was a medium for the masses.

An era is passing. Today, from the director to the stars to the technicians, everyone on the sets speaks English. The dialogues have more and more English words and phrases. '*Rahul, main tujhse mohabbat karti hoon*' has given way to 'I love you, Rahul'. The stories have always been aspirational—it could be argued that the nouveau riche aesthetic was fashioned by Yash Chopra in *Waqt* (1965)—but now more than ever they look above and beyond the immediate skyline. No one plays to the masses.

Everyone is playing to the multiplex. Ram Gopal Varma put it explicitly to *Time* magazine: 'With my films, I'm targeting the urban multiplexes, the sophisticated media-savvy young crowd. Frankly, I couldn't give a f*** for the villages.'

He could as well have said that he couldn't give an F for Dharavi.

Moving to Bombay

AAKAR PATEL

I came to Bombay, as it was then called, on 14 December 1994, one day before my twenty-fifth birthday. I had with me 1,550 rupees that my father gave me. My mother gave me a little idol of Ganesh, which I lost.

I rode the train from Surat, Gujarat's second biggest city. Our family business of manufacturing polyester collapsed after Manmohan Singh's reforms opened up imports in 1991. Our incompetence may also have contributed.

I came looking for a job in the stock market, which was then, as it is now, not hiring. A friend's sister, married in Bombay, hosted me for nine months till I made enough money to move out. She took no money from me—I had none to give—and never complained. She understood. Bombay is like that.

Mornings and afternoons, I spent looking for work in the British part of Bombay, the civilized part of the city. I spent some time training in the business of export. I learnt little, but I noticed the efficiency with which money was passed around between officers and clerks, and the joyless acceptance of bribes taken as entitlement.

I ate on the streets. A *vada pav*—a batter-fried potato ball stuffed in a bun—cost two rupees, as did a glass of iced sugar cane juice. That was lunch, and it was a very good one.

The Shiv Sena won the elections of 1995, and promised one-rupee meals for the poor, handing out stall space across Bombay to its cadre. I went to these stalls but the one-rupee meals were never available.

Four months after I arrived, I had found no job and had run out of money. A visiting uncle, whom I had looked down on in Surat because he was poor, took me to lunch and gave me a thousand rupees and a bar of smoky glass made by Lalique. He was a part-time dealer in antiques and had interesting acquaintances.

I was surprised at the lack of awareness of caste in Bombay. People didn't care about your caste in Bombay, or who your father was. My ears were alert for caste names, so I could place people, as I had to do in Surat. The people of Bombay did not speak of caste and, when they did, confused it with religion or, more commonly, language. 'I am a Punjabi,' one might say to the question: 'What's your caste?'

I understood the cleansing aspect of the city, its ability to purge caste through assimilation, only later.

Once, after I got a job as a journalist, a man came to me with a press note. He was a union leader in the municipal sweepers' department, and I placed him immediately. The note had the words 'Jai Bhim' on top, and that was the first time I saw someone invoke the name of one of the Pandav brothers from the Mahabharata. Later I learnt that the reference was actually to Bhimrao Ambedkar, who framed India's Constitution and was a leader of the untouchables.

His birthday was on 6 December, the day the Babri mosque fell, and it was marked every year by the pilgrimage of a million people to the site of his cremation in central Bombay. This mobilization display of the lower castes was new to me. In Surat they had no political standing. They were also embarrassed of their status and hid it.

When I applied for a job, they also didn't ask me what college I had been to—or even, often, whether I had been to one at all (I hadn't). I remarked on this to my friend. He said, 'There are only two things people ask you in Bombay: "What can you do for me?" and "How much will you charge?"'

I liked that very much.

This awareness that others were not looking at me the way I looked at them made me see myself in a new way. The ease with which my prejudices—nationalist, racist, sexist—switched off my thoughts and took over my views became obvious to me. But I realized also that just being aware that I was prejudiced did not free me—that an effort needed to be made with every thought and every conversation, and this was difficult.

Did it come without effort to others? This thought tormented me, and still does. Out to do some reporting, once I visited Govandi, a poor eastern suburb of Bombay. My source, an advocate named Shafi Sheikh, travelled with me as we took a local train from Victoria Terminus on the Central Line. As the train hurtled out of Bombay's business district, we stood in the crowded compartment. I noticed the men lying on the wooden seats, returning home from what must have been a full day's work. Thin bodies, sleeping with open mouths and shirts unbuttoned. Something about them bothered me, but I couldn't figure what.

'They haven't eaten since morning,' Shafi said. I had known the tiredness of hunger, but I had never seen it. I have tried to look at people differently after that, to see in them the ambition rather than just the poverty.

People in Bombay face south. Life in the city is a struggle to move a little more towards the south—those in the northernmost suburbs seek to move to the suburbs a little more to the south. Those in the southernmost part of the city—Colaba, Malabar Hill, Nariman Point—are its most privileged.

When I could afford to move to Bandra, easily the best of the suburbs, I lived, for the first time in my life, in a neighbourhood that was mixed: Christians, Muslims, Hindus. Bandra was one of the few places in India where you can buy both beef and pork. Here I learnt to cook, and to appreciate wine.

I worked for a while in entertainment and was surprised by how much hard work was involved in Bollywood, and how much skill there was in the business. I observed that the people truly different were the Christians and the Parsis. Their sense of order, community, cleanliness and decency was uncommon. And they had the urge to high culture.

In Bandra, I first heard the trill of pianos being played at practice. Not just '*Fur Elise*' and the theme from *Love Story*, but flowing rondos that I later discovered were written by Schumann. This discovery of classical music, of harmony, made me think of Western civilization. There was one key difference between Hindustani music, which I had been made to study as a child, and Western classical music. And it was that Western classical music did not always have to be sad. It could be joyous, like Beethoven's great Symphony No. 1 (much crisper than the corpulent, but deified, No. 9).

I grew to anticipate the midnight mass in our parish of St Andrew's Church, built in 1733. The solemn beauty of a thousand people singing '*Silent night*' together—and having sung it here for over 250 years—moved me deeply. Their hum carried gently but clearly across the winter air was one of the highlights of December. In 2001, courts banned all concerts outdoors after 10 p.m., meaning that midnight mass in Bombay now ended two hours before midnight. I resented the cruelty of that order which denied Christians the release of the moment.

In Bombay, I worked for the first time in my life with women. Having dealt only with men at business till the age of twenty-five, I was unprepared for having a woman as my boss. I thought of them, naturally, not militantly, as belonging at home.

My first job in Bombay was under a woman, who soon disabused me of my ignorance, and some of my stupidity.

I learnt here that it was possible to attract a woman using only words, which cost nothing (which was important); and I learnt that technique was involved in romancing women (still learning that).

I have found no fortune in Bombay, if that is measured by wealth—and it is by Gujaratis.

But Bombay helped me open my eyes. I do not understand much of what I see, but I am amazed by what Bombay has shown me.

This is the city of Jinnah (Karachi), of Manto (Lahore), Manmohan Desai (Valsad), Ustad Allah Rakha (Phagwal), Dhirubhai Ambani (Chorwad), Jamsetji Nusserwanji Tata (Navsari) and Shah Rukh Khan (Delhi). Amitabh Bachchan (Allahabad) and Rafiq Zakaria (Nalasopara). And Aakar Patel (Surat).

It does not embarrass me to put my name up with these men. Bombay taught them also.

Beauty in India

Racial, Reasoned or Random

AMAN NATH

INDIA: RESOLVING ITS PARADOXES AND POLARITIES

Whatever one says about India, as well as its exact opposite, can both be reasoned to be true. India can be called a very rich nation, but without any doubt it also has its 700 million poor that it cannot easily hide away. While India has demonstrated to the whole world that it is a very wise nation, yet, if you look at its press, you can continue, on a daily basis, to be amazed by its follies.

Yet again, while India was called the 'grandmother of all civilizations' by Mark Twain, it is a young democracy, still learning the ropes of governing such a diverse people. Broadly, the Indian people sublimate their daily existence on an ethereal level, disdaining the material as *maya*—only an illusion of possession—but this does not, in any way, mean that an average Indian will ever ignore the mundane in all its details.

If Charles de Gaulle, finding the French 'an ungovernable nation', had called them '*les veaux*' (cows), India can certainly be called a mock socialist, feudo-democratic, dynasto-oligarchic anarchy that continues to function within some unfathomable manner of cyclic, cosmic order!

BLACK, WHITE–AND GREY!

If whatever one says about India, as well as its exact opposite, can both be demonstrated to be true, then we get black at one end of the spectrum, and white at the other: both true. But within this dichotomous range, we have also got a long bar of grey, a third truth which links the two extremes, and within which a large middle class of some 500 million Indians live with their own honest brand of a 'grey'.

So where would 'beauty' figure in such a complex Indian context? Whatever one said about *beauty* in India could be reasoned from many different viewpoints. I believe that in our Indian democracy our Parliament was designed by the British to be round, so that all debates go full circle to return back to where they started from: a zero. And it may be of some interest that it was India which gave the world the concept of zero or *shunya*, a void which, in our convoluted Indian way, can be argued to be full! So nothing matters really–while all can also matter.

THE HISTORY OF 'LESS' AS MORE

Even the earliest travellers' records on India mention fakirs. The Indian fakir on nails was a curious nineteenth-century cliché for Europeans. The purpose of such isolated meditation, or exaggerated self-discipline and control of the body, was to gain *tapas* through renunciation or *tyaga*. This is a very Indian virtue, which translates quite simply as 'body heat', a pursuit of celibates and ascetics that won them more honour than the wealthiest men in the world! They had understood that an ultimate dispossession of worldly things was the best way to possess the whole cosmos. The American writer Saul Bellow echoed this when he wrote that possessing anything expensive was not just 'dangerous for the soul—it was even a threat to one's sanity'. It is not for nothing that those who choose monastic lives, in no matter which religion, live with less rather than more. For true Indian ascetics, non-violence, non-possession, non-touching, non-speaking and even refraining from gestures and facial expressions is imperative.

What is different about India is that no book of the twentieth-century European etiquette had cared to mention the honours due to a fakir in a palace. It was probably considered an inconceivable proposition. But the implications of the respect traditionally due to ascetics and holy mendicants has always remained more than self-evident to even the most dispossessed people of India.

In India there has been a long tradition of emperors and kings visiting fakirs in their modest abodes to seek their blessings or to ask for boons. If, however, a sadhu or a fakir visited a royal court, he was welcomed into the durbar hall and the king always rose to receive him, although this would not be customary for him while greeting nobles and ministers of ordinary rank—or even kings who had lesser fortunes or states than him. There is great symbolism and philosophical wisdom for conferring this honour on ascetics and saints because Indians understand that an ascetic, with the spiritual strength acquired through abstinence and austerity to renounce the material world, deserves far greater respect than a mortal who remains bonded to the illusionary hierarchies of wealth, title, ambition and power.

A lady writer friend travelling with me in the mountains had lost her bag. When a beggar approached her to beg for alms, she explained her plight with a shrug of her shoulders. The beggar offered her some coins saying, 'So we are in the same state!'

Poor India has many lessons in humility to teach the rich and arrogant.

FAKIR VS THRONE

In 1568 Akbar visited the Sufi saint Sheikh Salim Chisti at Fatehpur Sikri to thank him for the victory over the Sisodias of Chittor, and he later named his son after him (Salim, known to history as Jahangir). The saint actually shunned patronage and is reported to have said, 'If the king walks in from one door, I walk out of the other.' Akbar's reverence for the saint did not deter him for building his new capital at Fatehpur Sikri. In 1570 Akbar walked to Ajmer to ask for the boon of a son at the *dargah* (holy tomb) of Khwaja Moin-ud-Din Chisti, a fourteenth-century Sufi saint. The great Mughal's battle cry, '*Ya-Muin*', recalled the memory of this Sufi ascetic, whose power was proportionate to the degree of his sacrifice and austerity. This tradition of venerating simplicity continues.

GANDHI—THE POWER OF INNER BEAUTY

Much later, when in 1930 Mahatma Gandhi visited London for the Round Table Conference, he met His Imperial Majesty King George V at Buckingham Palace dressed in his usual way, in a loincloth reminiscent of Kipling's Gunga Din, with 'nothing much before and rather less than "arfo" that behind' as Churchill described him. On being questioned if he was indeed sufficiently dressed to meet George V, Gandhi is reported to have replied, 'The king was wearing enough for both of us.'

The difference in the East–West approaches was not understood easily. In 1931 New Delhi, at the Irwin–Gandhi meet at Viceroy's House, Gandhi's disregard for official protocol appalled some observers—Gandhi sat on the floor eating 'some filthy yellow stuff'. Robert Grant Irving writes: 'When the viceroy's dogs bounded in, they sniffed all around him as if they had never seen the like in the whole of their lives.' At another meeting in 1947, Gandhi had his lemon soup, goat's curd and dates before Mountbatten, offering the 'porridge-like sludge' which Mountbatten was trapped into tasting. He thought it 'ghastly'. 1n 1931 London, Sir Winston Churchill displayed his lack of understanding in pouring scorn on the image of Gandhi visiting Viceroy's House. He commented on the 'nauseating and humiliating spectacle of this one-time Inner Temple lawyer, now seditious fakir, striding half-naked up the steps of the Viceroy's palace'. 1932 New York: Robert Bernays published *Naked Faquir* with Henry Holt, which helped in institutionalizing Mahatma Gandhi's curious ascetic appeal against the mighty British Empire. Churchill had intended to use the term 'fakir' with its derogatory connotation of an itinerant wonder-worker or quack, but it had the reverse effect, elevating Gandhi to the level of a Sufi and strengthening his following amongst Hindus and Muslims. In the Orient of dervishes, sadhus and yogis, fakir is an honorific title borne out of an understanding that poverty is necessary—even desirable—to achieve proximity to God.

This tradition of 'less' as more gave Gandhi the power to wear just a loincloth, and it empowered him to disrobe British Europe of all its protocols, trappings and regalia.

WHITE—AS A COLOUR

In Udaipur the Lake Palace floats like a white Indian swan in the translucent waters like an ultimate, but need-based, fantasy of a maharana. There, where hot winds blew over the countryside for eight long months, a noble Thakur had once explained to me the logic of white simplicity.

'Why are our houses whitewashed clean after every monsoon? Not just because Rajasthan is so warm or because white reflects the sun away.'

'Then why?' I asked in ignorance.

'Our homes are all white from the outside, as also from the inside—white mattresses and bolsters for low seating—because it is the guest who must bring the colour!'

To acknowledge white as the king of colours is not just tropical wisdom, but great aesthetic refinement as well as a heightened sense of honour for guests. Homes with too much colour and art are spaces that residents design for themselves, demonstrative of their self-obsession with taste, or to show off their variegated lives, full of their collected memorabilia—not necessarily aware that if their guests wore fuchsia to their home, it may clash with the red.

UNDERSTATEMENT AS A STYLE

Le Corbusier had noticed great beauty in the simplicity of India's landscapes and its people, which his modernism mirrored in the buildings of Chandigarh. He placed the horns of the Indian bull iconically over the Secretariat building like a large crescent moon etched on the skyline.

Similarly, in 1958, Charles and Ray Eames made a very sharp and pertinent observation on a simple object of everyday use—the *lota*, or water pot, used for daily ablutions in every Indian household: 'Of all the objects we have seen and admired during our visit to India, the *lota*, that simple vessel of everyday use, stands out as perhaps the greatest, the most beautiful . . . no one man designed the *lota*, but many men over many generations—many individuals represented in their own way through something they may have added or may have removed.' The aesthetic of a lota, a simple brass water pot, will find place in the design museums of the West, both for its simple form and its functionality, its rim turned out so well that nothing ever spills away as you pour out of it.

The great Indian saint Kabir, who lived by the Ganges in Benares, wrote many a couplet on the earthen pot called *matka*, used in the north of India. Besides seeing the void as full, likening it to our bodies, he also likened the lowly potter to God, as he moulds our bodies on his wheel of life. Artists and photographers today continue to see much more in an earthen pitcher that their counterparts in the West would.

But Coomaraswamy, the great Sri Lankan Indologist, had a very different take on this. He commented that the more advanced civilizations of the world imagine themselves more civilized when they take an object of daily use from a living civilization and put it under a spotlight in a museum! Isn't the truth quite the contrary?

SIMPLICITY WINS OVER OSTENTATION

Just as India's society is designed for continuity rather than for change, simplicity has been one of the great safeguards of India's continuity.

If one looks at the excesses of the French court and nobility—its attention to fashion, etiquette and frivolity—and compares it with that of the British royalty, it is not difficult to understand why Louis XVI and Marie Antoinette were defamed and decapitated, while England managed to maintain its monarchical tradition. But, ironically, it was the British who taught the Indian royalty how to revel in luxury and excess, so that they would be so finally alienated from their own citizens, even to become ridiculous in their own land! Finally, history was to make both the French and Indian royalty and nobility socially redundant—though the Indian process happened without any bloodshed.

Trailing the Tongue

WENDELL RODRICKS

The mango groves stretch for miles along the coast. In the hot, humid month of May, Maharashtra sizzles on the Deccan Plateau. But here, near the sea, in Ratnagiri, a cool breeze blows the luscious perfume of the world's best mango, the Alphonso, through the palms and well-tended orchards. Then, suddenly, wafting on the wind, I hear it. The lilting melodious sound of my ancestral language.

Yes, it is Konkani indeed. There are few local words that I do not understand. I speak to the man in my native tongue. He is a Konkan Brahmin, he tells me. And his dialect of Konkani is called Chintapawani. We bond in an ancient brotherhood of the Konkan coast. It happens to me everywhere on this coastal strip. Further south, the people of Malvan speak Malvani, the Goans speak Gomantaki. Tipu Sultan's influence has resulted in Konkani with Urdu words in places as far flung as Mysore, Coorg and Srirangapatnam, and even in Calicut I was astonished to hear Konkani in a jewellery shop. There were some Malayalam and Tulu words thrown in. The owner recognized me and spoke in Konkani at length. How his 'family left Goa twice . . . in the thirteenth century fleeing the forces of Alauddin Khilji and later escaping the horrors of the Portuguese inquisition in 1560. There have been Konkan people here always. Before the Malabar coast, this was the Konkan coast.'

Surely he was misinformed! I had never heard of this before. 'But let me take you home for lunch and share more about our common lineage.' Over lunch that comprised steamed red rice, a fish curry and local pickle, I realized that it was not just language but food that was also common. So I set about discovering the Konkan coast—with my tongue.

Dr Krishnanand Kamat has a website that recounts the history of the Konkan. 'The seven kingdoms of the Konkan, as per Hindu mythology, mentioned in the Hindu history of Kashmir, included the entire west coast of India.' The Pandavas of the Mahabharata, Lord Krishna, Goddess Durga and later the Mauryas, the Marathas, the Muslims from the plateau and the Portuguese arrived on this coast. Due to the pious nature of the people this strip of land by the sea has many temples, with people faithful to 'their' temple gods. Annual pilgrimages all over the Konkan are common and the events surrounding them colourful and festive. The capital of the Konkan is supposedly Chandrapur. Is this the present village of Chandor in Goa?

The Konkan coast may have vanished today, but the Konkani language lives on. You can hear it in Karwar, Ankola and Kumta-Honavar. Away from the Mangalore coast, in the valley of Siddapur, I attended a wedding where villagers from far and wide spoke fluent Konkani. The Nawayatis of Bhatkal speak melodiously with Persian words thrown in. This did not surprise me. In Goa, the famous Chapora fort area was occupied by the Persians. The ancient name was Shahpura, the town of the Shah of Persia.

I settle down to a breakfast in Karnataka with a Konkani family. Steaming *undi* rice balls flavoured with ginger, curry leaf, chilli and coconut appear. They have a delicious sweetness as well. Is it the local molasses? This addition of a sweet ingredient in savoury or spicy dishes is popular from Gujarat to Kerala.

There are other commonalities. The simple broths made with lentils, the humble dishes using local bananas, rice and vegetables.

Here, in what was once Canara, a region of the Konkan, sour *ambat* and fiery prawn *gassi* find common ground with the hot and sour *ambotik* shark curry and the spicy Portuguese-influenced pork *vindaloo* of Goa. Rice is a staple. It is powdered, ground to a paste, steamed, fried or cooked as is. The *neer dosas*, the *idlis*, the *sannas*—rice preparations—grace most Konkani tables in their various avatars. Fruit like banana, jackfruit, cashew nut, mango and sour *kokum* flavour dishes in numerous ways. Mangoes are eaten raw in water pickles, ripe as dessert and sun-dried when raw as a souring ingredient. With a limited range of spices such as turmeric, asafoetida, cumin, mustard, fenugreek, chilli and pepper, a wondrous array of Konkani cuisine has evolved over the years.

Local ingredients are abundant due to the landscape that permits agriculture during the torrential rains which lash the coast in the monsoon, and the fertile earth that makes it easy to grow crops. On my trail of the tongue for language and food, I discovered a rare natural phenomenon. Along the entire Konkan coast, near the ocean and on the islands in the Arabian Sea, there are natural spring wells with fresh water. While in Arambol, Goa, a freshwater lake almost touches the ocean, the Fort Aguada derives its name from this natural wonder. The hill was called 'Mae de agua' (mother of waters). There were, and still are, so many springs on Aguada Hill that mariners would anchor at the base of the hill while barrels of freshwater rolled down into the ships embarking on long journeys across the globe. In Sindhudurg, Maharashtra, the stunning fort covers an entire island. Thirteen families live on the twenty-three-acre island surrounded by a raging ocean. But within are three freshwater springs.

It is the presence of these springs all along the Konkan that makes for easy cultivation of vegetables such as pumpkin, drumstick, ladies' finger, *tendli*, cucumber, tomatoes, eggplant and ridged gourd which have different names in different coastal areas.

There is in Goa an unusual astringent spice call *teflam* or *teofam* that flavours the curries of oily fish like sardine and mackerel. Non-Goans ask for teflam. They must have this spice that grows wild on the hills. But they possibly have another name for it.

And this is something remarkable about Konkani as a language. Because of the various influences, words appear in the language across the coast that seem alien to Konkan's neighbouring areas. Goan Konkani is peppered with Portuguese. For the most part, the items of daily life that the Portuguese introduced to Goans stayed in the original language. Spoon and table became localized to *culer* and *mez* (from *colher* and *mesa*). Similarly, traders who touched the coast introduced Arabic and Persian words such as *dukan* (shop), *karz* (debt), *fakt* (only), *dushman* (enemy) and *barik* (thin).

The most remarkable transformation of the Konkani language is that Konkani people introduced local words to be understood by non-Konkani-speaking people. Hence, a Konkani person from faraway Alappuzha or Kasargod in Kerala can understand what a Konkani person in Ratnagiri, Maharashtra, is saying but will not understand business terms.

Konkani is often denounced as a dialect of Marathi. Nothing can be further from the truth. Konkani, because of the sea trade, has more connections with Gujarati. There are many common words between the two languages that are not found in Marathi. The *lo*, *li*, *le* case terminations in Konkani find resonance in the *no*, *ni*, *ne* of Gujarati. In both languages, the present indicative have no gender. Similarly, the termination *ke* in Gujarati is the same as *ki* or *kir* in Konkani—for example, *kartoke* in Gujarati is *kartoki* or *kartokir* in Konkani.

There is a strange link away from the Konkan coast to the east of India that connects the Konkani language to Bengali. There are theories that suggest that Konkani is a language with Bengali as the mother language. Just as Hindi is from Sanskrit. This connection has found credence due to the migrations of the Gaude Saraswat Brahmins along the Saraswati river, whose origins are disputed, but it is believed that the Saraswat Brahmins travelled to Goa via this river while another group travelled to Bengal.

In Goa, on a journey to see the magnificent Betal statue in Loliem, I met a teacher, Raul Bose, who had played a part in the famous opinion poll in 1967 when Goans were fighting against being joined with Maharashtra. Mr Bose told me that there were migrations from Bengal since ancient times. European travellers to Goa in the seventeenth century mention about 'beautiful Bengali' women in their travelogues.

On the highway from Goa to Mangalore, about twenty-three kilometres before the city approaches, we stop regularly at a restaurant called Pallavi. The local fish, dusted in spices and drizzled with rice flour, is deep fried in coconut oil. It is crunchy, spicy and delicious. The prawn gassi curry is to die for and the lacy rice neer dosas light as air. They also make a Konkani dish: *vadde*. It is a small, deep-fried fritter that can be made with potato, grated vegetables or seafood. Here it is made with local clams. When I speak to the owner and ask to pay my bill, he chatters away in Konkani but presents the bill in the Kannada script. Another fact about Konkani sinks in. As it is a Prakrit (spoken) language without a script of its own, the melody of Konkani is written in the Devanagari, Roman, Kannada, Malayalam, Persian and Arabic scripts. How many living languages in Asia can claim to be written in six completely different scripts?

It would take the tiny state of Goa and its Konkani-proud people to make Konkani one of the official languages of India in 1986. A language that once trailed the length of the Konkan coast has found its space in many places dotting the western coastline of the country. But in Goa it has found its official home.

Gond Art

Of Mysteries and Market Forces

NISHA SUSAN

On 2 July 2001, on the Japanese island of Honshu, Jangarh Singh Shyam hanged himself from the ceiling fan in his room. He had been living at the Mithila Museum on an arts residency. He was thirty-seven. Two worlds mourned Jangarh: artists and central India's Gond community. The rest of us barely noticed the passing of the prodigious Adivasi artist who had made Paris gasp. Nine years later, when I set out in the direction of Jangarh's village, I had only a dim sense of how much his life and death had wrought.

On the morning of 12 July 2010, Mayank Shyam steps out of his black Santro and waits for his mother Nankusia to emerge in her best sari. The twenty-four-year-old had driven twelve hours from Bhopal to Patangarh village the previous week.

Patangarh is the bright green village in the hills of eastern Madhya Pradesh, where his father Jangarh Shyam came from. Several admirers have gathered here to unveil a bust of Jangarh.

A local DJ, instructed to play items with gravitas, has unleashed his Independence Day playlist—'*Aye mere watan ke logon*' is blaring over the village. Everything has been organized by Jangarh disciple Suresh Uruveti, and while everyone is polite, standing on the main street, the event has boiled up all the intense rivalry in this mother lode of Gond art. Who is Suresh to take all the decisions by himself, Jangarh's clan wants to know. Why aren't their names on the invitation card? They all want Jangarh honoured. Haven't they too—all of them—been transformed by what Jangarh had done?

The market for Gond art is swelling—everyone wants a piece. Sotheby's auctioned a Jangarh painting for Rs 6.3 lakh last March. Nankusia is antsy that right now, someone somewhere might be selling her husband's work. Mayank, insouciant in his dark sunglasses and jeans, chats about this and that—his big car woofers and the post-monsoon landscape here—seemingly nonchalant about the unveiling today or the larger battle for his father's legacy.

It seems easy enough to be Mayank Shyam. His name has cachet. Buzz around his work has grown. His juvenilia was auctioned for Kolkata Museum of Modern Art (KMoMA) by Sotheby's for over $5,000. He'll have his first solo in Paris next summer. It seems to be easy—easy enough—to be the heir apparent of an Adivasi art that's beginning to make money. Except for a few catches.

First, the 'tradition' is only thirty years old. Second, Mayank's art bears little resemblance to the tradition. And third, if he's unwilling to do the dance of ethnicity, he may not be able to sell his work. Even now, the most global Indian arts and literature still require some stylized elephants to sell internationally. Even two decades after his father's Paris launch, the response to indigenous art remains patronizing. Mayank may be a prince, but he may yet become a prince of nothing. What is a twenty-four-year-old to do?

You may not have heard of Jangarh but you'd recognize Gond art if you saw it. Step up close. Dot after dot of brilliant colour, needle-fine lines mesh into light and shade. Step back and the Morse Code bursts into fables, cityscapes, big-eyed figures. Step back further and you feel the fierceness—every playful figure leaps tiger-like at you.

Perhaps you had heard of the 2010 Adivasi art exhibit—showcasing Jangarh's work—at the Musée du Quai Branly in Paris, curated by Dr Jyotindra Jain. You may have seen Bhajju Shyam's travelogue *The London Jungle Book*, or snippets about Venkat Shyam's solo US show, or Sukhnandi Vyam's sculptures showcased in Delhi. Perhaps you have seen *Bhimayana*, a stylish graphic novel about Ambedkar's life with its beautiful art from the Gond couple Subhash and Durgabai Vyam.

At the Patangarh event, Nankusia speaks of her husband gravely. Suresh watches nervously as everything goes smoothly, although Mayank has disappeared just before the event begins. Jyothi, a farmer who lives across the street, has sold two paintings to visitors. A younger artist circles nervously around a collector with a reputation for rapaciousness.

At last, the bust is unveiled. It gleams, it is unmistakably Jangarh, but rather amateurish. No one, not even Suresh remembers the Kolkata sculptor's name. Why not a Gond sculptor? Subhash Vyam, Jangarh's brother-in-law, squirms a bit. 'None of us knows fine art,' he says. A statement that baffles till you realize he means that theirs is not the realistic style that village squares demand. The odd moment makes you reconsider what your eyes expect to see, and how little you want to be challenged. Gond art is almost on the verge of becoming a household name. So why is it still treated like a precocious child—with either piousness or condescension?

Mayank can trace his current situation to its roots more easily than most contemporary artists. The history of contemporary Gond art is the history of his family, of his father. What we know as Gond art is not a traditional art. Like the rice powder kolams drawn every day in south Indian homes, the wall drawings in Gond houses were not thought of in terms of art, before Jangarh. Today, you see the drawings very occasionally in the villages—simple in line and usually in white or yellow. What we know as Gond art is a whole new beast called Jangarh Kalam— the style of Jangarh. Jangarh's clever dots, delicate lines and lively menagerie of animals catapulted dozens of artists to the façade of the Madhya Pradesh legislative assembly building. Udayan Vajpayi and Vivek argue in their book, *Jangarh Kalam*, that if Jangarh's style came from anywhere outside his fertile mind, it came from the pointillistic tattoos that Gond women sport.

As a Pardhan Gond, Jangarh was supposed to be a bard—to remember and sing the Gond history. But the highly musical Jangarh was desperately poor. In the village everyone tells comic tragic stories of Jangarh's and Nankusia's several attempts to elope while still in school. They married at fifteen. The youngest of a large family, Jangarh tried everything to make some money. He quit school and tried his hand at farming. He grazed buffaloes and sold milk in the nearest town. Then and now, these Gond villages, staggering in their beauty, had little opportunities or conveniences cherished by modernity. Even today, there is a severe shortage of water and electricity. You can spend the day in a haze of mahua and memories of Gond glory or work very, very hard at farming. Or you can take your genes for granted and follow in Jangarh's footsteps. In Patangarh, Sanpuri and Gaar-ka-matta, many young people pick Door No. 2, Jangarh's door.

In 1981, Nankusia had never dreamt that her husband's wall drawings would change the destiny of everyone she knew. That year, seventeen-year-old Jangarh's turn for art was discovered in his village by a team led by the artist J. Swaminathan. He was brought to Bharat Bhavan, the cultural centre in Bhopal, and encouraged to try new (and traditional) materials and techniques. He became an international hit when his work was shown at the Pompidou Centre in Paris. Money followed fame and he encouraged cousin after cousin to apprentice with him. If you meet a Gond artist, it is highly unlikely he or she is unrelated to Jangarh. Every one of them has a story of being found in the shy shadows, as a five-year-old, or as a fifteen-year-old, by a teasing Jangarh.

Jangarh's death is still a mystery. It was not his first time abroad. Generous with time, money, music and good humour, he made friends wherever he went. In the beginning he wrote home. He was enjoying himself, he said. He missed them, he said. He would be back soon, he said.

Outside his family, there are those who have tried to understand his death with what little they knew or assumed about Adivasi culture. Some worry, even now, that he had not been culturally equipped to deal with loneliness. Others speculate he must have felt enslaved by the Mithila Museum, which paid him a small stipend and held his passport. Still others comment casually, unthinkingly, 'that these Adivasis are impulsive and tend to think of consequences later'. Among Gonds, whole villages mourn him.

Jangarh's death created a fresh surge of interest in the art, and today there are nearly a hundred Gond artists in Bhopal. Today, Gond art is sold in galleries and auctions, not obscure handicraft shops. Gond painters are not anonymous. They've crossed the artificial ravine between craft and art largely because Jangarh, groomed in Bharat Bhavan amidst modern artists, put a signature to his work and encouraged other artists to do so too. The idea that the modern art market demands individual identity is strong among the group. It is the market that demands individualism, though the artists themselves don't mind younger people (untested except by their genes) trying their hand at their canvasses.

And sometimes it is simply necessary to have extra hands. In the new house in Bhopal where Subhash and Durgabai Vyam live with their massive clan, everyone is an assistant. Upstairs, downstairs, anyone who can hold a brush paints. The Vyams have an eye on the demand curve. In Delhi, even recently, respectable collectors have tried to buy their work at bargain-basement prices, arguing, 'I used to buy Jangarh's work for Rs 500!' Faceless buyers ordering in bulk on the phone or email are much easier to deal with than the seemingly well-intentioned promoters who want free samples.

Back in the villages where Jangarh's clan lives, every lane has an artist. Take for example, twenty-three-year-old Dwarka who has trained with Nankusia in Bhopal. He has come home to Gaar-ka-matta to swiftly assemble a portfolio between grazing cows and farming. Right now, he depends on the arrival of the curious, the determined and the acquisitive. One story he tells is illustrative: 'Once a collector came here looking for me and I was grazing buffaloes far away. There had been no electricity for days, so my cellphone was dead. By the time I came back at dusk, she was gone. Never heard from her again.'

Like any other art world, the Gond artist community is a potent mixture of talent, avarice, in-fighting, self-fashioning, transcendence—and bullshit. Not that there aren't enough facile characterizations of Adivasi art coming from outside the community. In Mayank and his younger sister Japani's Bhopal home, with its trendy orange-and-purple walls, it's embarrassing to remember the KMoMA website which describes Mayank's cityscapes as 'confrontations of the ancient with the modern'. At home, the siblings talk endlessly about art and technique. They giggle at the aberration their younger brother is. Bablu has no interest in art and has recently found hip hop dance classes in Bhopal.

The Gond artists may in the future become savvy enough to avoid the exploitative. But it is difficult to avoid the tendency to self-exoticize. Man Singh Vyam (twenty years old and city-slick) frantically tells fables of simplicity, sentimental tales about how his art is inspired by the memories of playing on the swing in his grandmother's village. These stories can make you wince. So can meetings with old people in the impoverished Gond villages. Calloused by decades of greedy researchers, they now catch the unwary and say, 'Don't you want to hear traditional Gond songs? Turn on your recorder, buy me mahua and I'll sing for you.' The feeling of being stuck in porn for anthropologists—a pool of excessive and perhaps fake ethnographic display—is unavoidable. This is a distinct departure from Man Singh's mother, the award-winning Durgabai Vyam, who slips from prosaic conversation into the story of the River Narmada's failed wedding as if she were a compassionate eyewitness, so real is the myth of Narmada *maiyya* in her imagination.

Mayank is not an obvious victim of self-exoticization. He and Japani are, on the surface, untroubled by questions of identity or politics. Mayank recently met the artist Subodh Gupta and admires him for using the innocuous steel *bartan* to create spectacle. Sprawled in shorts and a T-shirt that says, 'I have a drinking problem. I can't afford it', Mayank gently mocks the art world. In Kolkata he told people that 'Nice to meet you' is a phrase one should use only when one is saying goodbye. When Shireen Gandhy of Chemould Prescott Road gallery, Mumbai, asked him to stop calling her 'madam', he asked if he could call her *bua* instead. He has a taste for short-circuiting what he perceives as the polite nothings of the gallery-opening party.

'I am an Adivasi *bachcha*,' Mayank says as often and as casually as he talks of Paris. He is sure that Paris—the site of his father's first international success—is waiting. His butter smoothness is upset only by ignorant people who assume his art is primitive. 'When I heard people saying, "Even I can draw this", I became determined to develop a style that stumps people.' His first innovation is the absence of primary colours. Also, unlike the others' free-floating figures, Mayank's black-and-white drawings are anchored in a sea of tightly packed grains of ink that takes months to create. His human and animal figures emerge out of a lush, modern imagination. There is no sense of the harried workshop in Mayank's house as in the Vyam household. Mayank's sights are not set on the anonymous buyer on the phone.

But he too is complicit in why his art is condescended to. He tells an intriguing story about the young Jangarh. 'For his first show, my father bought a safari suit and felt great. But when he arrived, someone yelled at him, "Why aren't you wearing traditional clothing?" He ran and changed.'

What would he have done in his father's place? He and
Japani smile pragmatically. 'If someone thinks that for a show
we should wear our traditional clothes, we'd wear it. No problem.'
Japani says she has dressed up for shows and enjoyed it. How
often do they wear their traditional clothes otherwise? Almost
never, says Mayank.

For Mayank, what he wears or the extreme challenges of
rural living—a transition he makes effortlessly whenever he
visits Patangarh—has nothing to do with being Adivasi. But he
knows that the occasional performance of cute 'authenticity' is
what the world wants.

Jangarh Kalam is often described as 'simple' and addressed in
annoyingly unsophisticated terms, as if all of it is equally pretty
or dull. I certainly wished, over the course of this journey, that I
had the intellectual apparatus to understand contemporary
Gond art on its own terms, in its visual vocabulary, with its own
inventiveness.

The way in which the form has rapidly developed in Bhopal
in just under three decades can show a way forward for fading
traditional arts. Beginning with Jangarh, every Gond artist has
taught younger people to paint. Perhaps this convention came
about from back-breaking deadlines. One need not ascribe
altruism here but the practice makes the form fertile. Painting,
as critics wandering through Delhi and Mumbai galleries will
tell you, is dying because successful artists cannot or will not
spare the time to teach the young. Mayank, who has so far not
allowed anyone else to dabble on his canvases, may be the next
big thing in Gond art, but if he does not teach younger artists,
he will cripple the art form.

The social conventions among Gond artists have larger implications. Until recently, they shared everything they knew—brushstrokes, homes, learning to deal with cities, government institutions and galleries. It is a generosity Jangarh Shyam put into place. In a hive of bees, what one bee knows the whole hive knows. However, like the rest of India, Gond artists too are increasingly subject to the competitive demands of modern living. It is a juggernaut one cannot deplore or quarrel with, only watch. It might well improve the work of individual artists but whether the form will stay robust without the communal backbone is questionable.

I press Mayank again on what is difficult about being him, being a young Adivasi in a Bhopal house with purple walls, with an eye on Paris. When he is not thinking about art, kinship is what is on his mind. 'What I sit and think about is how we should be dealing with people. How can I speak with sweetness, deal correctly with my family, my elders, my people? Things are changing but I want to know how to behave. This is what I think about.' Mayank's future and whether he will have to 'do ethnicity' depends on how we value contemporary Gond art. Jangarh Kalam is important beyond the pleasure afforded by its piquancy.

Tirupati

The God for a Modern Age

KOTA NEELIMA

It is known both practically and intuitively that every karma or action of every human is accounted for and balanced. However, it is the nature of Kali Yuga, where time moves so swiftly, that it renders this knowledge useless. Modern lives, crowded as they are with a bewildering variety of karma and experience, make it impossible to sift through each thought, word or deed to know the quotient of sin.

Religion in the modern age, therefore, must be capable of existing outside its own realms; it must possess a truth that can survive the scientific temper, and include freedom of choice in a world bred on democracy and free will. By controlling thought and desire in the mind, cause and effect can be controlled in life. By addressing what is human, one can make the choice towards that which is divine. But to do that, human beings must rise above the natural instincts and live by a superior set of rules that direct mankind's two most important endeavours for finding God: the internal and the external journeys.

The external journey has been mapped with landmarks of good and bad, right and wrong, *dharma* and *adharma*. These have been the basis of organization of our societies and nations. The system of crime and punishment easily extends to heaven, or hell, helping to choose the right desires, or causes, with the right effects. The internal journey, which is far more individualistic, has been more difficult to direct.

As all thought originates in question, the external influence has to govern the inner question. It has to be a question with the power to change destiny and, thereby, bring the nature of man closer to the nature of God. One of the most significant questions of the human mind has been: What is sin? With this question, the human mind becomes aware of its conscience, a crucial landmark in the internal journey to find God.

The memory of sin stays forever with a person, at levels of high or low recall, depending on the degree of goodness a person is willing to adopt. These are levels that an individual can seek to improve upon, creating another landmark on the inner way to God. The desire to be freed from past and present sins, to live a purer life in future, inevitably influences cause, choice and effect. That is yet one more landmark in the internal journey of the mind.

Religion connects all these internal landmarks to external ones in the physical world since all journeys need points of reference. In Hinduism, temples serve this purpose, but few address modern issues the way the god of Tirupati does. By cleansing the soul of the darkness of sins, the cause is changed, thereby changing the effect and changing destiny. By granting justified desires, the cause can be chosen so that the effect can be chosen and destiny too can, in turn, be chosen.

THE SACRED HILLS

Hills and mountains have always held a strange fascination for the human imagination. And, even though most of these lofty heights have been scaled, they still seem to invite comparisons with the imaginary heaven, the abode of the gods. That might be one of the reasons why places of worship are often to be found on hills and mountains.

The seven sacred hills of Tirumala lie about ten kilometres north-west of the town of Tirupati in Chittoor district of Andhra Pradesh. At an altitude of 2,500 feet, the seven hills are named Seshachala, Vedachala, Garudachala, Anjanachala, Vrishabhachala, Narayanachala and Venkatachala; the last has the temple of Lord Sri Venkateswara.

These hills are endowed with an unusually large number of *tirthas* or sacred water bodies. Some of them, in the order of importance, are Swami Pushkarani lake, Akasha Ganga, Paapa Vinasana, Asthi, Kataha, Ghona or Tumburu, Jabali, Kumara Dhara, Kapila, Chakra, Pandava or Go-garbha, Ramakrishna and Vaikuntha tirthas. The Venkatachala mountain is worshipped as a divine entity in its own right.

The greatness of this pilgrimage, or Venkatachala Mahatmya, is described in detail in the second part of the Skanda Mahapurana, called the Vaishnava Khanda, which is devoted to Lord Vishnu. Here,[1] Sage Sri Suta explains why the Venkatachala mountain is of such importance and states that all pilgrimages of this earth and the universe (*brahmanda antargathani*) are to be found here, as this is the abode of Lord Vishnu. The Venkatachala mountain, the sage says, is more significant than other pilgrimages, just as knowledge of the Vedas is the most

---

[1]*The Skanda Mahapuranam (Part-2: Vaisnava Khanda)*, Rashtriya Sanskrit Sansthan, New Delhi, 2006, chapter 17.

important knowledge of all (*vidyanam vedavidya*); just as Om is the most sacred among all mantras (*mantranam pranavoyatha*); and life, among all things, dear.

In the past, and even now, the most valued way of reaching the temple of Lord Sri Venkateswara has been by foot, but there is a procedure to be followed before walking up these pristine hills. Daily, hundreds of people climb over 3,500 steps to the summit, covering a distance of about nine kilometres. The Skanda Mahapurana describes the best way of undertaking this exercise.[2] At the foot of the mountain, a devotee must pray for the permission of the mountain to ascend it. The mountain that is venerated by gods, the mountain as pure and precious as gold, should be petitioned for permission for stepping on it. The devotee should plead for forgiveness for committing the sin of climbing the mountain in search of God. He must pray to the mountain to reveal the path that leads to a *darshan* or a vision of the god, Lord Sri Venkateswara, who resides at the summit. After this prayer, the devotee must place his foot tenderly on the mountain and gently proceed forward.

THE TEMPLE

While the idol of Lord Sri Venkateswara is self-manifest, the temple may have been established in the seventh century AD, according to the stone inscriptions on the temple walls. The inscriptions and their study have thrown a great deal of scientific light on the origin and history of the temple, the main credit for which goes to the eminent scholar Sadhu Subrahmanya Sastry.

The first temple is believed to have been small and compact, with limited scope for any other activity except basic worship.

---

[2]Ibid., chapter 19.

Inscriptions dating back to AD 614[3] on its stone walls prove
that the temple was already in existence then and that it was
considerably popular in the region. Puranic texts mention that
King Tondaman, a legendary king of the region, may have built
the first temple. However, even these accounts show that the
idol of Lord Sri Venkateswara was already present where it can
be seen today. Sastry[4] mentions that the early shrine may have
been a twelve-foot square room with a 'front room' ahead of it.
This 'front room' is known at present as the Sayana Mantapam
or the divine bedroom, where one of the moveable images of
the god rests at night. During the day, this is the room from
where the devotees get a darshan of Lord Sri Venkateswara.
Round the sanctum of this early temple was a corridor for
devotees to perform the circumambulation or *pradakshina* of
the temple. This passage was later closed when the original
shrine was extended.

Gradually, through the centuries, galleries such as the Mukha
Mantapam and outer corridors were added to the temple.
These additions were mainly in response to the increasing
popularity of the shrine and the need for accommodating more
devotees at the time of worship. On special days, queues of
devotees snake around the temple walls for kilometres. Although
the queues of pilgrims are shorter on regular days, the crowds
who wait patiently for darshan always number in thousands.
The image of Lord Sri Venkateswara can be viewed throughout
the day except for a few hours at night. According to Tirumala
Tirupati Devasthanams (TTD) statistics, 50,000 to 80,000
devotees visit the temple every day, with the numbers reaching
lakhs on special occasions.

---

[3]Sastry, Sadhu Subrahmanya, *Tirupati Sri Venkateswara*, Tirumala Tirupati
Devasthanams, Tirupati, 2004, p. 101.

[4]Ibid., p. 79.

The temple plan is based on concentric rectangles around a square sanctum. There are three major rectangular corridors for circumambulation. The innermost corridor is called Mukkoti Pradakshina and remains closed. The middle corridor, called the Vimana Pradakshina, goes round the inner temple and the Mukkoti Pradakshina corridor. The outermost one, called the Sampangi Pradakshina, encloses the inner temple, the Mukkoti Pradakshina and the Vimana Pradakshina. A Maha Pradakshina is laid outside the temple, through which the devotees perform circumambulation of the entire premises before entering the temple. The circumambulation is an important part of darshan of God, as it lets one get into the rhythm of the temple. It allows the devotees a moment to gather their thoughts, check whether they have all the material necessary for worship, and then, with complete focus, enter the main temple.

Three boundary walls or *prakarams* surround the temple, with inner and outer gateways, which are marked by tall towers or *gopurams*.

THE SANCTUM

The innermost area of the temple is approached through the Bangaru Vakili, or the Golden Courtyard, which leads to the Snapana Mantapam and the Ramar Meda.[5] Bangaru Vakili houses the sculptures of the gatekeepers of God, the two *dwara palakas*, Jaya and Vijaya. They are said to screen the devotees who enter through the courtyard to go into the temple. The doors they protect are covered in gold, and devotees walk between them towards the heart of the temple. These are also the doors in front of which the melodious hymns of

---

[5]Ramesan, N., *The Tirumala Temple*, Tirumala Tirupati Devasthanams, Tirupati, 2004, p. 95.

Suprabhatam are sung to wake up the god every morning. The doors have depictions of Lord Vishnu in the five manifestations of *para*, *vyuha*, *vibhava*, *antaryami* and the *archa* form, the form that can be seen in the main sanctum of the temple.

From the Golden Courtyard, one enters the Sayana Mantapam, the 'front room', and through that, to the main sanctum or the Garbha Griham. Not many have crossed, or are qualified to cross, any further than the Sayana Mantapam to enter the main sanctum, which houses the main idol or Dhruva Murti of Lord Sri Venkateswara. The walls of the main sanctum and those of the Sayana Mantapam are said to be seven feet thick, making them the most intriguing structural feature of the temple. Attributed to the many renovations of the temple, the reason for the unusual thickness of the sanctum walls has invited close study by scholars.

And yet, it is not more mystifying than the idol itself. There is a sensation of the intangible that a devotee feels as he or she gets closer to the main sanctum. The flickering oil lamps and the shifting shadows of the sanctum heighten the sense of isolation and provide each devotee with a private moment for connecting with God.[6]

THE IDOL

The idol of Lord Sri Venkateswara in the main sanctum is the focus of a million prayers every day. No other feature, aspect or

---

[6]Sastry, *Tirupati Sri Venkateswara*, p. 79: 'In accordance with the time-honoured principle of Indian Silpa Sastra, the Garbha Griham, and the Ardha Mantapa (ante-chamber) were constructed with limited space and limited light so as to infuse a sense of mystery and a feeling of respect, fear, awe, divineness, and devotion in the worshipper in serene atmosphere; and the oil lamps too in the sanctum afford only a dim vision of the Godhead, together conducing to the elevation of the worshipper's soul.'

practice of the temple is sought after as much as a glimpse of the god. There is no known sculptor of this idol and the self-manifest idol is eight feet tall and stands right in the centre of the sanctum, directly under the golden dome of the well-known Ananda Nilayam Vimana.

There are many aspects of Lord Sri Venkateswara that are iconic. Like the tall crown or *kireetam*, made of gold and diamonds with a large emerald set in the front; the white mark on the forehead with a red *kasturi tilakam*, a mark made of musk and camphor; and another unusual white mark of camphor on the chin. His right hand is held as *varada hasta*, the gesture of granting wishes of devotees; the left hand is placed on the waist; the conch or *sankha* and the discus or *chakra* are held in the other two hands. The feet are sheathed in layers of gold.

Images of goddesses are often seen next to the gods in Hindu temples. But the idol of Lord Sri Venkateswara carries the image of Goddess Sri Devi on His chest, close to His heart.[7]

THE GOLDEN DOME

Another feature special to the temple of Lord Sri Venkateswara is its dome or the Vimana located directly above the main idol in the sanctum. It is said in the Puranas that the day this Vimana shatters and falls, putting out the lamps that burn before Lord Sri Venkateswara in the sanctum, this manifestation or avatar of God will be over and the Kali Yuga will come to an end.

---

[7]Viraraghavacharya, T.K.T., *History of Tirupati (The Thiruvengadam Temple)*, vol. I, Tirumala Tirupati Devasthanams, Tirupati, 2003, p. 178. Goddess Sri Devi's image, seen on the right side of the chest, is an integral part of the image of Lord Sri Venkateswara; it has clearly not been put there subsequently and is not detachable.

Many important rulers, notably the great Krishna Deva Raya of the Vijayanagara Empire, have had the Vimana covered in gold. Though, at present, nothing can be seen of the internal structure, the golden dome is famous for its fine carvings and sculptures. About thirty-seven feet in height on a square base, the dome has a *kalasa* or a vase at the top and shows influences of architectural designs from the Pallava period.[8]

Under this great dome within the shrine are also present the different moveable images of Lord Sri Venkateswara, like Bhoga Srinivasa, Ugra Srinivasa, Bali Murti and Utsava Murti, also known as Malayappa Swami, which receive different types of worship daily.

THE STORY OF GOD

Perhaps the greatest stories of all are the stories that explain God and the nature of God, and which provide evidence that God resides in everyone at all times, the one supreme soul of which every living being is a part. This thought has opened up not only minds, but also societies across religions and the world.

One such story about the god of Tirupati is told in the Skanda Mahapurana through a dialogue between the legendary warrior Arjuna and the great sage Bharadwaja.[9] Arjuna is curious

---

[8]Rao, S.K. Ramchandra, *The Hill-Shrine of Vengadam*, Kalpatharu Research Academy Publication, Bangalore, 1993, p. 72: 'The figures and the ornamental decorations of this vimana are only in the gilt copper plates that cover the vimana. The actual vimana, which is in mortar and stucco, is devoid of figures; it has only the architectural features of Pallava vimana.'

[9]This dialogue is described in chapters 35 and 36 of the Venkatachala Mahatmya, Vaishnava Khanda and Skanda Mahapurana, as related by the sage Sri Suta to other sages.

to learn about the greatness of Lord Sri Venkateswara and the importance of Tirupati. When he questions Sage Bharadwaja, the eminent sage answers him that at Tirupati reside the two avatars of Lord Vishnu, Lord Varaha and Lord Sri Venkateswara.

Sage Bharadwaja speaks about the well-known (*vikhyate*) Venkatachala mountain, situated on the northern banks of the ancient river of Suvarna Mukhari. When Lord Vishnu assumed the form of the Boar God or Lord Varaha, He had chosen this mountain as His residence on Earth, a reason why this region is also known as Varaha Kshetra or the region of Varaha. Lord Vishnu had assumed this avatar to save the Earth, which had sunk to the deepest worlds and was covered in great layers of water. This avatar of God was generated from the sacred ritual, *yajna*, with the fire as His tongue; the Vedas as His four legs; the place where the yajna was conducted as His body; the mantras as His power.

There was darkness in the depths in which the Earth had submerged. But the Boar God brought light to the region with the brilliance of His curved tusks and found the Earth hidden beneath the seven worlds. Balancing the Earth between the snout and the curved tusks, Lord Varaha brought her out of the depths of darkness and the deadly waters. As He rose out of the waters with the Earth safe, those who witnessed the event praised God with gratitude. Then the Boar God placed the Earth amidst the seas and supported her with His power. Once the Earth was stable again, the process of Creation was restarted as before (*yatha purvam kalpayat*).[10]

---

[10]The story, as befits a Purana, speaks about the apocalypse and creation, the cycle of the birth and death of the universe. Just as everything is a reflection of the wish of God, His leela, so are human life, destiny and death.

THE AVATAR OF LORD SRI VENKATESWARA

Sage Bharadwaja then told Arjuna the story of King Sankha who was a great devotee of Lord Vishnu but failed to get even a single darshan of God. The king was deeply saddened by this and eventually lost all interest in life (*jeevitha nispruhey*). Aware of every thought of every human being and *being* Himself every thought of every human being, God was aware of King Sankha's thoughts as well.

Then Lord Vishnu spoke to the king, pleasantly surprising him. Lord Vishnu told the king to worship and mediate on the sacred Venkatachala Mountain, along with the legendary Sage Agastya, who was also seeking a vision of God. Following the instructions, King Sankha reached the sacred mountain and settled on the banks of the Swami Pushkarani Lake to meditate on Lord Vishnu. Sage Agastya also made his way to the lake and met the king. They together worshipped God, along with a number of other sages and devotees. On the third day, as they slept at night tired, they attained a vision of God in a dream. Delighted, they all awoke and knew they would very soon get a darshan of God. After bathing in the holy lake according to the prescribed procedure, the happy devotees continued their worship of Lord Vishnu. Then a light of great intensity lit up the sky, with the brilliance of a million suns, moons and fires merged together. Amidst that magnificent light, the men and women gathered there obtained the vision of God, Lord Vishnu.

They praised God as all-pervading, the One within the smallest atom, the One larger than the largest mass (*anoranun antaram sthulatsthulam sarvanatra sthitam*). Who could describe God who embodies the gist of Vedantas (*Vedanta saara rupam*), the One who was both within and without? How could people trapped in mortal forms and engulfed in maya describe God (*ko hi varnay ithum shakto mayaya theshu deheyshu*)? They trembled in fear at the fierceness of God's image and pleaded to Him to assume a more peaceful form (*shantam rupam*).

Lord Vishnu vanished and, within a moment, reappeared in a pleasant form, riding a celestial vehicle that was adorned with jewels. His face was a reflection of the moon, His manner was peaceful, His aura was the colour of blue lotuses, He wore garments of gold and ornaments of jewels. He held the conch, the discus, the mace and the lotus (*sankha chakra gada padma*).

He spoke to Sage Agastya and commiserated with him for the suffering caused by the harsh rituals he had undertaken and the severe penance. The Lord then offered that He would grant any wish the sage may have. Sage Agastya, thrilled, requested God to remain on the Venkatachala Mountain and grant His devotees the chance to see the image of Him in the physical form. The sage sought that He should stay forever on the mountain with a smiling countenance (*sadasminna sthitha*) and fulfil peoples' wishes (*prasada sumukho deva kankshith artha prado bhava*).

Lord Vishnu granted the request of the sage and stayed on the Venkatachala Mountain as Lord Sri Venkateswara to fulfil the desires of people and complete their destinies. That is the reason why there neither was nor will be another god equal to Lord Sri Venkateswara (*Venkatesha samo devo na bhutho na bhavishyati*). There neither was nor will be another place like Venkatadri (*Venkatadri samam sthanam na bhutham na bhavishyati*).

ADDITIONAL REFERENCES

1. Raghavacharya, Pandit V. Vijaya (ed.), *Tirumala Tirupati Devasthanams Inscriptions*, vol. III (*Inscriptions of Krishnaraya's Time from 1509 A.D. to 1531 A.D.*), Tirumala Tirupati Devasthanams, Tirupati, 1998.

2. Sastry, Sadhu Subrahmanya (ed.), *Tirumala Tirupati Devasthanams*

Inscriptions, vol. I (Translated and Edited with Introductions), Tirumala Tirupati Devasthanams, Tirupati, 1998.

3. Sastry, Sadhu Subrahmanya, *Tirumala Tirupati Devasthanams Inscriptions, Report on the Inscriptions of the Devasthanam Collection with Illustrations*, 1998.

4. Bhatt, G.P. (ed.), *Ancient Indian Tradition and Mythology*, vol. 52, Motilal Banarsidass, Delhi, 1993.

A Muslim Goddess

Sunderbans, West Bengal

SABA NAQVI

A journey into the Sunderbans is to venture into a terrain that lives by its own rules. Made up of little islands linked by waterways, they have no infrastructure for travellers who have to spend the night in boats or in the villages. There is a great stillness in the night at the edge of the land that disappears into the Bay of Bengal. There is a dark rustle of the forests, the gentle ripple in the water, the clouds moving swiftly across the moon and the stars. There is a strange goddess who is believed to be the keeper of these parts. She is called 'Bonbibi' and the locals say she is a Muslim goddess.

Even an 'impure' or ignorant Muslim knows there are no gods and goddesses in Islam. Idol worship is strictly banned. There is only Allah and his last prophet Mohammad and even he cannot be depicted in a picture or idol. Yet, the people of the Sunderbans have created a curious creature in the form of a Muslim goddess. In imagery and form, Bonbibi strongly resembles the several Shakti figures so popular in the state. Her devotees insist that she is not a metamorphosis of Goddess Durga or Kali, and are convinced that she is a Muslim.

Such a curious divinity could only have come into existence in an extraordinary landscape. Bonbibi's home is an unsual terrain: the Sunderbans, a vast tract of forest and swamp, is now divided between India and Bangladesh. A cluster of four-hundred-odd islands linked by a network of waterways form the largest estuarine delta in the world. The Sunderbans is also the largest mangrove forest in the world, much of which is exclusive tiger territory. Even the tigers here are distinct from their brethren in other parts of India—they are smaller, accomplished swimmers, and most significantly, maneaters. Studies have tried to determine whether the salinity of the water has caused the Sunderbans tigers to develop a taste for human beings, but no conclusive answers have been found. So lethal are these tigers that their appetite for man has led to numerous deaths every year. There is a village called Bagher Vidhava Gram, which literally translates into 'village of the tiger widows'—its inhabitants are all women whose husbands have had the misfortune of being eaten up.

Much of the region comes under Project Tiger where human habitations are banned. But there are several villages on the edge of the waterways and forests where a mixed population of Hindus and Muslims struggle to eke out a living through subsistence-level farming, a very basic form of fishing where villagers stand submerged in water for hours with their nets, cutting wood and collecting honey. The people are desperately poor and life in the delta is harsh. The rivers are constantly in flux and the islands change dramatically with the monsoons. Cultivated land is frequently flooded while the forest, the other source of income, presents many perils, particularly the tigers that claim at least fifty human lives a year.

In response to their environment, the locals, both Hindus and Muslims, have evolved a religion that is a curious mix of animism, the Hindu Shakti tradition and a typically Indian brand of Sufism, which is described by some scholars as the phenomenon of 'Pirism' in Bengal. The Sufis are commonly described as wandering Islamic mystics who have spread Islam through much of the continent. 'Pir' is a Persian word that means 'spiritual guide'. In Bengal, it covers not only the Sufis but a range of holy men, some of whom appear to be completely mythical and represent various *natural* forces. All of them have been deified as pirs.

The three most popular gods of the Sunderbans are Bonbibi, the Muslim forest goddess who is a Durga-like figure; a 'tiger god' named Dakshin Ray; and a legendary pir named Ghazi Miyan. The legends of the three deities are inextricably woven together. In his landmark work, *The Islamic Syncretistic Tradition in Bengal*, historian Asim Roy, referring to the Sunderbans divided between India and Bangladesh, says that Hindu Ray–Mangal literature depicts Dakshin Ray as a Hindu chief who battled Ghazi Miyan, the Muslim, for control of the forest. He writes: 'An even battle. It was ended, we read, by a happy compromise based on territorial divisions dictated by God, appearing in a significant form, half-Hindu and half-Muslim.'

But the legend that I found most common in the district of 24 Parganas covering the Indian side of the Sunderbans was somewhat different. In this version, Dakshin Ray is a tiger god who wages a mighty battle with Bonbibi, the protector of humans. Finally, Ghazi Miyan is forced to intervene and he works out a compromise where the forest is equally divided between the two, human beings and tigers. The locals even perform an elaborate dance theatre based on this legend. It is a colourful event with villagers donning tiger masks, some dressing up as the goddess, and others putting on a very primitive beard and skullcap to depict Ghazi Miyan. This legend is enacted in a simple folk theatre style to a riotous beating of drums and blowing of conch shells. The Bonbibi puja is a huge celebration in the forest and a delight for any visitor.

So who exactly is Bonbibi? She is definitely a less evolved Shakti deity, the female divine so worshipped across Bengal. Makeshift temples of Bonbibi line the edge of the forest and no local ventures inside without seeking her blessings. These temples are crude structures that usually have a clay image of Bonbibi. The more elaborate temples are found in the villages. Here, the goddess stands alongside many consorts, who are usually a happy mix of Muslims and Hindus. Bonbibi also appears alongside the 'tiger god', Dakshin Ray, who also has to be appeased. At times she is merely standing beside him; in other temples she is vanquishing him, looking remarkably like Goddess Durga destroying the demon. The Bonbibi tradition clearly draws from animism, once popular across India but now found only in the Sunderbans. Animistic cults have died out because of large-scale deforestation across the country but survive in the Sunderbans because of the rare terrain. Equally popular in this region is the Mobrah Ghazi or Ghazi Miyan tradition that survives not just in the forest area but throughout the entire 24 Parganas district. This tradition, too, originates in the need to seek protection from tigers, other animals and the vagaries of nature.

In the Sunderbans, Ghazi Miyan is worshipped alongside another figure called Kalu Ghazi and five Hindu deities. Some fakirs from the region, who claim descent from the Ghazi, accompany the locals into the forest where they perform an elaborate puja. The fakirs clear a space where they build seven small thatched huts in a single row. The first three huts are for the Hindu deities Jagabandhu (friend of the earth), Mahadeva (the destroyer) and Manasa (the snake goddess). The fourth hut houses Goddess Kali and her daughter Kalimaya, while the fifth hut has two compartments: one for a goddess called Kamesvari and the other for Budi Thakurani, a local deity. The sixth hut is dedicated to Ghazi Miyan and his brother Kalu Ghazi and the seventh to Sawwal Ghazi, the son of Ghazi Miyan, and Ram Ghazi, the son of Kalu Ghazi. It's quite an intricate and elaborate pantheon.

After these preparations, offerings are made to all the deities and the fakir spends the whole night praying to Ghazi Miyan and his consorts to protect the party from tigers and other dangers. The legend of Ghazi Miyan is basically similar throughout the 24 Parganas, though there are some local variations in the names of his consorts. Santosh Chaudhary, a local teacher, says there have been attempts to create divisions and raise the issue of Bangladeshi refugees here. 'But here in the Sunderbans, who can tell a Muslim from a Hindu, a Bangladeshi from a Bengali? They are so alike that they have even entered into a joint enterprise over their gods. How can you separate the people when you can't separate their gods?'

Mohammad Sheikh is a woodcutter of great fame in the region. He has the scars of two tiger attacks: on his right shoulder and the back of his neck. This is the price he has paid for repeatedly venturing into tiger country in quest of the famed Sunderbans honey. As his name suggests, Mohammad Sheikh is a God-fearing Muslim. But he does not credit Allah for saving him from a gruesome death; it is the blessing of Bonbibi, he believes.

She does not appear to be doing a very good job of it, I suggest, what with so many humans becoming a meal for the beasts each year. Wouldn't it be better to trust in Allah and his last prophet after whom you have been named? Mohammad Sheikh sees the world in black and white: 'Allah has too many human beings to deal with. Tigers are better left to Bonbibi.'

The Persistence of Memory

URVASHI BUTALIA

On 11 March 1947, Sant Raja Singh of Thoa Khalsa village in Rawalpindi district picked up his sword, said a short prayer to Guru Nanak, and then, with one swift stroke, tried to bring it down on the neck of his young daughter, Maan Kaur. As the story is told, at first he didn't succeed: the blow wasn't strong enough, or something came in the way. Then his daughter, aged sixteen, came once again and knelt before her father, removed her thick plait, and offered him her neck. This time, his sword found its mark. Bir Bahadur Singh, his son of eleven, stood by his side and watched. Years later, he recounted this story to me: 'I stood there, right next to him, clutching on to his kurta as children do . . . I was clinging to him, sobbing, and her head rolled off and fell . . . there . . . far away.'

Shortly after this incident, Bir Bahadur's family fled Thoa Khalsa, heading towards the Indian border where they hoped to find safety. India was being partitioned, and large-scale carnage, arson, rape and loot among Muslims, Hindus and Sikhs had become the order of the day. In many families, like Bir Bahadur's,

the men decided to kill the women and children, fearing that
they would be abducted, raped, converted, impregnated, polluted
by men of the other religion—in this case Muslims. They called
these killings the 'martyrdom of women'.

It was only two years earlier, in 1945, that Bir Bahadur's
family had moved to Thoa Khalsa. Talk of a possible partition
was in the air and they were worried for their safety. Saintha,
the village in which they had lived for many years, was a
Muslim-majority village and theirs was the only non-Muslim
family there. It was this that had made Bir Bahadur's father,
Sant Raja Singh, decide to move to Thoa Khalsa, where there
were many more Sikhs than Muslims. Everywhere, at this time,
people banded together with their own kind, believing that
safety lay in numbers. Ironically, and tragically, it was in Thoa
Khalsa that the real violence took place. In retaliation for
attacks by Hindus and Sikhs on Muslims elsewhere in India,
villages in this part of Rawalpindi—inhabited mainly by Sikhs—
came under concerted attack for several days. Shortly after Sant
Raja Singh killed his daughter and several others, he asked a
relative to take his life—perhaps the burden of what he had
done was too heavy to bear. A single shot from a gun ensured
that he joined the ranks of the martyrs.

Forty years later, Bir Bahadur told me these stories. I had met
him while researching a book on oral histories on the partition
of India. In the lower-middle-class area of Delhi where he lived,
Bir Bahadur was someone people looked up to—he came from a
family of martyrs. Not only his sister, but several other women
had been killed on that day. Bir Bahadur had been a young boy
at the time, but his memories were crystal clear and sharp. He

remembered the fear and the violence and remembered too that when the attacks had begun to seem imminent, people from his 'home' village of Saintha had come to Thoa in a delegation to offer his family protection. They were led by Sajawal Khan, the village headman. But his father had turned them away. They were Muslims and, even though he had lived among them in safety and peace for many years, he no longer trusted them. Bir Bahadur has never forgotten this rejection.

Stories of such violence—and more—are routine when Muslims and Hindus speak of the partition of the Indian subcontinent in 1947. The British decision to partition the country into two, India and Pakistan, led to the displacement of millions of people, a million deaths, and nearly a hundred thousand incidents of rape and abduction. Women were particularly vulnerable: not only was there mass rape and abduction but hundreds were killed by their own families, ostensibly as a form of 'protection', some had their breasts cut off, others had symbols of the 'other' religion tattooed on their bodies. But while stories of violence are routine, what is less known are the stories of friendship that cut across the rigid borders drawn by the Indian and Pakistani states. In the year 2000 Bir Bahadur and I embarked on one such journey of reconciliation across what had till then seemed like a somewhat intractable border.

It all began with a phone call from Chihiro, a Japanese journalist. She was keen to make a programme featuring an Indian travelling to Pakistan on the India–Pakistan bus, visiting his/her relatives. She, and a crew, would travel along with this person and film the journey as well as the 'homecoming'. She asked for suggestions. I offered Bir Bahadur's name. For years he had wanted to go back to his village in Pakistan, but had never had the opportunity. Now it had presented itself.

Today in his seventies, Bir Bahadur Singh is a tall, statuesque Sikh with a white, flowing beard. Always dressed in white, with a black turban and a saffron head cloth showing through, he makes an arresting figure. His family was only one among the millions of refugees who fled from Pakistan to India. They carried nothing with them and Bir Bahadur's key memories of that time are of hunger, fear and cold. Once in India, Bir Bahadur and his family struggled to keep body and soul together. He tried his hand at different things and then, at eighteen, managed to put together enough to set up a small provision store. Later, his family arranged for him to marry a woman from a village close to his home in Rawalpindi, and together they brought up a large family. Bir Bahadur has never been rich, and he has worked hard all his life for the sake of his children. A might-have-been politician (he stood for municipal elections on a Bharatiya Janata Party ticket some years ago and lost), he now leads a retired life, dividing his time between his farmhouse close to Delhi, his extended family of children and grandchildren, and his old (ninety plus) mother who lives close by. He was beside himself with excitement at the news that he might get permission to travel to Pakistan and visit his home village.

With Japanese intervention visas were swiftly arranged and a few days later, we left for Pakistan. Bir Bahadur arrived at my house with a small bag and a sackful of hard, dry coconuts. These were to be his offerings to the people of his village. 'There are no coconuts there,' he explained, 'and the people love them.' He had also written two letters, one to the people of his village, and one to his school friend, Sadq Khan, son of Sajawal Khan. 'We were good friends in school,' he said, 'I am sure he will remember me.' These he carried with him, in the event that we did not make it to the village. He was convinced we would find someone, somewhere, who would carry his letters to the village, and people from there would arrive in immediate response, to see him. For days he'd been like a child, excited and nervous. He'd ring me up every day—sometimes twice or three times in a day—to check on this or that detail. Would we be staying in a hotel? How much money should he bring? Could we not persuade Chihiro to do a radio programme instead of one for television (we did)—it would be much less obvious. And now that we were actually on our way, he could not believe his luck.

Heavy rain had delayed the flight. We spent a long and tiring night waiting at Lahore airport, uncomfortable in plastic seats. Occasionally, Chihiro and I would doze off out of sheer exhaustion. But not Bir Bahadur. Every time I opened my eyes, he would be wide awake, sitting on his haunches in the airport chairs, recounting his story to someone or the other—now a family on their way to Karachi (also delayed), now two helpful employees of the airport (with whom he was quickly exchanging photographs and addresses) and now the toyshop owner or the man selling tea . . .

Islamabad is a city of wide boulevards and tree-lined roads. At night, speeding through the deserted streets, there was little to see. We arrived, exhausted, at our hotel at three in the morning after a twelve-hour delay in our flight. The time of our departure was fixed for ten the next day.

The morning rose clean and washed. Armed with some water and our passports and visa papers, we set off for Thoa Khalsa. A wide, straight road led through fairly flat terrain to the outskirts of Islamabad. We'd been driving for an hour or so when we arrived at a major turn-off. Clearly some sort of

junction, the wide road was bordered at this point with small
shops selling fruit, juice, cigarette, food and snacks and all the
small knick-knacks that travellers buy when they make stopovers.
On the other side was a bus and tempo terminal, with scooters
and tempo taxis shouting out their locations, picking up point-
to-point passengers and quickly shuffling men into separate
seats the moment they saw prospective women passengers: one
of the unwritten rules of tempo travelling in Pakistan (and
indeed often in India too) is that men and women do not
occupy the same seat lest they inadvertently touch each other.
We stopped to ask for directions and then turned off into a
narrower road to the left. A gate across the road proclaimed a
level crossing, and a small signpost gave the name of the station.
'This used to be our station,' Bir Bahadur told me excitedly,
'the train stopped here, and we'd have to take buses from our
village to get here!' We stopped in the marketplace to get a
better look at the station. Immediately the car was surrounded
by a crowd of people—tall, hefty men in salwar kameezes. They
were everywhere: at the doors, in front of the car, virtually
inside the driver's door. We couldn't move, and I began to
panic a bit. In such situations the enmity and rhetoric of hatred
that India and Pakistan constantly rehearse come back to haunt
us, and, although the situation is harmless enough, it suddenly
acquires overtones of fear. But Bir Bahadur was unfazed: 'Stop,
stop the car,' he told the driver unnecessarily, and wound his
window down. He leaned out, trained his gaze on a tea stall
across the road and said, to no one in particular: 'Bhai sahib,
bhai sahib, excuse me, can you help?' A cyclist stopped by to see
what it was he wanted, and the crowd of men surrounding the
car suddenly transformed from a threatening bunch to a group
of curious and helpful onlookers peering into the car at two
strange women, and an odd man, clearly from across the border

for he had on a turban and there were no Sikhs in the area. 'Welcome, welcome, sardarji,' they said, 'where have you come from? India? What are you looking for here? Can we help you to find it?' Bir Bahadur immediately launched into his story while Chihiro and I sat nervously, wondering if it was wise, in an unknown place in Pakistan, to recall stories of the violence of Partition.

'I'm from this area,' he told them, 'my father used to run a shop in Saintha, and I am looking for the road to Saintha. Do you know Sajawal Khan from Saintha?'

'Not Saintha,' I whispered to him, 'we need to know how to get to Thoa Khalsa.'

'Yes, yes,' he said, turning to the man, 'and we need to get to Thoa Khalsa as well. But first, I want to find Saintha.'

It was at this point that it became clear to me that Bir Bahadur had already decided on the itinerary for this trip—no matter that Chihiro wanted to capture the drama of taking him back to the place where he had seen such a bloody history, he was determined to go to Saintha, his home village. I felt a curious mixture of relief (that we may not now have to confront what could have been an unpleasant situation) and elation (that he had succeeded in doing exactly what he wanted) and concern (for Chihiro and her radio programme which, after all, had paid for us to be here). While these thoughts were turning around in my head and I was wondering how to break the news to Chihiro, I suddenly found that Bir Bahadur had invited one of the men outside into the car. Basheer, he told us, was a son-in-law of Saintha, and had offered to ride there with us and help us find the place and the people Bir Bahadur was looking for. 'Can you slide up a bit, beta?' he said to me, and I pushed myself into as small a corner as I could, to make room for a rather large and hefty Basheer. We were breaking the unwritten

code here: three of us in the back seat, one woman and two
men. The available space was tight, and it was up to me to
ensure that our bodies remained at least one inch apart.
Meanwhile, everyone on the road offered us advice for free, one
person ran off and came back with six bananas, another asked if
we'd like a cold drink, while a third offered us mithai. Finally,
they waved us off with good wishes, extracting a promise that we
would come back this way and stop for a cup of tea.

And so we set off, down a long, straight road, past large fields
and scattered homes, spotting the occasional tractor carrying
bales of straw and groups of women drawing water at village
wells, their faces partially veiled. And slowly the landscape gave
way to a gentle, hilly terrain. We could have been in India:
everything looked exactly as it would on the other side of the
border, in Punjab: the villages with their mud houses, the scene
at the well, the fields covered with stalks of wheat pushing their
way out of the earth. 'Son,' said Bir Bahadur to Basheer after a
few minutes, 'just keep telling me the names of the places we are
passing by, just keep reminding me.' Dutifully, Basheer did as
he was told, and at one point, as we were passing a small rise on
our left with stray houses scattered along its slopes, Basheer
said, 'That village is called Thamali.'

'Stop, stop,' Bir Bahadur said to Sain, our driver, 'please
stop. Thamali is where my wife used to live—it's her village.' We
swung over to the side of the narrow road, and Bir Bahadur and
Basheer leapt out of the car. 'I can't believe it,' said Bir Bahadur
excitedly, 'we used to come here to play. There—there's the
banyan tree we used to sit under, and over that hill was her
grandfather's house, the water pump. Please,' he said, turning
to me, 'please can you take a picture of me by the tree—I'd like
to take it back to my wife.'

As he stood there waiting to be photographed, the tree

behind him, a small knot of people—husband, wife, perhaps a brother or brother-in-law and two children—came out of a nearby house. Bir Bahadur greeted the children, affectionately patting them on the head, and waited as the parents drew up. They came, faces open with welcome: 'Where are you from Sardarji, how have you come here? Won't you come to our home and drink some sherbet with us?'

'No, no, my child,' said Bir Bahadur to the young woman, 'thank you for your welcome, my daughter. This village Thamali is where my wife comes from. I used to play here as a child fifty years ago, long before you were even born. See that tree over there? That was the tree we sat under. My wife's family home was over that hill, there was a pond and a water pump there . . .' The pond was still there they told him, but of course the water pump had gone. The school too—the building was there, but it was no longer used as a school. Thamali had been at the receiving end of the Muslim attack on Sikhs in March 1947 and large numbers of people had been killed. Looking at the small, peaceful village nestling in the July sun, it seemed hard to believe that such violence could have taken place there. I tried to picture the mobs everyone—not only Bir Bahadur—had told me about, the countryside resounding with the cries of murder and revenge, the thirst for blood. How would they have moved from village to village, I wondered inconsequentially—this thin ribbon of a road was probably not there at the time. How must people have felt to see hundreds, thousands of attackers coming over these gentle, almost sleepy, slopes? What protection did their houses offer? At which points did they negotiate? What do people do when violence breaks out in this way? The people of Thamali, I remembered being told, had refused to believe initially that they could be attacked. Then someone from another village had persuaded them to climb atop one of the higher

houses and look down at the area around them, and they'd
done so and seen the mobs and quickly started to evacuate the
village. Some 30–40 women and girls were abducted, among
them two sisters of a family I had spoken to when I was working
on my book. As with many Hindu and Sikh families where
women were abducted and almost certainly raped, this family
too refused to acknowledge the existence of these sisters, for
their history was a history of shame, best forgotten. And here
we were, fifty years later, standing on that very same spot, in the
slanting, late morning light, being welcomed by people from
Thamali. 'Please come,' a young woman who was there with her
husband insisted to Bir Bahadur Singh, 'please come and bless
our house.' Bir Bahadur took a drink of water from the woman,
touched his hand to his brow, and blessed his hostess and her
children. 'We don't have time to stop, daughter,' he said to her,
'but I would like to give you something small as a token of my
love for you who live in this village now.' Then he called out to
our driver and asked him to bring his bag out of the car. He
pulled out two dried coconuts and held them out to the young
couple, 'This is a small offering I know, but I would like you to
have it. I have lived here and I know that it's not possible to get
dried coconuts here. These are for you with my love, with love
from your mother, my wife . . .' and saying this, he embraced
these strangers he had met only a few minutes before, touched
the bent head of the young woman of the house, and turned to
us and said, 'Come, let us move towards Saintha.'

Twenty minutes later, we rounded a bend in the road and
Bir Bahadur let out a shout of recognition. 'Look there,' he
said, 'there's my old school. It looks just the same!' Atop a little
ridge stood a small, low-slung building, with a narrow veranda
running its length, green painted doors and windows giving on
to it. As often happens in villages when outsiders come, by this

time our party had acquired something of a following—a clutch of curious youngsters offering to help, a few scruffy-looking children, a stray dog or two. And as we made our way deeper into the village, this small crowd swelled with the addition of a few other young men. There were no girls of course, nor any women.

We began walking. Some distance in front of us, Basheer spotted three old people shuffling along, weighed down with heavy cloth bags full of provisions. Recognizing two of them as his parents-in-law he rushed up to them and stopped them. We followed. Bir Bahadur introduced himself—Basheer had already given his parents-in-law the background to the story—giving his father's name first. The old man recognized the name although he did not remember Bir Bahadur himself. The woman with them, who'd been standing around silently, suddenly opened her mouth in a wide, toothless grin and poked Bir Bahadur in the chest. 'Are you Biran?' she asked, using the nickname his friends had given him.

'Yes, yes,' said Bir Bahadur, somewhat surprised, 'who are you?'

But she wouldn't say. Instead, she looked at him, mischief glinting in her eyes, and asked, 'How is Santo? Is she still alive?' using the nickname of Bir Bahadur's mother Basant Kaur, 'And how is Maano?' referring to his dead sister. I realized that the villagers in Saintha did not seem to know about Maan Kaur's death, or the horrible way in which she had died, or if they did, they did not want to make any reference to it directly. Instead, they spoke as if she were still alive.

'Santo is well,' said Bir Bahadur, glossing over the second question, 'she's in Delhi with all her grandchildren, but tell me, who are you?'

'I am,' she said with a touch of drama, 'Sadq Khan's wife.'

Bir Bahadur gave a great whoop of joy and, in the next instant, had put his arms around her and lifted her off the ground. 'My sister, my sister!' he cried, as tears began to stream down his face. 'Oh my sister, where is my brother? Where is Chacha Sajawal Khan? I heard he had died, is this true? Where is my sister Taj with whom I used to play? I wrote a letter to you all some time ago. Did you get it? . . .' Questions and more questions. The old woman answered some, avoided others. Later, we learnt that her slight hesitation had been because she no longer had an 'official' status as Sadq Khan's wife. He had taken another, a younger woman, as his wife. But at that time, all we knew was that the first contact had been made. Sadq Khan was alive and he was in the village.

Sadq Khan's father, Sajawal Khan, had been the headman of Saintha. Although Bir Bahadur's family was the only Sikh family in a village of Muslims, they were considered important and given respect because they were both moneylenders and shopkeepers. Sant Raja Singh was respected and trusted by the villagers of Saintha. This is how Bir Bahadur had described it when he had spoken to me earlier:

> The Musalmaans used to believe in us, trusted us so much . . . if a money order came for someone, no one would go to their homes to deliver it . . . [The post office] was in Thoa Khalsa and the postman would not reach people's mail to them or get money orders to them. That was why when Musalmaans went away to work from their homes, they would give our address as the place to receive their money orders . . . My father used to make entries in his register scrupulously . . . and then people used to come and buy their provisions out of this . . . those people trusted us so much.

In return, however, the Sikhs did not extend the same kind of trust to the Muslims. They practised the customary untouchability of Hindus towards Muslims, refusing to eat anything cooked or touched by them. In Bir Bahadur's words:

> If there was any function that we had, then we used to call Musalmaans to our homes, they would eat in our houses, but we would not eat in theirs and this is a bad thing, which I realize now. If they would come to our houses we would have two utensils in one corner of the house, and we would tell them, pick these up and eat in them; they would then wash them and keep them aside and this was such a terrible thing. This was the reason Pakistan was created. If we went to their houses and took part in their weddings and ceremonies, they used to really respect and honour us. They would give us uncooked food, ghee, atta, dal, whatever sabzis they had, chicken and even mutton, all raw. And our dealings with them were so low that I am even ashamed to say it. A guest comes to our house and we say to him, bring those utensils and wash them, and if my mother or sister have to give him food, they will more or less throw the roti from such a distance, fearing that they may touch the dish and become polluted . . .

In 1945, when Sant Raja Singh decided he wanted to move his family and business to Thoa Khalsa because he felt it would be safer, the villagers of Saintha tried hard to dissuade him. But Sant Raja Singh was afraid—he no longer trusted his Muslim friends. There were just too many stories of friends turning into enemies, of old, trusted relationships being betrayed. Once in Thoa, he felt, the family would be safer—should anything happen, the Sikhs could band together and fight. The tragedy, of course,

was that it was in Thoa Khalsa that the Sikhs became most
vulnerable to attacks spread over several days. I quote from Bir
Bahadur's description:

> When the trouble started, the people came from there
> [Saintha]. You know that Ma Hasina whom I mentioned
> to you, her son, Sajawal Khan, he came to us and said
> we could stay in his house if we wanted to. He came
> with his children. But we were doubtful, and today I feel
> that what he was saying, the expression on his face, his
> bearing—there was nothing there but sincerity and
> compassion and we, we misunderstood him. We had all
> been through so much trouble and they came to give us
> support, to help us, and we refused.

In many ways, Bir Bahadur's journey to Saintha now, fifty years
later, was a journey of penance and reparation. For a half-
century he had carried within him the guilt of the burden of his
family's refusal. He wanted, in some way, to appease this guilt,
to lighten the load. 'I just want to go to Saintha,' he had said to
me, 'and take the soil of my village and touch it to my head. I
need to ask their forgiveness.' What if they will not forgive, I
had asked, doubtful. 'Of course they will,' he said, confident,
'after all, once you fight, what is there left but reconciliation,
what is there left but forgiveness?'

Forgiveness, of course, is not so easily asked in something
like this. All the time that Bir Bahadur spent in Saintha, neither
he, nor anyone else, could bring themselves to refer to the
violence that had taken place in Thoa Khalsa. I could not
understand at the time, and I am still unable to do so, whether
the villagers of Saintha knew of what had happened to his sister
Maan Kaur, whether they knew that so many women in Thoa
had jumped or been pushed into a well and died . . . and yet,

surely they must have known. But whenever anyone asked Bir Bahadur about Maan Kaur—and a few did but others did not, again making me wonder if they knew—he somehow evaded the question. Only once did he say to an old woman who asked: 'She died.' Perhaps this is the way silences build up: Maan Kaur's absence hung in the air in virtually every encounter we had, and yet, apart from the odd question or two, no one explicitly mentioned her.

We made our way further into the village. A group of young women had gathered and begun talking to us. The conversation was interrupted by the sudden arrival of a tall, emaciated, scruffy-looking old man in a brown salwar kurta, and sporting a pencil-thin moustache and short beard. He hesitated for a moment, listening. Then he fixed Bir Bahadur with a sharp, direct stare and asked, 'Are you Biran?'

'Yes,' said Bir Bahadur, 'and who are you?'

'You don't remember me?' he said, 'Really, you don't remember me?' I couldn't tell whether he was angry or amused— there was a glint of something in his eyes.

'No, I'm trying,' said Bir Bahadur, 'but I can't. Tell me your name.'

'You bastard,' said the old man, 'you nearly strangled me to death one day! You jumped on me and almost tore my throat into ribbons,' he said, gesturing wildly at his throat, and then he leapt onto Bir Bahadur!

There was one of those moments of perfect stillness. I realized, in a moment, that no matter that it was more than fifty years after the event, we had, after all, carried the history of a bitter division with us. I felt a stab of fear. And then we saw that the old man was chuckling quietly to himself. He had made a joke! He told us his story. 'You crazy,' said Bir Bahadur, once he'd been reminded of the story, 'and I'll tear your throat again!' and he leapt on him in mock attack, as the two tangled and laughed and cried at the same time.

The story ran like this: He and Bir Bahadur had been at school together. It was during that time that Aslam had accepted a dare from his schoolmates to 'pollute' Bir Bahadur's drinking water by putting the earthenware pot in which it was stored to his mouth. It seemed incredible to me that, being the only non-Muslim family in the village, Bir Bahadur's family could keep these taboos, but they did. The young Aslam had drunk from the pot and then teased Bir Bahadur about it, at which the incensed young Sikh attacked his friend. The boys had fought, and had then been gently pried apart by the village elders who had explained to Aslam that he should not have done what he did, that it was important to respect the customs of others. Something, I thought, that we would do well to remember today.

Bir Bahadur had not remembered this particular instance but water and food played a major part in his journey home. 'There are two things I want to do if we make it to Saintha,' he had earlier told me, 'drink water from the village well and eat in the home of a Musalmaan.' This was his private penance, his reparation, his way of asking forgiveness for the harshness and cruelty of Hindu 'untouchability' and its pollution taboos. Now he turned to Aslam and said to him, 'Brother, can you take me to the village well? I want to drink the water from there.' Wordlessly, almost as if he divined what it was that drove Bir Bahadur to make such a request, Aslam led us further down the road, to a half-covered well. Two young men from the village were dispatched to find a couple of tumblers, while others lowered the bucket into the well and drew up a bucketful of clear, cool, sweet water. Bir Bahadur took the tumbler and touched it to his forehead before drinking deeply. He closed his eyes and seemed to pray as he drank—I could not make out the words, but I thought he was asking forgiveness, not so much for himself but also on behalf of his people. And then be bent down, took up a fistful of earth, touched it to his forehead and ran it over his turban. There was silence all around: all of us watching, sharing in this most private of rituals and yet feeling a bit like intruders. I could feel my eyes prick with tears—how, I thought, how could we have done this to ourselves? How could we have allowed ourselves to be divided thus? And then the spell was broken as two old women, watching us from a balcony above the road, spoke up and asked Bir Bahadur if he was Biran. And he was off again. But not before he had turned to me and offered the remainder of the water: 'Here child, you drink also,' he said. After a moment of doubt about how clean or otherwise the water was—after all, the well was open to the sky, even though the water in the bucket looked clear—I decided that there were times when considerations of bacteria and health simply did not matter. I put the glass to my lips and drank.

News of Bir Bahadur's visit had spread in the village and we had collected quite a large following. We moved on, Bir Bahadur and Aslam in the lead, talking about this field and that crop, and this hillock and that house. We were heading, I guessed, towards Sadq Khan. Bir Bahadur, meanwhile, did not know whether to laugh or cry as each new person came up and enfolded him in an embrace—his tears fell with abandon, drops of moisture glistening on his white beard. 'These are tears of joy, beta, don't worry,' he reassured me every time I looked at him. 'I am so happy. Did I not tell you we would be welcomed?'

We crossed a small bridge over a nullah, skirted slushy wet mud still recovering from the previous night's heavy rain, and made our way through some low bushes up a green, grassy slope. Just above us, to the left and right, stood two houses, and between them ran a small lane, leading to another house further back. As we wound our way up, people came out of their houses to greet Bir Bahadur. I suddenly became aware that, for the first time since we had entered Saintha, he was distracted. He was not listening. Instead, he was looking at the narrow lane which led to the house at the back. Through this, now, came a small, stocky man, a two- or three-day stubble on his face, shuffling along with difficulty. As he drew closer, a sort of silence descended on our group and we watched as he made his painful way towards us. His face held a smile but his eyes shone with tears. I think both of them knew instantly who the other was, but for some moments it seemed as if we were all caught in a state of suspension. No one could move.

Then he came within a few steps of Bir Bahadur and said to him in a whisper, 'Biran, is it really you? After all these years?' And Bir Bahadur, laughing, crying at the same time, thanking God, begging forgiveness, opening his arms wide and saying, 'Sadq, my friend Sadq . . . the gods be praised . . . Vahe Guru.' Lifting his eyes heavenwards he said, 'Vahe Guru, my cup is full . . .' With his arm around Bir Bahadur, Sadq Khan turned him gently towards the house and said, 'Come, let me take you to your home.' It was then that I realized that the house at the end of the lane, Sadq Khan's house, was the house that Bir Bahadur had grown up in.

As if on cue, the group of women and children broke into loud chatter. We entered a large courtyard, followed now by our entire entourage, and there was a great deal of good-natured banter: 'So Biran,' they said to him, 'have you come to take over your house? Do you want your property back? You'll have to tussle with us first, you know.' And Bir Bahadur laughing, 'No, no, this is yours, not mine—it's yours . . .' At one end, some young women were cooking, their heads covered and faces hidden. We were shown around the house and I thought of the young Maan Kaur, playing with friends here, little knowing the terrible fate that awaited her.

But we were here on work. Suddenly, reminded that we should be paying attention to the radio programme we had come to make, Chihiro thought that this might be a good moment to capture: the two friends meeting after all these years. So she tried to shoo everyone out of the room in which we now sat—a dark, cool room with only one window. She then turned the fan off: it was making too much noise, she said, and would disturb the recording. Someone immediately turned it back on. She tried to get the children to go out and the two men to respond to her questions, without success. Eventually, she gave up and decided to just capture the scene. She'd do her interview with Bir Bahadur later.

Outside, charpais were now laid out in the shade of the old banyan tree and people began to congregate there. 'Did you ever receive the letters I wrote?' asked Bir Bahadur of no one in particular. Yes, he was told, two letters had arrived, one addressed to the village and one to some of the village elders who were now dead—so for a while, they had lain around in the village post box and no one knew what to do with them. Then they decided to open them and the letters were shared among all those in the village who were there at the time of Partition.

'I wrote you two more,' said Bir Bahadur, 'I was not sure I would be able to come here, so I thought I would send you the letters from Thoa.'

Where are they, he was asked, and he produced them from

his pocket. So that everyone could know what was in them, Sadq Khan asked Bir Bahadur to read them out. Meanwhile, he and another man with a black scarf tied turban-like on his head went into the house and came out holding sitars. They strummed gently, as Bir Bahadur read:

THE FIRST LETTER

I greet all my brothers and sisters of Saintha village and offer you my salutations. I am Bir Bahadur Singh, son of Sant Raja Singh, who used to run a general merchant (kirana) shop in Saintha. I have come to Pakistan from India to fulfil a long-cherished dream. All my life I have had but one dream—that is, to be able to come here and meet with all of you, and now I have come to realize this dream. I wanted to come back, to visit again the places where I played as a child, to meet with all of those people who gave me so much love; I knew that if I could do this, it would give me real happiness. I have forgotten the names of so many of you who were my childhood friends—it has been fifty-four years since I left Saintha village—but in my memory I have kept the names of some of the village elders I remember, and I am putting them down here: Chacha Mohammad Zaman, Masi Barkat, Masi Noor Jehan, Chacha Sajawal Khan, Chacha Sarwar Khan, Chacha Muran who was lame in one leg, my dear sister Taj, my elder sister Sultana who was given in marriage in Khodiwala village, Dari who became my friend at the time of his circumcision. So many of the children of our elders went to school with me. Chacha Sajawal Khan's mother, Ma Hussaini, or Dadi, in whose lap I used to play and under whose loving care I grew up. I have come to renew my friendship with the families of our respected elders. I request you to come from Saintha to meet me [the letter was written when he did not know whether he would make it to Saintha]. *I will be ever grateful to you for this. If you can, I will be found at the address given below. My visa is valid for only four days and I will be waiting for you. I have full faith that you will surely come.*

My mother is still alive and it was also her desire that I come and meet with you once. When you think back on those old times, you will remember me. I have drunk the water of the Dhela Dhulla stream and the village well, I still have the taste of Chacha Sarwar's guavas and the fruit from Khojiwala on my tongue. I remember my teachers, Sargat Ali and Saif Ali, from whom I learnt so much. They lived in Sadda village. I studied in Skot School and was the only Sikh there. Those of our elders who are alive, please give my salutations to them, and those who have passed on, I ask you to pay my respects at their graves. For those of you who are alive, I hope you will accept once again the hand of true friendship that I extend to you. I am waiting for you. When you come, please bring me a handful of earth from our beloved Saintha and some water from the Dhulla stream where we played as children. Please also bring some photos and then we can sit and talk here.

God be with you and may He protect you.

THE SECOND LETTER

My brother Sadq Khan,

My beloved Sadq Khan, son of Sajawal Khanji, please accept my greetings. My brother, I am the son of Sant Raja Singh, who used to run a kirana store in Saintha. I have written you letters before this, and have also received replies, but for some time now I have not written. Please don't think that I have forgotten you and everyone else in Saintha. Every day in my dreams I taste the delicious figs of Dadi's gardens, and I swear to you on God's name that when the dream breaks, and I awaken, I can still taste the sweetness on my tongue. I remember Dadiji, Chacha Sajawal Khan and everyone from the village—your memories are still fresh in my mind. I remember Arif Bhai, who lost his life while trying to save me from snakebite—perhaps it was that God loved him too much and took him away. My sister Taj and I used to play in Dadi's lap, we used to fight over who had the right to sit there. I would say Dadi belongs to me and Taj would insist that she *belonged to her and Dadi would take us both in her lap and give us abundantly of her love. I have memories of the kharboozas (melons) Masi Barkat fed us, the fruit Chacha Sarwar Khan gave us, and so many others . . . It is with these memories in my heart that I have come from India to see you. I want to greet you and all my friends with whom I studied in Skot School. I have come to Thoa Khalsa and this evening I will return to Islamabad. My visa is only for four days. I beg you to come and meet me. I will do my best to come to Saintha but it may be that I will not be able to come. I am sending you this letter from Thoa Khalsa—please come here to see me.*

 Your brother

 Bir Bahadur Singh (Biran)

The letters read, Bir Bahadur handed them over to Sadq Khan. As his voice faded, the strumming grew louder and soon, a clear, strong voice rose above the noise of the conversation, singing songs of loss and joy, welcoming long-lost friends, come from afar. Others joined in, and gradually a silence descended over the gathering, each person thinking his or her private thoughts. The shadows began to lengthen, the sun making its way to its resting place and quietly, tactfully, as the singing continued, we were drawn aside and taken into the house to be fed.

As we began to move, we heard a voice say, almost as if in jest, 'Our cup is so full we have even forgotten to eat! But the guests must be fed, for us this is enough . . .' Sadq Khan put his sitar down, and followed us into the house where he ate with us, and then we said our goodbyes and set off. A long train of people followed us through the village, some singing, some talking, some just holding Bir Bahadur's hand.

But while one journey had ended, the other—to Thoa Khalsa— still remained incomplete. Should we go there or not? Bir Bahadur's clever sleight-of-hand that morning had initially served to sideline the issue. And now it no longer seemed that urgent. Chihiro had her story—a happy one. In Saintha, they advised us against going: the people of Thoa Khalsa are not good, they said, they do not like strangers. They were being polite of course—they meant Indians, or more precisely, Hindus and Sikhs. And who could blame them? Every such stranger must have been a reminder of that terrible and violent history of a half-century ago. And I? I wasn't sure. I wondered what kind of reception we would get: in 1947 the population of Thoa had been mostly Sikh. But now, there wasn't a single Sikh left there. Instead, they'd been replaced by Muslims, many of whom must have carried their own tales of violence at the hands of Hindus and Sikhs. Would they even want to see us?

And then, there were other things. I have known Bir Bahadur for more than ten years now. I've interviewed him extensively for my research and we have kept in touch. In all that time, Maan Kaur's story has always remained only at the edges of our conversation. Or perhaps that's not quite true. Bir Bahadur has never hesitated to speak of Maan Kaur, but he has always described her as heroic, a martyr to the cause of the religion, someone who embraced death willingly. I find this difficult to believe. She was sixteen years old. What could she have known or understood about the troubled politics of Partition? Of the hate and rage that suddenly seemed to have consumed people who had, until then, lived as friends and neighbours? Could she really have believed that the cause of making a new nation would be better served by her death? Or indeed by the deaths, the rapes and abductions of countless other women?

For Bir Bahadur these were not the questions that troubled

him. Maan Kaur had brought honour to his family, she had done them proud, and he admired her for that. Instead, it was his father towards whom he extended his understanding and compassion. He said as much to me once. 'Imagine,' he said, 'imagine, a father who kills his daughter, how much of a victim, how helpless he must be . . .'

We did not make it to Thoa Khalsa in the end. Not that we did not try. We did, in a half-hearted way. But it turned out that Thoa Khalsa now fell inside the Pakistan atomic ring and was banned to foreigners. We returned to Delhi the next day, our journey done, the radio programme made, a sort of forgiveness asked and given, Maan Kaur's story once again relegated to the realm of silence.

'The Door to His Hospice Was Never Closed'

NAVTEJ SARNA

Muinuddin Chisti laid the roots of the Chisti *silsila* in India based on the principles of contentment and compassion, abandonment and abnegation, generosity and truthfulness. While Muinuddin stayed for the most part in Ajmer, his disciple, Kaki, moved to Delhi where he began to command a huge spiritual gathering, including the Slave King Illtutmish. Kaki's closest disciple was young Farid.

Farid, or more properly, Sheikh Farid ud-din Masud Ganj-i-Shakar, was born on the first day of Ramzan in 1173 in the Punjab town of Kothiwal in a family which could trace its lineage to Caliph Omar. The legend goes that it was a cloudy night and people had no way of finding out if Ramzan had begun or not. A dervish then said that a great soul had been born and the people must look to him for their answer. If the child drank milk, then Ramzan had still not begun. As it happened, the child Farid refused his mother's breast and the people knew that it was the first day of Ramzan.

219

Several stories explain how he got his name. One goes back to the time his mother, Bibi Miriam, taught him to pray. When he inquired what it would get him, she replied that he would get sugar. She would hide a lump of sugar under the prayer carpet and hand it to him when he completed his prayers. One day she forgot to put the sugar but yet it appeared after the prayers. From that day on, she started calling her son Shakar Ganj and that was how he would be revered for centuries. Another story talks of the time when as a young man given to rigorous abstinence in worship, he fasted for three days. Finally, overwhelmed by hunger, he placed some pebbles in his mouth and found that they had turned to sugar which he could eat and continue to pray. This was seen as a special blessing from the Almighty on Farid. Yet another story talks of a time when he met some sugar traders travelling on camels. He asked them what they were carrying. Not wanting to tell the truth, lest they had to share some of the sugar with him, they said that they were carrying salt. 'Then it will be salt,' he replied. On reaching their destination, the traders found that indeed their sugar had turned to salt. They travelled back to Farid, confessed their deceit and apologized at which he turned it all back into sugar.

The child was sent to follow his studies in Multan where his spiritual aptitude was noticed by the visiting saint Bakhtiar Kaki, who immediately accepted him as a *mureed*. When he was sixteen, his mentor advised him to tour the Islamic countries and meet leading mystics of the time. For the next eighteen years (1196–1214), Farid travelled to Ghazni, Baghdad, Afghanistan, Syria, Iran, Mecca, Medina and Jerusalem, recently opened to Sufis from all over the world by the conquest of Saladin. And in Jerusalem he would fast and meditate, perhaps in his favourite way—hanging himself upside-down for forty days in a dark room.

When Muinuddin and Kaki passed away in quick succession, Farid was presented with the latter's robe, turban, stick and wooden sandals. The mantle of the Chisti order had fallen on his shoulders. Finding that the intrigue-ridden atmosphere of Delhi did not suit his contemplative personality, he shifted to the quieter cantonment town of Hansi in Punjab. As his reputation grew, he left Hansi too for the remote town of Ajodhan which would soon become an important spiritual centre. His students studied, ate and slept in his humble home. Devoting themselves to spiritual development and contemplation the master and his students lived at subsistence levels, refusing to borrow money for food. Occasionally, they would circulate the *zanbil*, the basket made of palm leaves in which the townsfolk placed food for the dervishes and they would divide what came as charity. All Farid had was a small rug on which he sat during the day and with which he covered himself when asleep. He fasted all day, eating dried grapes with a glass of sherbet at the time of *iftaar*, following it up with his evening meal of millet bread. Any provisions donated to the *khanqah* were distributed amongst the needy. The khanqah was open to wandering dervishes and many were attracted to him, to pray and to study, to listen to his discourses, and to hear his poetry in Persian, Arabic and Punjabi.

So Baba Farid lived on into his nineties, surrounded by his children and grandchildren and his favourite mureeds. Thousands of Sufis, supplicants, students and dervishes passed through his khanqah in Ajodhan. The mureed who would succeed him and under whom the silsila would reach its pinnacle of glory and influence was Nizamuddin Auliya, whose dargah in Delhi remains one of the holiest places in India, revered by Muslims and non-Muslims alike. Nizamuddin wrote of his spiritual master: 'The door to his hospice was never closed.

Silver, food and blessings due to the kindness of the Almighty Creator—all were distributed from there to all corners. Yet no one came to the sheikh for material assistance since he himself possessed nothing. What marvellous power! What a splendid life! To none of the sons of Adam had such grace been available.'

And this power, I cannot help thinking in the twilight, came all the way to Jerusalem and touched it so indelibly that I need to go searching for it after so many centuries.

I could have begun this account at the Mount of Olives, whose graves, forever waiting for the Messiah to raise the dead from their slumber, are bathed even now in the warm light of the sinking sun. Instead, I find myself standing on the Hill of Evil Counsel. Its name is diabolical, irresistible. Here it was that two thousand years ago, High Priest Caiaphas and his colleagues decided to arrest Jesus and give Judas the thirty pieces of silver that would be the price of his betrayal.

I look at the stunning vista from this promenade on the escarpment that runs to the edge of the gardens of the old Government House, once the residence of the British high commissioner in the days of the Mandate and since 1948 the UN's headquarters in Jerusalem. A smoky twilight is beginning to settle down in the lightly wooded valley just below me, which unfolds gently from this hill but rises more sharply on the far side to Mount Zion. This is the valley of Hinnom, or Gehanum, or Jehanum. Or simply, Hell. Nasir-i-Khusrau, the Persian traveller of a thousand years ago, wrote that 'the common people state that when you stand at the brink of the valley you may hear the cries of those in hell, which come up from below. I myself went up there to listen, but heard nothing.'

Meeting it at a sharp angle is the narrower Valley of Kidron, at the base of the Mount of Olives, in whose far reaches I can make out the faintly glistening five golden onion domes of the Orthodox Russian Church of St. Mary Magdalene, each adorned with its Orthodox cross. The church opens for severely restricted hours but I have managed to see its meditative nuns walking, hunched in their habits, in the green surroundings in the shadow of the white sandstone building marked by arches and gabled roofs. Just one twisting street below it is the Garden of Gethsemane, where an exhausted Jesus was arrested as he rested under the olive trees. The descendants of those trees, their trunks swollen with the passage of centuries, their shoulders burdened with having seen too much, are still there. Next to the olive grove is the grand Church of All Nations, believed to enshrine a piece of bedrock where Jesus prayed alone on the night before his arrest.

The old city, with its walls built by the Ottoman Sultan Suleiman the Magnificent five hundred years ago, rises out of these two valleys, as if out of an abyss. Houses scramble up and down the slopes of the valleys, roads snake into their depths. And beyond the old city spread the proud buildings of West Jerusalem, each of the same stone.

The lights begin to come up in the windows one by one and at this hour it is not possible, nor necessary, to figure out which is Israeli or Arab and which stone is holy to the Christians, or the Jews, or the Muslims.

At this hour of the lighting of the lamps, it is difficult to imagine the desert wilderness that this must have all been not that very long ago. A time when the bleak paths that came from Damascus and Jaffa, Bethlehem and Hebron, would have led the caravans of travellers, happy and relieved to see Jerusalem's walls, after surviving weeks of the hostilities of nature and raids of bandits, to one or the other gates of the old city. All manner of travellers and adventurers, pilgrims and priests, Christian crusaders, Islamic warriors, Jews of every hue drawn to this lodestone helplessly.

And even more difficult to imagine a time before these Ottoman walls. A time of other walls that have long been buried under the dust, that show up only tantalizingly in some archaeological dig, enabling some heat-crazed archaeologist to die at peace, one more line added to an obscure map. In some other city, those old stones may be carried away, used to build some peasant hut, or serve as a rough step, or be chipped away and thrown by careless boys. But here each stone that is unearthed is a piece of history, a triumphant political statement, an affirmation or a decrial, one more microscopic addition to the jumbled jigsaw of kingdoms—temporal and spiritual—that is Jerusalem.

The seventeenth-century Turkish traveller Evliya Celebi, who travelled twice through Palestine in his wanderings through thirty countries, is my observant guide on many walks through this land. His first sentence on Jerusalem says it all: 'It is called in Greek the Province of Aelia, in Syriac *Maqdisha*, in Hebrew *Has*, and in Arabic *Beit-ul Maqdis* or *Quds*. It contains the shrines of one hundred and twenty-four thousand Prophets. Before and after the deluge it was the *qibla* of mankind.'

The sun is sinking fast and the rich yellow light is weakening, able to catch less and less in its faltering grasp. Only the tops of the trees on the hill are visible—the pines and the olives through which rustles a cool breeze and the golden Dome of the Rock, in the centre of the massive platform that the Jews call the Temple Mount and the Muslims call the Haram-al-Sharif, the Noble Sanctuary, the place which concentrates within itself a world of conflict, a sea of faith, history and fable, longings and aspirations. It is on that Dome that the eye always settles when looking upon Jerusalem, as it rises above the platform of ageless flagstones. That is, according to so many Prophets, where it all began. So I watch it as the sun sets and as the rays of light shorten. The burnished gold of the Dome seems to grow brighter, as if it is gathering them within itself, to exude them all night at will.

To find Herod's Gate I have to go to the other side of the old city, to its northern wall. Beyond this wall lies the crowded commercial centre of Arab East Jerusalem, pierced by Salahdin Street with its shops, Internet cafés and small hotels. The crowded pavements, where fresh kebabs are roasted next to mounds of shoes and underwear, give the whole place the bustling look of an authentic Arab market, very unlike the quiet, orderly streets of Jewish West Jerusalem. On this side lie the buildings of the American colony and the houses of the Jerusalem notables that came up in the late nineteenth and early twentieth centuries.

It is difficult on any day, and impossible on a Friday, for a car to navigate the road that separates the old city from this neighbourhood or to find a break in the constant stream of pedestrians, women in *hijab* and men in *keffiyeh*, many walking with canes, heading to the old city to pray at the Al-Aqsa Mosque on the Haram, the third most holy of Muslim religious sites.

I look for flower-sellers as I enter Herod's Gate; it has also been known as *Bab-al-Zahira* or the Gate of Flowers down the centuries. Instead, there are fruit-sellers lining its substantial archway. It is the beginning of March—the last pomegranates, the early oranges, watermelons and melons are piled up inside the gate. As I enter the archway I am greeted by a man of medium height, with alert grey eyes and a polite, easy and genuine smile.

'I am Nazeer,' he says, 'Nazeer Ansari.'

Quickly he leads me through the gate and up a few steps into the street inside the old city. Before I have had time to look around, I find myself staring awestruck at a green iron gate with its two stone pillars. The words 'Indian Hospice' are carved on one of them and on the other, in Arabic, *Zawiya al-Hindiya*. An indescribable excitement grips me: an Indian presence in the middle of old Jerusalem. Nazeer smiles gently and unobtrusively at my surprise and opens the gate.

'You are in India now,' he says as we start walking up the broad path from the gate. Tall *saru* trees with their tight pine cones line both sides of the path. 'My father is waiting for you.'

I look up. At the end of that path of broad steps stands a tall, erect man, dressed elegantly in an overcoat with a woollen scarf round his neck, a soft, peaked woollen cap protecting his head.

Finally, several months after I had first heard mention of the place, I am about to meet Sheikh Mohammed Munir Ansari, the director of the Indian Hospice.

'You are welcome,' Sheikh Munir takes my hand warmly in both his hands. When we get to know each other better, he will always embrace me, thrice, Arab style. We stand for a few minutes at the entrance to the Hospice. I try to gauge his age. He looks younger than the eighty he turns out to be. He smiles easily and the eyes behind the gold-rimmed glasses are lively. Behind us a steady stream of Palestinian women and children are coming up the path and entering a complex of two buildings that seem part of the Hospice.

'Those buildings are the UNRWA clinic,' Sheikh Munir

says by way of explanation in his clear, deliberate manner. 'For the refugees of 1948. This building,' he points towards part of the clinic, 'was built by Indian soldiers during the Second World War. It is called the Delhi wing. And this,' he points to his left, 'is where we live now, the Travancore wing. It was also built by the soldiers.'

As if on cue, the gate to the Travancore wing opens and a tall woman steps out. She is stylishly dressed in trousers and high heels and her hair is pulled back in a French knot. Confidently, she extends a hand to greet me. Her eyes shine with the same elemental playfulness that I have seen on her father's face.

'This is my eldest daughter, Najam,' the sheikh introduces us. 'And this,' he points to another smartly dressed lady who comes out of another door, 'is my other daughter, Nourjahan.'

'You can call me Jani, everybody does,' she introduces herself.

'And this,' Nazeer adds, pointing to a third lady who has joined us, 'is my Wafa, my dear wife.'

I don't know it then but this is going to be the pattern of so many meetings: Nazeer outside, his father at the top of the steps and then the ladies who happen to be at home . . .

Together we enter a short, narrow corridor with its chequerboard of black-and-white mosaic tiles. A large map of the old city of Jerusalem fills one wall.

'This is a rare map from the early twentieth century,' Nazeer points out. 'On this you can see the city as it was before the takeover of 1967. You can see how close the houses were to the Wailing Wall. After 1967 they were all cleared up. And this, on the right, is our office.'

The office is a small room with a large writing desk behind which stands an Indian flag. Large iconic photos of Gandhi and Nehru adorn the walls surrounded by several smaller ones.

'This is my father,' Sheikh Munir points at one of them,

'with Maulana Muhammad Ali of the Khilafat. And here he is alone, with a different turban, the Indian one.'

I take a quick look at the photos of the tall, bespectacled Indian figure, the elder sheikh, Nazir Ansari of Saharanpur. But this, I realize, is not the time to ask about his story; there will be time enough. So we step out into the sunlit courtyard of the Hospice, where the women are waiting, making idle talk around a grove of lemon and orange trees. It's a pleasant young sun of early March and I enjoy the little orange that Najam hands me. I can bite right into it and eat it, peel and all. A small mosque opens out into the courtyard and through its half-open door I can see the bare room with its arched walls and a *mihrab*. A full carpet covers the floor. On the far end of the courtyard are a number of rooms, several in a state of dereliction. Sheikh Munir points out two graves—perhaps of pilgrims or earlier sheikhs—that mark the furthest end. A visitor's room contains more photographs and a table with a visitor's book and details of people who have stayed at the Hospice in recent years.

Finally, I ask the question that has brought me here: 'Why is this known as Baba Farid's Hospice?'

'You are right, this is also called the Zawiya al-Faridiya. They say Baba Farid came here from India, meditated here and then his followers began to come here, stay here. A long time ago. They were given a *waqf*, first the mosque and those two rooms. And then the property expanded through the centuries as a place for Indian pilgrims to stay.'

Sheikh Munir leads me to one of the rooms at the far end of the courtyard. An attendant brings out a bunch of keys and unlocks a low door. I have to bend low to step in. Cobwebs flutter in the sunlight that streams in and a dank smell rises from within. He points towards an opening in the floor, barely visible at the far end of the room.

'There are some rooms below this room,' Sheikh Munir says. 'It is believed that those are the rooms where Baba Farid meditated. And in this room my wife and children hid when the bombs fell here in 1967 and the Israeli soldiers entered the Hospice.'

It is our first meeting, so I do not push for details. But I know that I must know.

In the long drawing room in the Travancore wing, I meet the sheikh's wife, Ikram. She speaks little but her presence is pleasing. There is tea, Indian style. 'Lipton is the best,' someone says. And *bourekas*, fresh pastries stuffed with spinach and cheese, and carrot cake and poppy-seed cake. Each of the women has made something and wants me to taste it. There is even a fruit salad. 'This is a French salad, in the name of Nimala, our sister who lives in Switzerland,' Nazeer explains. Someone mentions that on an occasion like this they miss Nazer, the eldest brother who lives in Saudi Arabia.

They are a graceful and charming family and I hate to tear myself away. I know I will obsess for weeks and months about this little Indian corner in the old city, about the underground chamber of Baba Farid, about Indian soldiers during the World War, about shells raining down on children huddled in a dark, dank room, about the man who came here mysteriously from Saharanpur and about the family who laugh and smile and tease each other.

Maps for All Times

MANOSI LAHIRI

The idea of *Hindoostan* is old, but the first maps to define this land were made by European cartographers, as recently as the sixteenth century. Intrepid travellers carried home tales of their journeys and these formed the basis of the early maps of *Hindoostan*. These maps were in response to Europe's curiosity about the Orient, and later, the necessity to ensure safe voyages for their merchant mariners to coastal trading ports in India. Ancient India had active maritime communities on its coasts; it traded with Africa, Arabia and the Persian Gulf countries in the West, and, Indochina, Indonesia and China in the East. Yet its adjacent seas and ocean remained uncharted until Vasco da Gama's voyage around the Cape of Good Hope to India in 1498.

European cartographers gave form to the idea of *Hindoostan* or India from information gathered from mariners' and travellers' yarns, much before it was scientifically surveyed and its true shape and dimensions determined. They used their discretion to highlight or subdue known facts well before these

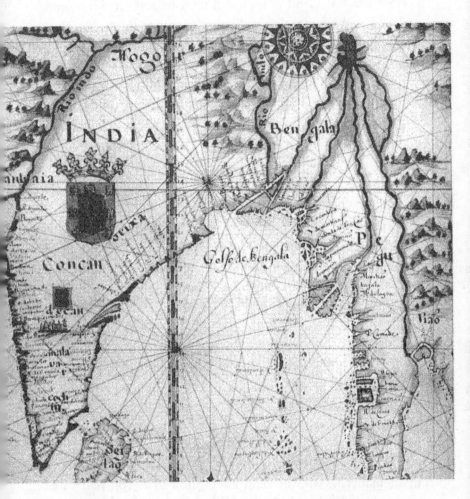

Portalan chart of Southeast Asia by Antonio Sanches, 1642.

became accepted norms in modern mapping. The earliest maps were a magical blend of fact and imagination, of impressions culled from chronicles published by travellers and some anticipation of what a foreign land could be like. As was often the case, since the cartographers had not visited the places they were required to map, exotic rivers, mountains, lakes and places were introduced from stories based on well-perpetuated legends. Sometimes, these fanciful additions remained in the maps for several decades. The reliability of these maps was questionable and cartographers occasionally incorporated phantom features into the maps of India.

Indian cosmographers seem to have made little, if any, contribution towards defining the land known variously as *Bharat, Indae, Indoustan* and *Hindoostan*. Their 'maps' were imaginatively drawn on the basis of religious concepts and myths about the creation of the universe, but had little to do with realistic representations of land and sea. These cosmographs tended to be artistic representations showing man's place on earth as described in ancient tales, often bearing no relation whatsoever with existing ground conditions or the shape of islands and continents.

Two millennia ago, when Ptolemy (Claudius Ptolemaeus *c*.CE 100–178) wrote *Cosmographia* or *Geography*, little would he have known the impact his work would have on the drawings of the first maps of the world. The illustrious geographer and mathematician, who lived in Alexandria in Egypt, had listed many places by their latitude and longitude from astronomical observations. For the next 1,500 years, generations of geographers used these measurements to draw maps that perpetuated images of the known world, including *Hindoostan*.

Ptolemy's *Geography* was the source of the first maps of South Asia made in the West and in use till as late as the fifteenth century in Europe. In this map, *Indiostena regio* was the approach to *India Intra Gangem* from the west, enclosed between the two rivers, the Indus and the Ganges. From his observations, cartographers drew in the the Indus (*iindis f.*) and the Ganges (*ganges flu*) originating from lakes in the high northern mountains. They drew in the *naua gimna flu* (Jamuna river) and several places like *maddura* (Madurai), *Sorethe* (Surat) on *thebe flu* (Tapi river), *mananda flu* (Mahanadi river) and *Mesolus flu* (Masulipatam river). Ptolemy's Indian peninsula was smaller than we know it to be today and his concept of the Indian Ocean was that of an enclosed sea. A striking feature of the map of South Asia was the enormous island *Taprobana* (*Tamraparni* in Sanskrit), mistakenly placed on the south-west of the Indian peninsula. Today we know this island as Sri Lanka.

This is not to say that Indians did not have a mental image of their land. In the eighth century, the great Indian sage, Shankaracharya, had defined the *Char Dhams* or Four Abodes of God at the farthest ends of Bharat. The mother country extended from Dwarka in the west to Puri in the east, and from Badrinath in the north to Rameswaram in the south. And long before that, pilgrims went to the *peeths* or religious places as far west as Hinglaj in Baluchistan, Amarnath in Kashmir, Kamakhya in Assam and Kanyakumari at the southernmost tip of India. But cosmographs did not identify these places in images to guide people to reach them. Indigenous maps that well represented the land and charts of surrounding seas began appearing around the seventeenth century. If others existed earlier, they have not reached us.

Arab geographers had developed Mecca-centric maps more than a thousand years ago to show direction of places to the holy city. The astronomer and scholar Al-Beruni (c. 973–1048) made an exhaustive table of coordinates of 600 important places of the world. But unlike Ptolemy's tables, these were not used by later Arab cartographers to make maps and add toponyms. His world maps, with the south oriented to the top of the sheet, showed the distribution of land and sea. It also depicted eastern Africa smaller than widely accepted during his time.

There was always much movement of goods along the Indian peninsular coast and this trade was controlled by the Indian states adjoining the coastal belt, as well as by merchants commanding large coastal fleets. By the sixteenth century, in the Mughal period, the Portuguese had established several settlements, maintained armed patrolling fleets and charged fees (protection money) to ships that approached Goa, Diu, Daman, Cochin along the Arabian Sea, Chittagong along the Bay of Bengal and Bandel on the Hooghly river.

The Siddi, who had a base off Janjira Island, south of Bombay, were successful as pirates and mercenaries. They are believed to be the descendants of Ethiopian slaves sold to Indian merchants and princes by traders from the seventh century onwards. Escaped slaves built the almost impregnable Janjira Fort on the island around 1500. They were able to defend their island fort successfully for three-and-a-half centuries against the Marathas and Europeans, till the British finally occupied Janjira in 1870.

On 31 December 1600, Queen Elizabeth I of England signed a royal charter that gave the East India Company exclusive trading rights in the Indies. Not long after, British ships found their ways to the west coast of India, following the Portuguese, Dutch and French in search of spices, textiles, opium, indigo, precious stones, coir, ivory, saltpetre, slaves and more. This brought them into conflict with strong Indian rulers who had merchant and military fleets. The many conflicts between the

British navy and Shivaji over Vijaydurg in the Konkan coast are now part of folklore. Later, in the Malabar coast, wars between the British navy and the Mysore rulers Haider Ali and Tipu Sultan are well documented in manuscript maps. In this period, European merchants also had armed conflicts with each other on Indian soil and in littoral waters. Port cities like Mangaluru, Masulipatam, Pondichery, Cochin, etc., were controlled by different merchant companies at different times.

So it was that the European trading companies created the first *portolan* maps of India from the sixteenth to the mid-eighteenth centuries. These beautiful sketches served three important purposes. They represented the 'factories' or trader's warehouses, roads, other important buildings and surroundings of the ports in map form. These were the city maps of the times and based on information gathered from factors. At the same time, the coasts of India were mapped diligently, primarily for piloting ships to protected harbours and for their safe landing. Most of this survey and charting was undertaken by the marine hydrographers of the various East India Companies.

Merchant ships needed dependable ocean charts to lead them from their home countries to India and back. This was the beginning of the mapping of the ocean routes to India from the West. Not only information on the sailing routes but also on other aspects of importance to sailors—ocean currents, winds, cyclones, pirate-infested seas and more—was gathered. The navigation charts showing dramatic rhumb lines and sea monsters are a product of this period. Hydrographic charts improved over time with the understanding of geodesy and the introduction of marine chronometers.

Soon rivalry amongst European nations and local rulers led to armed confrontations and wars in India. From mid-eighteenth century, occupation of territories was closely linked to the mapping of the interior of *Hindoostan*. Thus while the Battle of Plassey in 1757 put the English EIC in a commanding position in Bengal, it was the Battle of Buxar in 1764 that brought the most significant change in the mapping of India. After gaining large tracts of land in Bengal, the first survey maps of the Ganga delta were made by James Rennell, the surveyor general of Bengal. In the next decades, as the British marched across the land, they surveyed, documented and mapped *Hindoostan*. The emphasis had shifted from sea to land and from commerce to war and administration. Maps were now made to support the armies as they occupied new territories, increasingly beyond the control of the Mughal emperors.

Many maps in the repository of the National Archives of India point to the enormous mapping effort by the British in a bid to define boundaries of occupied, ceded and annexed territories and for the purpose of assessing revenues in the acquired territories. One may postulate that were it not for the purpose of engaging in India through commerce, Great Britain would not have mapped India on such a grand scale in the late eighteenth and nineteenth centuries. Since maximizing profit was possible only by military subjugation and control, extensive modern mapping of India was a consequence of the wars that resulted in the colonization of the country.

On examining scores of maps of India, spread over five centuries, it is my view that war and commerce were the main drivers of map-making in this country. If that were not the case, would we not have seen a significant number of maps expressing alternative images of the country? The question is not really a rhetorical one. This is to suggest that there were alternative approaches to mapping which were never exploited. Maps resonate with information of the areas they represent and map-makers selectively represent themes of their interest. The map-makers of the Company and the Raj had little interest in documenting subjects beyond strategic–military requirement, and their direct interest in administration and exploitation of their territories. They undertook these enormously complex and spatially extensive mapping missions with great success.

We know that in the past sketch-maps were made for the use of kings and other patrons. The enormous Panoramic Sketch of the Valley of Kashmir (227cm x 407cm), scripted in Persian, is remarkable in its size and detail. This 1836 sketch-map by Abdool Rahim, a resident of Bokhara, is at present in the Map Library of the British Library. Maharaja Jai Singh (1688–1713), who established the city of Jaipur, naming it after himself, was a collector of maps and plans. His extensive collection has remained in the *pothikhana* (manuscript library) of the City Palace. The Kachwaha dynasty of Jaipur also boasted of having the earliest native makers of modern city plans in India. The museum's collection includes a number of city sketch-plans of Jaipur, Dhundhar, Amer, Agra and Surat in the traditional indigenous style.

Could there have been maps of pilgrimages, migrations and famines? There are, after all, many maps made of the Holy Land by cartographers of different countries. Why do we not see maps of the many *dhams*, *jyotirlingas*, *peeths* and other religious places in India? Traditionally, Hindus and Muslims in India went on pilgrimages to religious places. Pilgrimage maps have been traced in the records of the Jaipur princely state as well as in Benaras (Varanasi). Few in number, these are more of sketch-maps. Pilgrims would usually carry these back home and hang them up on the walls and worship them. Many pilgrims travelled annually to the Kumbh Mela at the confluence of the Ganga and Yamuna, to the Sagar Island at the mouth of the Hooghly river, to Rameswaram in the Gulf of Mannar, or went on Haj to

Mecca. Yet there seems to have been no attempt by Indians to make maps of these religious places and the chief routes leading up to them—even in Bengal, where modern cartography had an early beginning.

Migrations of people have been closely associated with wars and annexations. There are very well-documented movements of people from one part of the country to another over the last five centuries—for instance, the migrations of Maratha groups to Bangalore, Indore, Gwalior, Bhopal and even within Maharashtra from before and after Shivaji's times. Why are these not recorded in the many maps made during the British Raj? After the Partition of British India into Pakistan and India in 1947, millions of people moved from one country to another in one of the greatest migrations in the history of mankind, in the shortest possible period of time. Yet, I have still to come across maps that depict this phenomenal movement of people. It appears that the collection of relevant data to create the maps was never undertaken. The only maps are small-scale illustrations using arrows to show from where the waves of people came and went over the new international borders. Similarly, indentured labourers moved from India to the various British colonies— were these movements ever mapped to show the connections of the original homes of the migrants to their eventual destinations?

How were the maps of the Partition of Pakistan and India made? How were the Radcliffe Lines drawn between West Pakistan and India in the west, and East Pakistan and India in the east? Were they drawn on the basis of the concentration of religious groups as recorded in the 1941 census, or were the geographical features on the ground taken into consideration— natural boundaries, communications, watercourses and irrigation systems? The Boundary Commission apparently drew the lines along administrative boundaries. Be that as it may, the maps were released two days after the two countries became independent—on 17 August 1947, and attached as annexures to the Boundary Commission's reports. They were not published and thus were not available for public scrutiny.

Famines in India are well documented and learned studies have been carried out in this area. Many famines were experienced in different parts of the country while it was a British colony. Yet, where are the famine maps of India? Surely they would have been made to enable administrators to give aid, just as revenue maps were made to enable collectors to gather taxes? My search led to one set of six manuscript maps of a lesser-known famine in the Doab and North West Provinces in 1861. This set of maps is in the repository of the National Archives of India, Delhi.

In the beginning, maps of India were aesthetic manifestations of the cartographer's imagination—beautiful, quaint and unreliable maps of an exotic or mythical land. Little more than sketches, they were creations of cartographers who had learnt of the country from others who claimed to have knowledge of it. Over the years, these maps gathered factual information. They were filled out with rivers, mountains, plateaus, plains, forests and important cities. Then the years of coastal and inland surveys provided additional details and some degree of correctness in terms of the positions of these places. Boundaries of different territories were added as were new places, roads, railway lines, canals and much more. Once the positions of places were satisfactorily determined, it was easy to make thematic maps of different kinds. As printing technology improved, it became possible to publish large wall maps and atlases from the maps that had already been compiled from surveys. It also became possible to replicate many maps and atlases over a short period of time, thus making them available to a large number of people.

The greatest beneficiary of early scientific mapping endeavours were the British traders and colonizers who used the services of their army engineers to conduct many different surveys to measure the territories gained from humbled adversaries. The early surveys produced by the Company surveyors and hydrographers were sent to England for map compilation, engraving and printing. Till the 1840s many of these maps remained for the exclusive use of the Company. It was only in the 1850s that more maps of India were published for public distribution. The later maps made after 1858, by the Imperial Government, reflected the accumulation of a variety of knowledge on India, with greater stress on depicting infrastructure, like railway and telegraph lines.

The nineteenth century was undoubtedly the century of Indian maps; the coincidence of several different circumstances made it so. The Company's need for reliable strategic information to plan campaigns, record territorial gains, identify sources of commercial products, estimate revenue collections—and sometimes, the Orientalist's passionate thirst for knowledge—led to an immense volume of maps being produced. For the very first time, the land was systematically measured and new ideas of geodesy introduced into mapping. A prodigious body of data on the subcontinent was collected; it was also compiled, mapped and published for distribution. By the middle of the nineteenth century, compilation and reprography of the maps were being increasingly undertaken in India, which enabled much quicker preparation of maps for publishing and distribution. While this happened, many other maps remained as manuscripts and were never published. Tragically, these maps are now old, in very poor condition, faded and degenerating. If they are not brought to the notice of the cartographic enthusiast and professional now, they will forever be lost to civilization. The National Archives has now scanned many of these and converted them to digital maps.

Cartography in India has come a long way. The early cosmographers had created paintings of our earth and that of India in the image of their own philosophies and beliefs. Early cartographers located places by taking astronomical measurements—positioning by reference to celestial bodies. These methods were then abandoned for the more methodical systems of terrestrial survey. After more than two centuries of extensive terrestrial surveys, an increasingly greater role was played by aerial photography and satellite imaging in mapping. And now the wheel of events has turned fully. The technology of survey and mapping has changed dramatically. With the use of Global Positioning System, the emphasis has now once more shifted to locating places with reference to bodies in space, with a difference: man-made satellites. At the same time, terrestrial topographical survey has been largely replaced by the use of satellite images of different kinds. All processes of map-making, including processing of surveyed data, designing and laying out the map and finally publishing it, are now computerized.

As the account of mapping of India comes to an end, we know that we are at a crucial crossroad: the era of mapping to support expansionist strategies has given way to the present times when the demand for maps for social and economic development of the nation state is on the rise. In the past, the expansion of overseas empires of the colonial powers was aided by reliable maps. With hindsight, we know that without the complex exercise of surveying the country and its extensive mapping, the territorial expansions of the British in India would have been severely hampered. But now the mapping environment has changed dramatically. The mapping needs of a democratic and independent nation are different from those of interest to trading companies or colonial powers. Now there is a demand for reliable maps not for war and commerce but for supporting administration of services or planning of social and infrastructure projects. At the same time, because of remarkable technological changes in the field of cartography, the era of paper maps is being superceded by digital mapping.

A map is an index of nationhood and sets the bounds of a nation. The map of India is not made of fragmented polities, as it was when we began with our story of *Hindoostan* of the imagination. The present map is of a visibly unified nation—India or Bharat—unmistakably of one country and one people. And just as the story of this nation has been chronicled by countless historians, travellers and storytellers, so too has this story been retold today in the cartographer's language: through the maps of India.

Armchair Travels

NAMITA GOKHALE

Home for me remains the tourist town of Nainital, where some part of me continues to live even though I don't visit it much any more. In the course of many, many summers, I haven't ever managed to climb up to either Tiffin Top (aka Dorothy's Seat, 2,619 m) or China (Cheena) Peak (2,278 m). Yet I have walked the High Himalayas, with Nain Singh Rawat, whose journals I encountered through a set of serendipitous accidents.

I had to travel back through time for this journey, return to 1863, when knowledge of the Himalayan terrain was restricted to either blanks or based on travellers' tales and vague pictorial Chinese maps. That was the year when Colonel Walker, the superintendent of the Great Trigonometrical Survey, recruited Nain Singh, then thirty years old, and his cousin Mani Singh, who was a little older.

Nain Singh Rawat was born in a Pundit family in 1830. They lived in the village of Milam in the Johar Valley, at the foot of the Milam Glacier, in the shadow of Nanda Devi in the high reaches of the Central Himalayas. This Kumaoni lad was an intrepid adventurer and natural explorer. Instructed by his colonial masters to travel as a simple pilgrim, he set out to map mountains, trace the course of rivers, and unravel the mysteries of uncharted cartographies. The Trigonometrical Survey equipped him with a sextant, a compass and a thermometer, which was to be placed in boiling water to determine the heights. To disguise the true purpose of his travels, Nain Singh was also given a Tibetan prayer wheel, and a rosary with only a hundred beads, as against the ritual one hundred and eight. Every tenth bead was larger than the others. Chanting the Buddhist prayer 'Aum mani padme hum', the Pundit would turn the prayer wheel with pious concentration and drop a bead with every hundred steps.

Nain Singh had been drilled by a sergeant major using a pace stick to take steps of a fixed and certain length, maintaining a constant, measured pace regardless of whether he was treading uphill, downhill or on level ground. A hundred beads of his cunningly modified Buddhist rosary represented ten thousand steps. Each step was three-and-a-half inches, and a mile was composed of two thousand steps.

The Pundit's survey notes, written out in secret on long strips of paper, were concealed in the drum of the prayer wheel. Mercury, used for measuring atmospheric pressure and calculating altitude, was hidden in cowrie shells, to be poured as required into the begging bowl he carried as part of his spy-explorer's kit.

Pundit Nain Singh Rawat's village of Milam, in one of the remotest parts of Kumaon, was habitable only for a few months, from June to October. He was acclimatized to the Himalayan heights, accustomed to the rough terrain. He knew the stars and constellations and could navigate the dark Himalayan nights with the brilliant starlit sky as his guide. But that is not enough to explain his story, of how and why he kept walking.

In the years 1865 and 1866, Pundit Nain Singh walked from Dehradun to Kathmandu to Lhasa, to Mansarovar Lake, and then back. He returned with information of the Tsang Po's course for 600 miles, and notes for a map detailing the southern trade routes to Tibet.

From 1873 to 1875, the Pundit travelled with his prayer wheel and rosary across the span of the Himalayas—Leh to Ladakh to Lhasa and onwards to Assam. Appreciative geographers lauded him, and he was described as 'a man who has added a greater amount of positive knowledge to the map of Asia than any individual of our time . . .'

Nain Singh Rawat was appointed 'Companion of the Indian Empire' (CIE). He was presented with two gold watches, from the Royal Geographical Society and the Paris Geographical Society, as well as the Founders' Gold Medal from the Royal Geographical Society in 1877. The first watch was stolen by one of his pupils.

But what drove him, pushed him, compelled him? What was it that kept him walking?

Pundit Nain Singh carried travel in his genes. Traders in the Milam Valley migrated seasonally to western Tibet, where the markets were dependent on Indian merchants for cereals, cotton, sugar and hardware. Tibetan traders in turn exported borax, wool and salt, and also gold, to India. There was a complicated system of trade covenants, where every Indian trader had a *mitra* or colleague in Tibet. These partnerships were marked by the splitting of a stone, one half of which was in the custody of each partner.

As the Russians and the British raced for control of Central Asia, geographical knowledge of the mysterious and unmapped Himalayan massifs was essential to the invincibility of the Empire. Nain Singh was but a pawn in the Great Game, a lowly servant of the Company Bahadur, but his passion for walking, for observing and mapping the crucial and strategic valleys and plateaus of Tibet and the High Himalayas, the mountains that were his home, led him on incredibly long and exhausting journeys.

On the 29th of October 1865, Nain Singh Rawat arrived in Shigatse, crossing a river bridge formed by iron chains and ropes. Not far from there, the fast-flowing currents of the Pen Nang Chhu meet the Nari Chhu, the mighty Brahmaputra river. The Gang Mar Dzong stands to the north-west of Shigatse. To the south-west is the Tra Sji Lhun Po monastery, surrounded by high walls a mile in circumference. Inside the stone walls there are temples and shrines and noble houses. Four gilded spires rise above the walls, hinting at the wealth and glory within.

I try to picture him, Pundit Nain Singh Rawat of Milam. 'Short, stocky and stubborn', the Pundit is hardy and well accustomed to the cold, dry air. His sharp eyes have noted the flow of the rivers, he has charted the currents from observing where they are weak and allow the water to freeze. His trusty thermometer has already graphed the atmospheric pressure several times. It is November and the temperature falls below freezing point at night, even indoors. The travellers sleep using their boots as pillows, to prevent them from freezing overnight. The lowest temperatures recorded are 25 degrees Fahrenheit, the highest 50 degrees.

This city on the roof of the world has a population of 9,000, another 3,300 priests inhabit the monastery. It is a cosmopolitan place, with several Nepalese traders, Kashmiri, Ladakhi and Chinese merchants, and the occasional white Russian. A force of 400 Tibetan soldiers guards the gold mines of Mauri Hill, fifteen miles to the south of the city; it is prohibited for anyone to dig or excavate there.

The chief priest of this magnificent monastery is the Great Lama, the Panjan Ring Bo Che, or the Pancham Lama. Through the length and breadth of Tibet, the Pancham Lama is considered a divine incarnation, who can read the thoughts of men and who will never die.

It is the 1st of November 1865. A Sunday. The waxing moon shines over the golden spires, gilding them with silver. The party of Ladakhi traders to whom the Pundit has attached himself seek blessings from the Great Lama. Their request has been granted. Pundit Nain Singh, who is with them but not of them, is a worried man. He is an outsider, a spy, a traveller with a hidden purpose. He has heard that the Great Lama, the Panjan Ring Bo Che, can decipher the hearts and minds of men. How will the Pundit steel his heart, conceal his mind, in the presence of a Realized One? What if the Lama asks him about Colonel Walker, or why his rosary counts to only a hundred beads?

There is no option but to go. The Ladakhi traders wear colourful woollen hats. They have thin moustaches and creased faces and reverence writ large in their hearts and sleeves. The Pundit, Nain Singh of Milam, in the employ of the Great Trigonometrical Survey, posing as a pilgrim, is carrying his rosary with the hundred beads, and his prayer wheel thick with concealed strips of paper, his notes and observations jotted in the most minuscule handwriting imaginable.

His gait is steady and his face impassive. He scrutinizes the carved doors, the holy scrolls, the *thangkhas* of divinities and demons, the rows of butter lamps that lead them to the Presence. In the hallways beyond, monks are muttering *sutras*, their chants rising and falling, echoing and resonating. The air is heavy with faith, and there is a sense of conviction and purpose everywhere.

But the Pancham Lama is just a child. A small-built boy of

about eleven, with a smooth, tender face and puzzled eyes. As the throngs of worshippers uncover their heads and bow before him, he bends over from his high throne, which is draped with tapestries of rich silk, brocades and shimmering weaves, and blesses them.

The Ladakhis then offer him their gifts, and the priests who stand guard behind the boy give them white scarves in return. Panjam Ring Bo Che beckons them to be seated. He breaks his profound silence to ask them three questions, as he does to all his visitors.

'Is your king well?'

'Is your country prospering?'

'Are you in good health?'

He does not wait for their replies, which in any case are confused and inarticulate.

The Pundit ponders the three questions. He serves no king, but the Malika-e-Hind, Empress Victoria, rules his land. He thinks of the half-sovereign gold coin that bears her plump profile. Her country is not his country, but he supposes, and hopes, it is prospering. And his health is now fine, he is strong and confident again, as he realizes that, in all places under the sun, the gods are the gods and no one can read the hearts and minds of men.

I have walked the high mountains with the Pundit. I put the books away, and the notepad where I have been writing. It has been a long journey, both fatiguing and exhilarating.

Notes on Contributors

M.J. AKBAR was born in 1951 and graduated with honours in English from Presidency College, Calcutta. He joined *The Times of India* as a trainee in 1971 before moving to *The Illustrated Weekly of India*, then India's largest-selling magazine, as sub-editor and feature writer. In 1973, he took over as editor of the news fortnightly *Onlooker*. In 1976, Akbar moved to Calcutta to join the Ananda Bazar Patrika Group as editor of *Sunday*, India's first genuine political weekly. In 1982, he launched what would be called India's first modern newspaper, *The Telegraph*. He left journalism for a brief stint in politics in 1989, contesting and winning the Kishanganj seat in Bihar on a Congress ticket in the general elections. He resigned from government in December 1992 and returned to journalism and full-time writing. He launched *The Asian Age* in February 1994 with editions in Delhi, Mumbai and London. During this period, he was also editor-in-chief of the *Deccan Chronicle*. In September 2010, he joined *India Today* and Headlines Today as editorial director. He resigned in October 2012. He launched *The Sunday Guardian*, a weekly newspaper in 2010, and continues to serve as its editor-in-chief.

Simultaneous with a full-time career in journalism, he has been a prolific and best-selling author of major political works that examine the conflicts and challenges of the last, disturbing century. His critically acclaimed books include *India: The Siege Within, Challenges to a Nation's Unity*; *Byline*; *Riot after Riot*; *Nehru: The Making of India*; *Kashmir: Behind the Vale*; *The Shade of Swords: Jihad and the Conflict* between *Islam and Christianity*; *Blood Brothers*, a novel, and *Tinderbox: The Past and Future of Pakistan*.

MARIE BRENNER is an author and writer at large for *Vanity Fair*. She has published five books, including *Great Dames: What I Learned from Older Women* and the bestselling *House of Dreams: The Bingham Family of Louisville*. She joined the staff of *Vanity Fair* in 1985; she has also been a contributing editor for *New York* magazine and *The New Yorker*, and has contributed articles to *The New York Times Magazine* and *Vogue*.

She is the winner of six Front Page awards for her journalism and the Frank Luther Mott-Kappa Tau Alpha Award for research. Her 2003 investigation of the rise of anti-Semitism in France ('France's Scarlet Letter') made international news.

Her expose of the tobacco industry, 'The Man Who Knew Too Much', was the basis for the 1999 movie *The Insider*, which was nominated for seven Academy Awards, including Best Picture. Her article 'Erotomania' became the Lifetime movie *Obsessed*. The director Alex Gibney is currently developing her article 'In the Kingdom of Big Sugar' for Tribeca Films.

She lives in New York City.

URVASHI BUTALIA is co-founder of Kali for Women, India's first feminist publishing house, and now runs Zubaan, an imprint of Kali. She is an independent feminist researcher and writer, and has written and published widely in books, newspapers and magazines at home and abroad. Among her best-known publications is the award-winning history of Partition, *The Other Side of Silence: Voices from the Partition of India*, which has also been translated into many languages. In 2011, she was awarded the Padmashree by the Indian government for her work in women's publishing.

IPSITA ROY CHAKRAVERTI is India's foremost authority on the supernatural. Her research into ancient cultures and civilizations started many years ago in a chalet in the Laurentians in Canada. It was upon return to India that Ipsita took up the cause of women battered and branded 'daayans' and revealed the true nature of a much maligned branch of learning—Wicca, or 'dakini vidya'. Over the years, Ipsita has spoken at forums such as the CII, IIT Delhi, IIM Calcutta, St. Stephen's College Delhi and United Nations bodies in Delhi on the subject.

Ipsita's stories and concepts have been picturized on the big and small screens. In 2006, Ipsita launched the Wiccan Brigade (renamed The Young Bengal Brigade in 2013)—a first in the country. This is a forum where people of all ages and from all walks of life come together to research old, esoteric knowledge. In 2012, Ipsita launched the Psychic Wing of the Brigade, which works on investigating places with a past and blends science and mysticism in decoding them. Ipsita is the author of *Beloved Witch: An Autobiography*, *Sacred Evil: Encounters with the Unknown* and *Spirits I Have Known*.

ASHOK FERREY is Sri Lanka's biggest selling author in the English language. He has written two books of short stories, *Colpetty People* and *The Good Little Ceylonese Girl*; also an anthology, *Love in the Tsunami*; and a novel, *Serendipity*. He is a guest lecturer at the Colombo School of Architecture and host of The Ashok Ferrey Show, an arts programme on Sri Lankan television. His latest book, *The Professional*, has just been released. Ashok Ferrey lives and works in Colombo as a personal trainer.

Writer and publisher **NAMITA GOKHALE** is the author of eleven books including several works of fiction. Her first novel, *Paro: Dreams of Passion*, published in 1984, created a furor with its candid sexual humour. Other novels include *The Book of Shadows*, *Shakuntala: The Play of Memory*, *The Habit of Love* and *Priya*, a sequel to *Paro*.

Gokhale has worked extensively with Indian myth. She has written *The Book of Shiva* and retold the Mahabharata for young readers. She has also edited *In Search of Sita: Revisiting Mythology*, a landmark anthology on feminine figures in the Indian epics.

A co-director of the Jaipur Literature Festival and of Mountain Echoes, the Bhutan literary festival, Gokhale is committed to showcasing literature from across the Indian languages. She currently curates *Kitaabnama: Books and Beyond*, a multilingual book show on Doordarshan.

ADVAITA KALA is a bestselling novelist and award-winning screenwriter. Her debut novel, *Almost Single*, has sold over a hundred and fifty thousand copies and has been translated into French, Hindi and Marathi. She writes a regular column for *Mail Today* and a popular food column, *Epicuriosity*, for *The Financial Express*. An avid traveller, she lives out of a suitcase painted with a one of a kind mural—it's not pretty but it ensures that she doesn't pick up someone else's bag. Yes, it's happened—more than once.

MANOSI LAHIRI studied at the Universities of Calcutta, Delhi and London, and holds a doctorate in Geography from Delhi University. While lecturing in geography after graduation, she came to the realization that the growth of computer technology would lead to new ways to make and use maps. So in 1993 she founded ML Infomap, in New Delhi, to develop digital maps and provide services in geographic information systems. Digital map products and IT solutions developed by the company, which she heads as chief executive officer, are widely used by corporations and research institutes. Dr Lahiri has contributed to several prestigious projects of the Government of India as well as a number of UN organizations. She is also the author of the Understanding Geography series of text books for Indian middle-schoolers, published by Oxford University Press India. Her latest work is *Mapping India*.

SABA NAQVI is a Delhi-based journalist. She writes extensively on politics, governance and current affairs. Beyond her role as a reporter and political analyst, she follows issues of identity and polarization. *In Good Faith: A Journey in Search of an Unknown India* is her first book.

AMAN NATH is a historian by education but from an early age he has painted, written poetry and practised graphic design and copywriting for several advertising campaigns. He has co-written/authored fourteen illustrated books on art, history, architecture, corporate biography and photography that include *Jaipur: The Last Destination*, *Dome Over*

India: Rashtrapati Bhavan, Brahma's Pushkar: Ancient Indian Pilgrimage and *The Monumental India Book.*

He is involved in the restoration of India's unlisted architectural ruins, now run as the twenty-eight Neemrana 'non-hotel' Hotels, which have won awards from UNESCO, the Indian travel trade industry and several national awards. Aman Nath wrote the catalogue and the publicity campaign for the first Indian contemporary art auction by Sotheby's sponsored by *The Times of India* for their sesquicentennial celebrations in 1977. He was the curator of Art Today, the art gallery of India Today.

As an inveterate traveller—after walking 400 km to Mount Kailash and sub-Antarctica—he has contributed to several travel magazines.

KOTA NEELIMA is a political journalist and author, and writes about religion and social issues. Her book, *Tirupati: A Guide to Life*, which was published in November 2012, is a national bestseller and has been translated into Hindi and Tamil. Neelima has also written three novels—*Riverstones*, *Death of a Moneylender* and *Shoes of the Dead*—which are critiques of mainstream journalism and its neglect of issues of rural India.

Presently, Neelima is a research fellow for South Asia Studies at SAIS, Johns Hopkins University, Washington DC.

RAHUL PANDITA was born in the Kashmir Valley; at the age of fourteen, in 1990, his family was forced into exile, like thousands of others, by Islamic extremists. He lives in a Delhi suburb now. A journalist by profession, Rahul works as associate editor with the Indian news weekly, *Open* magazine.

Rahul Pandita is the author of *Our Moon Has Blood Clots*, a memoir on how Kashmiri Pandits became victims of a brutal ethnic cleansing at the hands of Islamist militants in the Valley of Kashmir. He has also authored the bestselling *Hello, Bastar: The Untold Story of India's Maoist Movement* and co-authored the critically acclaimed *The Absent State*. He has extensively reported from war zones that include Iraq and Sri Lanka. In the last few years, most of his work has been focused on India's Maoist rebellion in central and east India. In 2010, he received the International Red Cross Award for conflict reporting.

AAKAR PATEL is a writer based in Bengaluru. His translations of Saadat Hasan Manto's non-fiction will be published in early 2014; his book on India will also be published in 2014. He is a former editor with several newspapers including the Gujarati daily *Divya Bhaskar* and the afternoon tabloid *Mid Day*. He oversaw the Urdu Inquilab during his six years at *Mid Day*. He writes weekly columns for *Mint Lounge* and *Deccan Chronicle*, and for Pakistan's *Express Tribune*.

DEVDUTT PATTANAIK is the author of twenty-five books and 400 articles on the relevance of mythology in modern times, including *Myth = Mithya: A Handbook of Hindu Mythology*; a novel, *The Pregnant King*; *Jaya: An Illustrated Retelling of the Mahabharata* and *Sita: An Illustrated Retelling of the Ramayana*. Trained as a medical doctor, he worked for fourteen years in the pharma and health care industry before becoming business advisor in Ernst & Young. He then turned his hobby and passion into his profession to become Chief Belief Officer of Big Bazaar Future Group. He consults Star TV and Epic TV on storytelling. He is advisor to the television shows *Devon ke Dev Mahadev* and *Mahabharat*. His radical yet accessible views on leadership, management and governance on TV shows like *Shaastrath* on CNBC Awaaz and *Business Sutra* on CNBC have made him a popular speaker in corporates and business schools.

JERRY PINTO lives and works in Mumbai. He is a journalist and a writer of poetry, prose and children's fiction. His works include *Surviving Women, Asylum and Other Poems, Helen: The Life and Times of an H-Bomb* (which was awarded the National Film Award for Best Book on Cinema in 2007), *A Bear for Felicia* and *Mumbai Meri Jaan*. His first novel, *Em and the Big Hoom*, was published in 2012 and won The Hindu Lit For Life Prize for Fiction in 2013. He is the translator of *Cobalt Blue*, published in 2013.

WENDELL RODRICKS is India's Guru of Minimalism who pioneered resort wear, minimalism and eco-friendly fashion before the words were coined. Working from a remote village in Goa, his work has attracted a growing clientele and he has been invited to show in the world's most important garment fairs, including IGEDO, the Salon Pret-a-Porter Paris and BIOFACH Nuremburg. Known for his whites and use of cut and colour in special handwoven weaves, the Wendell Rodricks style is unique in India and is recognized for its fluid emotion and lack of embroidery. He has done three grand finales for the Lakmé Fashion Week and his work has earned respect in the corporate world in India. Wendell Rodricks has written two books: *Moda Goa: History and Style* and *The Green Room*, both released in 2012. Apart from writing, he has done various design projects ranging from designing for the Goa Police to designing the packaging for the Blenders Pride carton for the festive season 2012.

MISHI SARAN was born in India and spent her first decade in New Delhi. She has also lived in Switzerland, Indonesia, USA, China, Hong Kong and Korea. She majored in Chinese Studies at Wellesley College (USA) and returned to Hong Kong in 2014, after eight years in Shanghai. Her first book, a travelogue, *Chasing the Monk's Shadow: A Journey in the Footsteps of Xuanzang*, was shortlisted for the 2006 Hutch Crossword Book Award. Her novel, *The Other Side of Light*, was shortlisted for the 2013 Commonwealth Book Prize. Her third book is a novel set in 1930s' Shanghai. She can be contacted at www.mishisaran.com.

NAVTEJ SARNA is the author of the novels *The Exile* and *We Weren't Lovers Like That* as well as the short story collection *Winter Evenings*. His non-fiction works include *The Book of Nanak*, *Folk Tales of Poland* and a translation of Guru Gobind Singh's *Zafarnama*. His most recent work is *Savage Harvest*, a translation of Punjabi Partition short stories. He contributes regularly to *The Times Literary Supplement*, *The Hindu* and other journals. A member of the Indian Foreign Service since 1980, he has served as a diplomat in several capitals, as the foreign office spokesperson and most recently, as India's ambassador to Israel.

AVEEK SEN is senior assistant editor (editorial, books and arts pages) at *The Telegraph*, Kolkata. He studied English literature at Jadavpur University, Kolkata, and University College, Oxford. He was a lecturer at St. Hilda's College, Oxford, and was awarded the 2009 Infinity Award for writing on photography by the International Center of Photography, New York.

ALI SETHI is a writer and musician living in Lahore. A graduate of Harvard College, he is the author of the novel *The Wish Maker*, a nominee for the 2010 DSC Prize for Literature. He has written opinion pieces, reportage and literary essays for *The New York Times* and *The New Yorker*, and is currently working on a novel.

Ali is also a classically trained vocalist in the Hindustani Khayal tradition, a disciple of Ustad Naseeruddin Saami of the Delhi Gharana. Though his *riyaz* consists of exercises in *vilmabit asthais* and *bandishes*, he is happiest when singing Urdu ghazals and Punjabi folk songs. His cover of Farida Khanum's 'Dil jalane ki baat karte ho' was featured in Mira Nair's *The Reluctant Fundamentalist*, and he has recorded two songs—a ghazal of Ghalib's and a duet written by author Mohammed Hanif—for Sarmad Khoosat's upcoming biopic on Manto.

BULBUL SHARMA is a painter and writer. Her works are in the collection of the National Gallery of Modern Art, Lalit Kala Akademi and Chandigarh Museum as well as in private collections in India, UK, USA, Japan, Canada and France. She has held solo exhibitions of her paintings in Mumbai, London, Delhi, as well as participated in group shows in India and abroad from 1987 till 2013.

She has published several books which include *My Sainted Aunts*; *The Perfect Woman*; *Anger of Aubergines*; *Banana Flower Dreams*; *Shaya Tales*; *Devi*; *Eating Women, Telling Tales*; *Now That I Am Fifty* and *Tailor of Giripul*. Her books have been translated into Italian, French, German, Chinese, Spanish and Finnish.

Her books for children are *Fabled Book of Gods and Demons* and *The Children's Ramayana*. She conducts 'story painting' workshops for special needs children and is a founder member of Sannidhi, a NGO that works in village schools.

DAYANITA SINGH is an artist who works with Photography and Books. She was born in 1961 in New Delhi. She studied at National Institute of Design, Ahmedabad.

Singh has published eleven books: *Zakir Hussain* (1986); *Myself, Mona Ahmed* (2001); *Privacy* (2003); *Chairs* (2005); *Go Away Closer* (2007); *Sent a Letter* (2008); *Blue Book* (2009); *Dream Villa* (2010), *Dayanita Singh* (2010); *House of Love* (2011) and *File Room* (2013). Her works have been exhibited and collected worldwide, shown most recently at the Venice Bienale 2013 and at Hayward Gallery, London.

MAYANK AUSTEN SOOFI is the author of *Nobody Can Love You More: Life in Delhi's Red Light District*. He also wrote four guidebooks available under the title *The Delhi Walla*, which focuses on the city's monuments, food, hang-outs and people respectively. The boxed set of these guidebooks were called by the UK-based *Guardian* newspaper as one of 'the best quirky guidebooks from around the world'. Soofi runs the popular website, thedelhiwalla.com, in which he details Delhi's lives and loves. He is also a photographer and his archives include more than 20,000 photos of Delhi's monuments, people, food, streets and gardens.

NISHA SUSAN is a senior commissioning editor for Yahoo! Originals. She is a founder editor of the women's zine *The Ladies Finger!*. She was features editor at *Tehelka* magazine where she wrote on silent cultural phenomena like online sex tapes, why young women choose the hijab, how the poor take stock of the absurd poverty line and the rule book of appearing Indian. Her short fiction has been published by n+1, *Caravan*, *Pratilipi*, *Out of Print*, Penguin and Zubaan. For the past few years her fiction has been exploring the way technology, particularly the Internet, leaves its imprint on relationships. She is currently working on a novel. She lives in Bengaluru.

HM THE QUEEN MOTHER, ASHI DORJI WANGMO WANGCHUCK is the author of *Treasures of the Thunder Dragon: A Portrait of Bhutan*. The book provides unique intimate insights into Bhutanese culture and society. She is also the author of *Of Rainbows and Clouds: The Life of Yab Ugyen Dorji As Told to His Daughter*.

Acknowledgements

Appreciation and gratitude to my editors, Krishan Chopra and Debasri Rakshit, for their patient encouragement and constant support. To Shuka Jain for her imaginative help in giving graphic shape to the book.

To all the contributors who provided the orchestra of perspectives that made the anthology come together.

To Shubhda Khanna and Chhavi Malik for their help in early days. To Rita Peter Bakht for always being there when needed. And to Anisha Lalvani for her keen ear and gentle suggestions.

Copyright Acknowledgements

'A Retreat to Holy India' by Marie Brenner
This first appeared as 'Finding Marie' in *Departures*, January/February 2009.

'In Search of Lost Time' by Mayank Austen Soofi
This first appeared in *Livemint*, September 2011.

'The Land of Seven Hundred Hills' by M.J. Akbar
This first appeared in *The Penguin Book of Indian Journeys* edited by Dom F. Moraes, Penguin Books, 2001.

'Hello, Bastar' by Rahul Pandita
Taken from the essay 'Hello Bastar', in *Hello Bastar: The Untold Story of India's Maoist Movement* by Rahul Pandita, Tranquebar, 2011.

'Lost without a Trace' by Aveek Sen
This first appeared in *The Telegraph*, Kolkata, 12 April 2007.

'F for Dhravi' by Jerry Pinto
This first appeared in *Dharavi* edited by Joseph Campana, HarperCollins India, 2013.

'Gond Art: Of Mysteries and Market Forces' by Nisha Susan
This first appeared as 'Jangarh Shyam Committed Suicide Nine Years Ago. Now, As His Clan Pushes His Legacy, Gond Art Is Becoming a Rage Abroad' in *Tehelka*, July 2010.

'Tirupati: The God for a Modern Age' by Kota Neelima
This essay has been compiled with extracts taken from the book *Tirupati: A Guide to Life* by Kota Neelima, Random House India, 2012.

'The Muslim Goddess: Sunderbans, West Bengal'
by Saba Naqvi
Taken from the essay 'A Muslim Goddess', in *In Good Faith: A Journey in Search of an Unknown India* by Saba Naqvi, Rupa Publications, 2012.

'"The Door to His Hospice Was Never Closed"'
by Navtej Sarna
Excerpted from the author's forthcoming book, *Indians at Herod's Gate*.

'Maps for All Times' by Manosi Lahiri
Excerpts from *Mapping India* by Manosi Lahiri, Niyogi Books, 2011.